PENGUIN BOOKS

# WARRIOR OF THE FOURTH ESTATE

B.G. Verghese (1927–2014) studied at Delhi and Cambridge universities and was a columnist and author. He served with the *Times of India* for many years before becoming the information adviser to Prime Minister Indira Gandhi. He was later the editor of the *Hindustan Times* (1969–75) and the *Indian Express* (1982–86) and was with the Centre for Policy Research, New Delhi, thereafter. His books include *Waters of Hope*, *India's Northeast Resurgent*, *Reorienting India: The New Geo-Politics of Asia*, *First Draft: Witness to the Making of Modern India*, *A State in Denial: Pakistan's Misguided and Dangerous Crusade*, *Post Haste: Quintessential India* and *Breaking the Big Story* (edited).

Verghese wrote extensively on education and population and was associated with NGOs in these fields, as well as in human rights, the environment, regional cooperation and security. He was a member of the Press Council and chair of the Media Foundation. He received the Magsaysay Award for Journalism in 1975.

PENGUIN BOOKS

# WARRIOR OF THE FOURTH ESTATE

B.G. Verghese (1927–2014) studied at Delhi and Cambridge universities and was a columnist and author. He worked with the *Times of India* for many years before becoming the information adviser to Prime Minister Indira Gandhi. He was later the editor of the *Hindustan Times* (1969–75) and the *Indian Express* (1982–86) and was with the Centre for Policy Research, New Delhi, thereafter. His books include *Waters of Hope*, *India's Northeast Resurgent*, *Reorienting India: The New Geo-Politics of Asia*, *First Draft: Witness to the Making of Modern India*, *A State in Denial: Pakistan's Misguided and Dangerous Crusade*, *Post Haste Quit: Essential India* and *Breaking the Big Story Retold*.

Verghese wrote extensively on education and population and was associated with NGOs in these fields, as well as in human rights, the environment, regional cooperation and security. He was a member of the Press Council and chair of the Media Foundation. He received the Magsaysay Award for Journalism in 1975.

# WARRIOR
## OF THE FOURTH ESTATE

# Ramnath Goenka
## of the Express

B.G. Verghese

PENGUIN BOOKS
An imprint of Penguin Random House

PENGUIN BOOKS

USA | Canada | UK | Ireland | Australia
New Zealand | India | South Africa | China | Singapore

Penguin Books is part of the Penguin Random House group of companies whose addresses can be found at global.penguinrandomhouse.com

Published by Penguin Random House India Pvt. Ltd
4th Floor, Capital Tower 1, MG Road,
Gurugram 122 002, Haryana, India

First published in Viking by Penguin Books India 2005
Published in Penguin Books by Penguin Random House India 2017



10 9 8 7 6 5 4 3 2



ISBN 9780143429159

Typeset in GoudyOld Style by SURYA, New Delhi
Printed at Repro India Limited



www.penguin.co.in

# Contents

## Copyright Acknowledgements

Grateful acknowledgement is made to the following for permission to reprint copyright material:

Aroon Purie for excerpt from 'On the Firing Line', *India Today*, 30 September 1987.

Joseph Mathai for excerpt from *Indira Gandhi: Reminiscences* by K.K. Birla, Vikas, 1986.

While every effort has been made to trace copyright holders and obtain permission, this has not been possible in all cases; any omissions brought to our attention will be remedied in future editions.

# Acknowledgements

A very large number of people have contributed towards the writing of this volume.

First and foremost, thanks are due to Vivek Goenka, chairman, *Indian Express* Pvt. Ltd and Shekhar Gupta, its editor-in-chief, for inviting me to undertake the task. They placed the resources of the *Express* at my disposal and spared no effort in facilitating the task. Manoj Sonthalia, chairman of the Southern Group, and Ms Saroj Goenka in Madras were equally welcoming. They spoke to me of their own recollections and the former kindly made available several valuable documents and photographs. These have supplemented those collected under the aegis of the Ramnath Goenka Biography Project led by V. Ranganathan, now sadly deceased.

V. Ranganathan and his colleagues Gita More in Delhi, Jaiboy Joseph in Madras and N.S. Jagannathan in Bangalore were generous with their time. I could only speak with C.P. Raghavan over the telephone as he is unfortunately not in the best of health.

The Biography Project material proved invaluable and covered the whole range of Ramnath Goenka's associates and interests. These had been stored in Bombay, where Ms Vaidehi Thakker, *Express* director, arranged for me to inspect them and move the bulk of them to Delhi and also helped organize a number of local appointments in the city.

In Delhi, Usha Uppal, special assistant to Shekhar Gupta, handled all the logistics regarding travel to Madras, Bangalore and Bombay and was good enough to set up several appointments in these places.

I was provided office space with the *Financial Express* in the Express Building in Delhi where I was able to sift through all the material and go through a large number of bound volumes of the *Express*. The librarian, Dharamvir, and his assistants were most helpful in locating specific files, photocopying hundreds of pages of material and procuring further reference material from other libraries. The Editor and staff of the *Financial Express* tolerated my poaching on their space with equanimity, despite sharp fluctuations in the Sensex.

My gratitude to all of them.

In addition, I thought I should endeavour to meet several persons personally so as to be able to draw them out over and beyond whatever they may have said earlier in their taped interviews. Most readily obliged; but some were not available or were unwell or abroad.

Thanks are due to Messrs V.P. Singh, Chandra Shekhar, the late Narasimha Rao, Inder Gujral, Jagmohan, Nanaji Deshmukh, Nusli Wadia, Venu Srinivasan, Dr Bharat Ram, Arun Jaitley, Fali Nariman, Sushil Goenka, Tarlochan Singh, S. Varadan, Vishwabandhu Gupta, Bhure Lal, Tony Jesudasan, B.N. Tandon, Kuldip Nayar, Ajit Bhattacharjea, S. Nihal Singh, Arun Shourie, Prabhash Joshi, S. Gurumurthy, Suman Dubey, Prabhu Chawla, Saeed Naqvi, Sitanshu Das, T.J.S. George, V.N. Narayanan, Dr J.K. Jain, H.Y. Sharada Prasad, Coomi Kapoor, Ashwini Sarin, Arun Sinha, P.C. Jain, Rajendra Nath, Sankaran Nair, T.N. Sethuraman, V. Mohan and S. Srinivasan.

Arun Jaitley placed his personal law library at my disposal and his juniors were most proficient and obliging in procuring several case histories and judgements relating to the *Indian Express*.

The list of those earlier interviewed on tape as part of the Biography Project is given in the Appendix.

All these many persons have contributed towards the writing of this biography. Hopefully they will find their reward in this volume.

My special thanks to Nandini Mehta, who edited this work at Penguin Books with meticulous care—ably assisted by Jaishree Ram Mohan—and to Sevanti Ninan, who took time off to read the manuscript. Both offered valuable suggestions regarding chronology, content and the need for expanding or clarifying statements that assumed an excessive recall of past events on the part of readers. Their suggestions have gone towards improving the book. Thanks also to Krishna Gopal, librarian, JNU, for his assistance in tracking down certain references.

# Preface

Soon after Ramnath Goenka passed away in October 1991, the *Indian Express* decided to collect and collate material pertaining to his life and work, as a precursor to assigning an author to write his biography. A Biography Project was launched, with V. Ranganathan, former business manager of the *Indian Express*, Bombay, an old associate and confidant of the late *Express* chairman, as chief coordinator, and considerable progress was made. However, the project, which had suffered a number of interruptions, had more or less stalled in 1999 for a variety of reasons and was thereafter put on hold in 2001.

Vivek Goenka, chairman of the *Indian Express* Newspapers Ltd, and Shekhar Gupta, the editor-in-chief, approached me in December 2003 to author the biography. I was honoured to accept the invitation to do so in view of my own connection with the *Express* and my long and happy association with Ramnath Goenka, or RNG as he was more usually known.

My task was made far easier by the work already done by the Biography Project group in gathering a vast amount of primary data in the form of over 320 interviews and collection of documents, reports, books, articles, references, clippings, obituary notices and photographs. The interviews had been taped and transcribed and classified under eighteen subject headings. I supplemented these with further conversations with a range of persons but was unable to meet some who might have shed valuable light or provided context and perspective or narrated the other side of specific events and episodes. I also pored over and culled out a good deal of material from bound volumes of the *Express* archives.

Three cells were set up in Bombay, Delhi and Madras under Ranganathan who, alas, passed away recently before seeing the project, on which he had laboured for so long with such devotion, come to fruition. M.G. Kochar, another old *Express* hand, assisted the Bombay cell, headed by Ranganathan himself. Gita More and C.P. Raghavan conducted the interviews in Delhi and some other centres, with Prabhash Joshi chipping in towards the end. In Madras and the South, Jaiboy Joseph undertook the task, with L. Seshan and N.S. Jagannathan joining him later.

Many of those interviewed were candid, though some of what they said was off the record or non-attributable. They portrayed Ramnath Goenka as they knew him, warts and all. These confidences have been respected and, except where the reference is innocuous, no source has been named though matter has been cited within quotations but without attribution. Obviously, the choice of material used had to be selective and, in case of conflicting accounts and contradictory assessments, I followed my own sense with regard to the weight of evidence. The responsibility for this is entirely mine.

Many who read this volume will recognize a phrase, idea or anecdote or comment scattered though the pages. I have not changed the language or sentiment in some cases as the original narrative was evocative of the time and mood surrounding events recalled in tranquillity.

I have quoted extensively from RNG's own writings as well as from the editorials and columns of the *Express* and reports in contemporary journals, as these best capture the flavour of the occasion. I have retained the names Madras, Bombay and Calcutta as this is what these cities were known as in his lifetime.

There is much that has not been included, partly for lack of space or because it relates to matters that would have detracted from the central focus of this biography. These provide interesting material for further writings on specific aspects of Ramnath Goenka's life. The editorial and news material available from the vernacular newspapers of the *Express* Group, their editors and staff was by no means missing but constituted the smaller part of the Biography Project archival collection. While the *Indian Express* is constantly cited, it must be understood that the term 'Express' in many cases refers to the *Express* Group as a whole.

Another point that needs emphasis is that this volume is a biography of Ramnath Goenka and not a history of the *Express*. That must be a separate endeavour and would be worth attempting. Yet much of the story of the *Express* comes through, as the newspaper was an intrinsic part of RNG's life. He wrote for the *Express* periodically, issued statements from time to time and had a 'war cabinet' or inner crisis management group that revolved around those in or otherwise closely associated with the *Indian Express*, his flagship publication. A.N. Sivaraman, editor of *Dinamani*, and Prabhash Joshi, editor of *Jansatta*, were among the insiders. A few other chosen outsiders were also called for counsel at different times.

The *Express* succession has been skimmed over lightly. This is because the matter was contested and settled after RNG's passing. However, in his own lifetime, he worried over the future of the *Express* after the sudden death of his son, Bhagwandas. The *Express* was not merely a newspaper empire but a mission to uphold the nation's freedom, unity and core values for the progress and prosperity of all its people. That is what he had imbibed from his understanding of the scriptures, and from Gandhi, ideals tempered through the struggle for independence. With Bhagwandas gone, he was unsure. He toyed with the idea of a trust, or even an editorial trust, but ultimately decided that the succession must follow his bloodline. The grandchildren were as yet untried, so he inducted them. There were the expected pulls and pressures from within and without, and his putative decision was only finally confirmed after his demise.

A word about the chapter contents. The narrative is by and large chronological. However, given events and episodes are carried forward in an unbroken narrative within a single chapter, rather than made to spill over into others, so that the thread is not lost. This has sometimes resulted in a particular chapter covering a chronological period that runs ahead of the chronology of later chapters.

The first two chapters tell of Goenka's early life, family and marriage. A Marwari from Bihar was led by circumstances to set down his roots in Madras, where he gradually gained acceptance as a 'Tamil Brahmin' (1922–48). This is where the *Express* was born. The narrative traces his rise to eminence in the South with some later events recounted here to fill out the 'Madras story'. Goenka was an active Gandhian worker and Congressman and sat in the Madras Legislative Council. The expanding *Express* empire then took him to Bombay, after an abortive interlude in Calcutta, and then to Delhi. Chapters three and four trace the 'Bombay story', including the founding of PTI, and then the 'Delhi story' and his membership of the Constituent Assembly. There is some overlap. Each story runs ahead of the principal events described, covering the period from 1946 to 1975, as the *Express* established new editions in the west and north.

Chapter five, spanning the period from 1946 to 1976, returns to Calcutta and recalls earlier episodes, but essentially centres on RNG's non-newspaper business interests. These relate to the stock market, his takeover of the National Jute Company, and his bid to acquire control over Indian Iron and Steel. These ventures evoked controversy and conflict with the authorities. RNG sustained heavy losses, which took time to recoup.

Chapter six, covering the years from 1969 to 1977, revolves around the Congress split and the JP movement, of which

RNG possibly was the principal financier and organizer, and leads up to the dark days of the Emergency. He came into confrontation with Indira Gandhi, who was determined to silence the *Express* and bring RNG to his knees. This is followed in chapter seven by the saga of the rise and fall of the Janata Government (1976–80), in whose formation RNG played a notable part, and the return to office of Indira Gandhi and a further time of travail (1980–84).

The next two chapters have a wider span. From small beginnings, the *Express* had grown into a vast multi-edition, multi-lingual chain. The Group underwent considerable technological modernization but lacked professional management or a coherent organizational structure. RNG's failure to delegate authority, his tight-fistedness over money and tendency to equate trade unionism with communism, which he abhorred, are discussed in chapter eight.

Litigation was central to RNG's life and being, and kept him going as it bought time. On the other hand, a vindictive government arraigned him on countless charges in a bid to stop or break him. Goenka fought more cases and spent more time in court than possibly any other person in India. This story, told in chapter nine, spans much of his career.

The next two chapters follow a certain periodization. Chapter ten covers the early honeymoon with Rajiv Gandhi, which soon degenerated into a bitter, no-holds-barred contest (1985–87). This intensified through 1987–89, ending in the formation of the National Front government under V.P. Singh, the short-lived Chandra Shekhar ministry, and the assassination of Rajiv Gandhi in 1991. These developments are the subject matter of chapter eleven.

Altogether this entire period from 1985 to 1991, covered in chapters ten and eleven, witnessed events and exposés galore involving Reliance Industries; V.P. Singh's crusade against corruption and his resignation as defence minister; the Fairfax and Thakkar–Natarajan investigations; the Bofors howitzer and

HDW scandals; the spat between President Zail Singh and Rajiv Gandhi; the political ascendancy of V.P. Singh; the St. Kitts affair and much else. All these got closely intertwined in the parliamentary debate, political controversy, litigation and headlines of the time, with Goenka and the *Express* playing leading roles, locking horns with a wrathful government under Rajiv Gandhi.

The story goes back and forth at the dizzy pace of a roller-coaster ride. Perhaps the reader may find it hard at times to keep track of the many sensational developments that were taking place simultaneously. But if these episodes were to be treated separately, the unfolding plot with its many sub-plots, would lose its dramatic flavour. Nor might it adequately convey the tremendous pressure under which RNG functioned, foiling an attack here, counter-attacking there, all the while taking counsel with his 'war cabinet' to carry the battle to Parliament, the courts and directly to the public at large through the *Express*.

RNG took seriously ill in 1989 and was in and out of hospital thereafter. Chapter twelve covers his declining years, the man and his legacy, and the anxious debates with and among a close circle of advisers over the future of the *Express*.

The *Indian Express* was Goenka's flagship, and it was the vehicle through which he primarily fulfilled his destiny and fought his battles. The Indian language papers and the *Financial Express* were secondary to his mission, except when regional issues cropped up, such as the anti-Hindi agitation in Madras, the separation of Andhra and the bifurcation of Bombay Presidency, when *Dinamani*, *Andhra Prabha*, *Loksatta* and other vernacular papers spoke up. But catering as they did to a regional readership, he permitted them to develop their own editorial stance on interstate controversies. It was the *Indian Express* that reflected his national perspective and, on economic matters, the *Financial Express* too.

Therefore, those looking for details regarding the vernacular papers or, indeed, about the *Financial Express*, might not find them in these pages. For this is a biography of Goenka and not of the *Express*.

Goenka had contemplated commissioning both a history of the *Express* and his own biography at various times. In 1976 he recruited V.N. Narayanan, then an assistant editor with the *Tribune*, to join a 'sinking ship' and write his biography. He sent him to Vijayawada to take charge of the edition and said he would be relatively undisturbed there to get on with this assignment. Narayanan had some conversations with RNG and got started. However, come 1977 and RNG got busy constructing the Janata Party and soon forgot about the idea of a biography! This seemed the wrong time to brood on the past when the future beckoned.

Then in 1978, V.S. Ganapati Sharma, chief reporter of the *Express* in Madras and later with the Express News Service, was asked to write the story of the *Indian Express* to commemorate its golden jubilee in 1984. He researched the topic, met various people in Delhi, Madras and Hyderabad and made exhaustive notes. However, he was later told that RNG wished the files to be passed on to Dom Moraes, then with the paper in Bombay, who would write the book. That was done and Sharma heard nothing further. It is doubtful if Dom Moraes did anything at all, and failed to return the files and material when he left the *Express*. The entire effort went waste.

Earlier, in 1967, R.A. Padmanabhan of the *Express* had been put in charge of a research unit to gather material for a history of the *Express*. He said he had completed a third of the project, up to Independence. This covered RNG's early life, his coming to Madras, the takeover of the *Express* from Sadanand and his first foray into Bombay. Several chapters were in fact drafted and some of Padmanabhan's work has been cited in the present volume. The work was not completed or published as a book. But the draft chapters were part of the archival material collected by Ranganathan.

There have been articles on Ramnath Goenka and a recent book on him in Hindi, among other publications. But a definitive biography has been lacking.

This volume is intended to fill that gap. I have deliberately avoided too much detail so as to make it readable rather than comprehensive. Nevertheless, there is quite a lot of detail too, for RNG lived a crowded life. What is attempted is a broad-brush portrayal of a fascinating and complex character, an enigma and bundle of contradictions, who presided over a newspaper group that not merely recorded the events of our time but made not a little history too.

# Introduction

## A Man for All Seasons

He was a man for all seasons. Tinker, tailor, soldier, sailor, rich man, poor man . . . the lot. Ramnath Goenka was metaphorically all of these, but quintessentially India's Mr Newspaper. Born to an ordinary trading family, he rose by dint of a native ability, grit, bluff and bluster to become a most powerful national figure and a patriarch of the Press. He presided over a media empire spanning the country in seven languages and read daily by some five million people. His mission was to open doors for information to flow and let the people know, especially that which those in authority would rather hide. As a newspaper publisher, he believed he had a great social obligation to provide empowering knowledge and continuing education.

He was more than merely a newspaperman. He was a freedom fighter who answered the call of Gandhi to awaken the people and unite them, liberate their minds and join the struggle for swaraj. He was a businessman too, trading in many commodities and speculating in the market. He even printed examination papers when he first acquired a press, to keep the business going. He was not impervious to making money. Of course, money mattered. But he was not in business for the money—he was in business to possess the wherewithal so that he himself might be independent and in a position to sustain his many endeavours. His newspapers entailed expenditure.

They yielded little or no profit. Property did. He was a man of property. He bowed to Saraswati but never forgot Lakshmi.

Newspapers were necessary to give voice to freedom. Hence they became his chosen instrument for struggle. He grew his own chain of papers but did not hesitate to assist other publishers, even possible rivals. He was one of the youngest Indians ever to become a legislator, being nominated to the Madras Legislative Council in 1926. He sat with the Opposition and was later to stake his all, as repeatedly in the future, in response to the Quit India call, supporting the underground and hundreds of Congress families whose breadwinners languished in jail. He fought to enlarge press freedom in the Constituent Assembly and India's first Parliament. Nehru and Patel were among his heroes and he remained a steadfast Congressman until Indira Gandhi split the Party.

Independence was meant to liberate the people and not bind them in the coils of a licence–permit raj that spawned corruption. He was attracted by the call to free enterprise by the Swatantra Party under Rajagopalachari, and was later to become an acolyte of Jayaprakash Narayan in his drive against corruption and big government. The Emergency spelt a Second Freedom Struggle for him and was to mark the beginning of a long and epic battle against the might of insolent State power cruelly bent to prosecute and persecute the *Express*. Goenka had to face a barrage of charges and restraints and a flood of litigation that perhaps none other in the annals of modern India ever had to suffer. Fortunately he loved a good fight and thrived on litigation. It rejuvenated him. The Janata interregnum provided some respite. But the battle assumed even wider and uglier proportions all round through the Rajiv Gandhi years, getting enmeshed in a bizarre political and corporate war as well. Some of this was surreal cloak and dagger stuff with sundry 'god-men' thrown in and elements of pure theatre.

In between, Goenka tried his luck in industry. He acquired considerable if passing prominence in the worlds of jute and steel, and thought nothing of siphoning *Express* funds into these essentially extra-curricular enterprises. His losses here ran into tens of crores, a tidy fortune for most, though the *Express* itself ultimately recouped its investments. However, he consistently put into the *Express* more than he took from it.

*

What manner of man was Ramnath Goenka? He was born into a Rajasthani bania family in Bihar, and grew up with little formal schooling in Darbhanga and Janakpur in Nepal. He was self-taught and, in a broader sense, well educated, being well versed in Sanskrit and the shastras. He was a stout nationalist and a believer in India's traditional values and culture. If unwell, he would turn to Ayurveda and nature cure. Kottakkal was his favoured health resort. He was an amalgam of Rajput and bania, Bihari and Tamil, an atypical Marwari who was of the community but not really part of it. He combined the attributes of a Vaishya, Kshatriya and Brahmin. He was always to say that his business instincts came from his Marwari genes: 'Send a naked Marwari into a desert and in a year he will be rich.' But there were only three honest Marwaris—one was his grandfather 'who has gone', the other (and this with a chuckle) was himself, and the third was his great-grandson 'who is yet to come'! The biggest drawback in any Marwari, he would say, is that he respects money more than himself. But he was different. He was an immensely proud man and would break rather than bend.

RNG was not a family man and whatever little held the family together disappeared with the passing of his wife, Moongibai. He never shared his life with his son and two daughters or with their children, and was in many ways closer to his friends and associates. He knew this but was somehow unable to bridge that divide. He created an empire but did not know how to build a family. He was too individualistic and domineering. Happiness eluded him. So too, good health in later life, though an earlier alarm about having the deadly Hodgkin's disease proved unfounded.

He was a loner and lived a frugal, almost ascetic life. Bound by Gandhian vows, he neither smoked nor drank, was a strict vegetarian, took little interest in any recreation other than bridge, wore khadi, eschewed clubs, lived in utter and even unkempt simplicity without pomp or show, and maintained a battered Fiat which he drove himself. He would walk, almost at a trot, five miles a day, eleven rounds of his penthouse terrace in Bombay making a measured mile. He would keep switching off lights and not tolerate waste and, despite his wealth, only travel economy class by air and never book himself into a five-star hotel. He was a very early riser and would go through the papers carefully and then get on the phone to his editors and contacts to dissect the news and plan the day. Work, he said, was entertainment.

But he had good reason not to keep a personal chauffeur. 'Should he know where all I am going?' he would say with a smile. He had his assignations. He was something of a philanderer, but many of the young women whose company he kept generally looked on him as a fatherly figure. He would sometimes have a bevy of girls around him and liken this to Krishna among the gopis. But some reports were less kind.

He was very tight-fisted but could at the same time be extremely generous, especially to those in need or who were ill. He laid the foundations of nephrology in India by donating a dialysis machine to the Vellore Christian Medical College Hospital. Though Cho Ramaswamy was a critic, Goenka never refused to print his satirical journal, *Tughlak*, in the *Express* press. Annadurai, the chief minister of Tamil Nadu, had not always been well disposed towards Goenka either. Yet when he was stricken with cancer, a famous surgeon was flown out from the United States at Goenka's instance. Annadurai died. The bill came to Rs 90,000, which the state government desired to reimburse. Goenka declined the offer, saying he had not acted in expectation of payment. On another occasion, he remonstrated with a friend for paying a Bombay railway porter as much as Rs 2 for carrying his bags. Overhearing this, the porter remarked that his son's examination dues had cost Rs 25 and he had some other expenses to meet as well. Goenka immediately gave him Rs 50. He patronized famous musicians and once presented a Fiat car to Musiri Subramanya Iyer, 'a gentleman among musicians and a musician among gentlemen'. Such stories were legion.

He was also a patron of letters. He not only printed and published Rajagopalachari's *Mahabharata* and *Ramayana* at loss to himself in popular, low-cost, soft cover editions, but gave the author a cheque as advance royalty. Likewise, he undertook to bring out Tamil editions of Nehru's *Autobiography* and *Discovery of India*.

He was a hands-on man in a hurry. Impatience translated into action. When his eldest granddaughter was getting married, some 200 guests from the groom's side needed to be accommodated in Madras. The plans went awry. The new hotel on which he had banked was incomplete and all the others fully booked. Undaunted, he coolly proposed buying a suitable hotel and selling it after the event, whereupon the astonished management decided that this was a client worth cultivating and provided him all the rooms he required!

He was a deeply religious man, steeped in the scriptures, nevertheless a staunch secularist. He respected all faiths as different pathways to the Almighty, believing in spirituality rather than religiosity. He was regular in his devotions, visiting temples and spiritual leaders to invoke divine blessings. His first call every morning, and sometimes at dusk, would be to the Kapaleeshwar Koil in Mylapore, Madras, the Hanuman Temple in Bombay and Delhi, the Kali Bari in Calcutta, and some other shrine wherever he might be. He would often be seen at Delhi's Hanuman Mandir on a Tuesday, clad in a simple dhoti, barefoot, stripped to the waist, patiently waiting his turn for darshan in the sanctum sanctorum, at the tail end of a long queue, marigold flowers and laddoos in hand. He made a donation towards reconstruction of the Somnath Temple, as also for renovations to the garba griha of the Krishna Janmasthan in Mathura. He had worshipped at all the great shrines and visited the holy places of pilgrimage at Tirupati, Guruvayoor, Sabarimala, Kanchipuram, Varanasi, Mathura, Chitrakoot, Shirdi, Badrinath and Dwarka. He was a patron of several temples, even built some himself, and was a trustee of the Tirupati Devasthanam for some years. He would regularly walk seventeen times around the parikrama of the Krishna Temple at Mathura on auspicious occasions. A friend once met him at Guruvayoor Temple to be told that over 200 cases had been slapped against him and he had 'come to submit them to the Lord'.

He was a devotee of the late Paramacharya of Kanchi, Swami Chinmayananda and Satya Sai Baba. He visited Rajneesh but was 'shocked' by what he saw at his ashram in Pune. He followed Maharishi Mahesh Yogi for some time, during which he cunningly pulled off a hilarious and not unprofitable coup against the government. The Delhi administration was at that time bent on seizing the Express Building in Delhi but found the Maharishi in occupation, with thousands of his foreign disciples in transcendental meditation, levitating in a state of bliss! He was for a time a follower of Amiya Roy Choudhury or 'Dadaji' but was soon disillusioned, as he was with Chandraswamy, the highly connected but controversial 'god-man' who was involved in various political machinations, in some of which Goenka perhaps had a collateral interest.

The Paramacharya's saintliness and piety and Swami Chinmayananda's depth of learning attracted him. He found great compassion in Sai Baba and was greatly impressed by his miraculous power, though he was later to confess that the Baba had lost some of that attribute by overuse. But he would always say that the Baba's benediction and forecast that Indira Gandhi would falter by March 1977 sustained him during the dark and difficult months of the Emergency when everything seemed lost. He believed in karma or fate but would also seek out astrologers and tantrics just in case they had something to say that might come in handy.

He encouraged his Sunday papers to run Vinoba Bhave's discourses on the Gita and permitted religious advertisements and letters by Anandashankar Pandya in the *Express* to propagate 'the sublime truth of Hinduism, a universal religion'. These were later brought out in a booklet entitled *In Defence of Hinduism*. Likewise, as chairman of PTI, he got the agency to provide extensive coverage for the second Dharma Sansad or conclave of Hindu dharmacharyas in Udipi. He was a proud Hindu and sometimes felt that secularism was being pushed too far. When his daughter-in-law, Saroj, wished to donate to a Christian charity in Kerala, he wrote warning her that public service by the Church was most often done with the underlying motive of conversion. But he left the decision to her. Nevertheless, he was not a bigot but eclectic in many ways and worked for an amicable solution to the Ayodhya dispute. Religion, he said, had nothing to do with newspapers.

He was expedient and used people. He had genuine respect for Jayaprakash Narayan and went to great lengths to build him up as a messiah. But he was sceptical about the practicability of his Total Revolution. He would as soon be drawn towards a person as be distanced from him or her as circumstances changed. Thus there were occasions when he poured scorn on men he otherwise respected or regarded as friends. Rajagopalachari was one, Kamaraj another. It was said of him that he was a good friend but a dangerous enemy. Yet he was a chivalrous opponent. He had a sneaking respect for Indira Gandhi, as she had for him. He saw her as Nehru's daughter while she remembered that he had given her husband, Feroze, a job in the *Express* at a difficult time for the couple. When the electorate cast her aside in 1977, he called on her and did not wish to see her humiliated. Again, when her younger son, Sanjay, was tragically killed in an air crash, he empathized with her as a parent who too had just lost a son. Likewise, he did not wish the differences between her and her younger daughter-in-law to be played up in the *Express* as family disharmony was not uncommon and not to be politically exploited. When Dhirubhai Ambani, his latter-day bete noire, was hospitalized, he was quick to send him a bouquet and wish him a speedy recovery.

He held Acharya Kripalani and Achyut Patwardhan in high esteem for their service to the nation, sagacity and self-abnegation. He canvassed for the latter's elevation to the office of President of India, an honour Patwardhan declined. He did not agree with Morarji Desai on all issues but admired his personal integrity. These were values he set great store by, at least in others, for he did not necessarily always live up to them himself.

Goenka was temperamental in the extreme and given to sudden eruptions of anger when he would shout and scream, beat his head, throw things around and flail his arms as though convulsed by an apoplectic fit. Those present feared such frenzied outbursts could burst a blood vessel or bring on a heart attack. But the storm would pass as quickly as it came and he would resume conversation as if nothing had happened. Sometimes these fits of anger were histrionic, to impress his startled audience as much as the target of his simulated wrath.

Often in banter, but certainly in anger, he would spew forth the foulest invectives from a wide repertoire in several languages. The more genteel, and those who did not know him, would recoil in horror and embarrassment. Those who knew him well would know that, at least in their milder forms, these were possibly terms of endearment! There is the famous story of RNG lying in a coma, all strapped and hooked up in the recovery room of a leading hospital, anxiously watched over by the nurses. The silence was suddenly interrupted by shrieks that brought doctors scurrying in to deal with what they thought must be a grave emergency. Concern and confusion reigned until a close friend who heard the commotion exclaimed, 'Thank God, the old man seems to have recovered,' deciphering the terrifying sounds as a volley of RNG's choicest imprecations promising to see his antagonists dead before he left this world! Apocryphal perhaps, but typical.

The man was a great raconteur and would regale visitors with delightful anecdotes from which he would derive pungent aphorisms that were as educative as they were amusing. He had tremendous powers of recall and a truly elephantine memory. He would remark that he had broken every rule in the book except traffic regulations. Prudence dictated such obedience, except when it came to instructing his drivers to spirit away sensitive records and documents in anticipation of a raid on one of his offices! He would also not mind speeding on the open highway. On one occasion, he was driven to Shirdi from Pune to visit Sai Baba. Finding the chauffeur going too slow, he clambered into the driver's seat and zoomed off, only to put the car into a ditch. Shaken but unhurt he reached Bombay in a relief car rushed to the spot by the *Express* office in Pune. Back home, he admonished the hapless manager. 'Look here, you wanted to kill me, is it? I asked for a very good driver but you gave me a useless man who was not even familiar with the route. I had to throw him out of the car on the way back and while I was driving I narrowly escaped death. You fellows do not care for me at all!' The king could do no wrong.

Goenka was politically influential and, in his own way, determined the course of events. He was instrumental in elevating Rajendra Prasad to become the first President of India, in preference to Nehru's choice of Rajagopalachari. Later he got Rajagopalachari made chief minister of Madras Presidency as the only way to keep out a Communist ministry after the first general election in 1952. He favoured Indira Gandhi's election as leader of the Congress Parliamentary Party and prime minister in succession to Lal Bahadur Shastri but did not have a decisive role in this as sometimes made out. He was, however, a central figure behind Jayaprakash Narayan and in the formation of the Janata Party in 1977 but would have preferred to see Jagjivan Ram as prime minister. He was, likewise, a key figure behind the making of the National Front under the leadership of V.P. Singh. He himself reportedly declined ministerial office in Nehru's time and preferred to operate behind the scenes.

His means of wielding power was not party politics but command and control through the power of his newspapers, which packed a considerable media punch. He used them and his personal contacts with a wide assortment of politicians and establishment figures to play political chess, moving a pawn here, a rook there, thinking many steps ahead. Yet, he had the capacity to free his papers from his own political beliefs. Views mattered. News mattered more, for that was the fountain and source of all opinion. He gave his editors considerable freedom but set the direction and remained firmly in charge. Some of the most illustrious names in Indian journalism were associated with the *Express* Group, though many were mere birds of passage. He could be whimsical, even arbitrary, and was a poor paymaster. He knew how to convey a message in a manner that suggested that the listener had taken an independent decision. As he would say, 'If you want to rebuke your daughter-in-law, scold your daughter first in her presence. She will take the hint.' He was a shrewd judge of character and soon saw through flattery, but respected those who stood up to him. He was a fighter himself, and respected those who stood their ground on principle.

Some editors were more equal than others. A.N. Sivaraman and Seshadri ('Master') were like family. S. Mulgaokar was a very close friend and bridge partner. He respected Pothan Joseph and Frank Moraes as professionals and stylists, and Kuldip Nayar as a newsman. Some of his vernacular paper editors were recruited as well-known literary figures. He treated Arun Shourie almost as a son, though they broke twice. Prabhash Joshi was a confidant, and he would swap stories with Saeed Naqvi, Hiranmay Karlekar and others. He enjoyed their 'mischief'. He was warm towards young reporters who brought in stories. He constantly kept an eye out for talent and when he thought he had found somebody worthwhile he would swoop.

Dina Vakil, now resident editor of the *Times of India*, Mumbai, relates how she was recruited by RNG to edit the *Express Sunday Magazine*, which was to be revamped and printed in colour. After a first encounter at the penthouse in Bombay he invited her again one evening and took her out to dinner across the road to the Oberoi Hotel, where he ordered her—but only her—a post-prandial glass of sherry. Dina Vakil joined the *Express*. In a piece she wrote many years later, she remarked that never again was she professionally courted in as canny a manner, 'at least, not by an old man in a dhoti'. His latter-day lament, however, was, 'Where is the talent? Where do I look for an editor?'

The *Express* often indulged in activism and strayed from the path of objective journalism. It was at times openly partisan. But he never allowed his papers to become party organs. He was, however, a poor manager and failed to build an institutional framework that would survive his lifetime. One of his early associates was to say that he was an 'earthy, hard-headed realist to whom no means was taboo and no task too great to accomplish'. He had no permanent friends or permanent enemies, only permanent interests. Like all pioneers and frontiersmen, who hewed a new path or took the road less travelled, he was unconventional and made his own rules. People are sometimes dismissive of their contemporaries. They see them from too close. However, they are remembered in history because they made a difference.

Goenka made a lasting contribution to Indian journalism. He pioneered multiple-group multi-lingual editions and 'van editions' that would carry his papers to distant nooks and crannies so that in sum they would sell more than older established papers from any given centre. He was also a leading figure in the creation of the Press Trust of India. He was a rare publisher and an effective brand manager for the *Express* Group. Indeed, he was the *Express*. In the final reckoning, he was greater than his paper or the causes he espoused.

It would be an exaggeration to say that he did not know fear, but he never showed it. If something went wrong, well, there was another day. Repentance was not in his nature. Whatever he did was right—at that moment. In the Gandhian manner, the difference lay not in his changing words and deeds but in changing circumstances, between then and now. Maybe he was amoral to that extent. There was not always sufficient time to weigh right and wrong, for it was not for him to tarry when the trumpet sounded for battle.

This he learned from the Gita. He would recite two couplets in particular, to himself and to others:

*Hato vaa Praappsayasi swargam jitvaa vaa Bhokshyase mahiim*
*tasmat Uttishta kaunteya yuddhaaya krta-nischaya. (Sloka 36)*

*Suhka-dukhe same krtva laabha alaabhau jayaajayau*
*tato yuddhaaya yujyasva naivam paapam avaapsyyasi. (Sloka 37)*

What fate could fall more grievously than this? Either—being killed—thou wilt enter Swarga's safety, or alive—and victor—thou will reign an earthly king.

Therefore arise, thou Son of Kunti! Brace thine arm for conflict, nerve thy heart to meet—as things alike to thee—pleasure or pain, profit or ruin, victory or defeat. So minded, gird thee to the fight, for so thou shalt not sin.[1]

# 1

# The Making of a Marwari Tamil

Rajasthan is rich in legend and history. Its proud forts and parched sands tell a story of war, heroism, chivalry, nomadism and a constant battle for survival against nature's odds. Harsh living on tight margins bred thrift and hardihood. The more venturesome would migrate to pastures new and, in course of time, Marwaris established themselves as an enterprising trading community in lands afar, wherever opportunity beckoned.

It is not known when first somebody in the Goenka family of Agarwal banias decided to seek his fortune beyond the confines of the ancestral home in Mandawa in Rajasthan's Churu district, in the Shekhawati region. The opening up of new lands to revenue settlement through the nineteenth century, in the wake of the Raj, fostered a mercantile economy that encouraged entrepreneurship. By the turn of the century, a branch of the Goenka family had settled in Dildarnagar, a village near Darbhanga, in Bihar. It was here on 18 April 1904 that Jankidas Baijnath Goenka's wife gave birth to a boy named Ramnath. His mother died when he was barely six months old, whereupon he was adopted by his aunt, the widow of Jankidas's elder brother, Basantlal, who had passed away in 1901.

Jankidas, himself an adopted son, was a modest piece goods merchant and sahukar; but Basantlal had a relatively thriving business and some property in Janakpur, just across the border in Nepal. It is this transfer of residence and homes that was later to cause some confusion regarding Ramnath's date of birth. This was assumed to be some time in 1902, until subsequently corrected.

Ramnath spent his early years in Janakpur but attended school later in Darbhanga until the seventh standard. His was obviously a traditional upbringing, with formal tuition being supplemented by the moral lessons imbibed from stories of the Ramayana and Mahabharata with which his adopted mother must have regaled him. The Gita was his guide. This early background, possibly coupled with some time spent at Kashi Vidyapeeth, laid the foundation for a depth of scriptural knowledge. Somewhere along the line, he learnt Sanskrit and would later readily recall a shloka for every occasion.

There is no record that Ramnath matriculated. The nationalist movement had gained impetus with Gandhi's return from South Africa. The Mahatma was soon to visit Champaran in north Bihar to wage satyagraha against the virtual bondage of hapless peasants to British indigo planters. It was here that Ramnath first set eyes on Bapu. The young Acharya Kripalani was also drawn into that movement. Whether Ramnath got to know the latter then is not clear, but they were to meet later in Kashi. The Acharya was both his teacher and his mentor at the Vidyapeeth and the younger man was always to address him as 'guru'. Whatever the beginnings of their acquaintance, it was to be a lifelong association.

Ramnath was married when only twelve years of age and his child bride ten. Moongibai was from a Bajaj family of Deoria in eastern Uttar Pradesh. Marriage was not a sufficient cause for him to interrupt his studies and leave without gaining a degree. Did other family circumstances intervene? He was essentially a self-taught man. However, around 1919-20, when just about sixteen, young Goenka joined the business of his adopted mother's well-to-do merchant brothers, Babu Prahladrai Dalmia and Babu Sagarmal Dalmia, in Calcutta. Ever restless, he was soon apprenticed to Surajmal Nagarmal, an associate of Sukhdevdas Ramprasad, an established yarn and piece goods dealer, on a far from princely but yet not inconsiderable salary of Rs 30 per month. Though there was probably much else to learn, endlessly manhandling, displaying and rewinding heavy bales of cloth for choosy customers must have been a tiresome chore for an awakening nationalist.

The Jallianwala Bagh massacre had aroused the nation, and national opinion was further outraged by the indignity of the Rowlatt Act. Ramnath was apparently rounded up for joining a protest against this draconian measure but was soon thereafter reported hobnobbing with Bengal terrorists. The staid Marwari community was alarmed. Politics and business did not mix.

One can assume that anxious family consultations ensued. Prahladrai Dalmia was one of the Calcutta Marwari *panch* or council of elders and enjoyed a status that could not be lightly endangered. It was accordingly decided to spirit away the young rebel to some distant outpost where he might learn the trade in a more politically tranquil clime. Madras seemed far enough. And so it was in 1922 that Ramnath, having just attained majority, found himself on his way to the southern metropolis that was to become his adopted home, there to be an agent for Sukhdevdas Ramprasad, a 'dubash' of Walker and Co.

Ramnath would later constantly tell himself and others that he came to Madras with no more than a lota and a nine-cubit-long dhoti, which he would have to leave behind when he departed this world. Therefore, it was for him to do his duty as he saw it and not look for material reward. This philosophy accorded with the shastras and recalled Tolstoy's famous tale of the avaricious count, who was ceaselessly intent on enlarging his estates, but was like all flesh finally interred in a grave measuring no more than six feet by three—which is all the land that a man requires.

*

There must have been an element of culture shock in Ramnath's transfer to Madras, a strangeness of language, dress, food and even climate. However, the ubiquitous Marwari community was quartered with Gujaratis and other North Indians in a prosperous settlement in Sowcarpet, in the heart of the city. It is to that bustling area, flanked by Armenian Street and China Bazar, redolent of its cosmopolitan character, that the new arrival repaired.

Ramnath initially took residence with a family named Chaudhry, which hailed from the village adjacent to his native Mandawa, at 23 Peria Naickar Street. Moongibai perhaps joined him a little later. He then moved to what may have been the more spacious Damani House next door, at No. 8 Chinna Naickar Street, and still later to another Sowcarpet residence at No. 1 (now No. 11) Ramanuja Street. By then his eldest child, Bhagwandas, was born, followed by two daughters, Krishna and Radha. This last abode was subsequently gifted to the Moongibai Girls School that he founded to foster education in what was a crowded and underserved locality. It promoted a measure of both vertical and lateral integration, partly through the grant of scholarships.

The *Indian Who's Who* of 1935 mentions 413 Mint Road as his address and this is probably where he maintained a business office. The entry reads: 'Goenka, Ramnath, Dubash, The Bombay Co. Ltd, Madras, b 1901 . . . Came to Madras 1922, Agent for Sukdesdas Ramprasad of Calcutta, Exporters and Bankers. Started independent business, 1926.' The young Ramnath was by now a familiar man about town attired in dhoti, silk jubba, Marwari cap and, sometimes, a Jawahar jacket or coat, chewing paan and sporting a vermilion pottu on his forehead, as a family friend recalls. By the early 1930s he had a car, still something of a rarity in those days.

Ramnath commenced his independent career in June 1926 as a partner in Murliprasad Mohanprasad & Co., 'dubashes' of the Bombay Company of 169 Broadway, though he dabbled in stocks and bullion on the side. 'Dubash' means one who knows two languages. The Sahibs obviously needed an interpreter to do business with the Natives. However, in a larger and more important sense, the term referred to a financial broker who would testify to the creditworthiness of a client up to a given monetary ceiling. Thus it was on the word or informal guarantee of the dubash that the Bombay Company would sell goods to its clients against after-sales reimbursement. The dubash's margin was one paise in the rupee or a commission of 0.5 per cent.

It must be assumed that Ramnath proved an astute and assiduous businessman as evinced by his rising fortune. He had earlier been invited to join the Dakshina Bharat Hindi Prachar Sabha through C.R. Rajagopalachari and Jamnalal Bajaj, and was thereafter named a life trustee by Gandhi. This brought him in touch with nationalist and other leading figures of the day. He must have caught the eye of C.P. Ramaswami Aiyar, Law Member in the Madras Governor's Council, and was nominated to the Madras Legislative Council on 30 January 1926 at the extraordinarily youthful age of twenty-two, as a representative of trade and commerce.

Nominated members were expected to support the Treasury Benches, but Ramnath sat with the nationalist opposition and left nobody in any doubt as to where his sympathies lay as secretary of the Independent Party in the Council. He straddled business and politics and was much sought after. A business associate, Gordhandas Gupta, recalls living with him and dining off silverware. His engaging ways and readiness to help those who approached him or those he himself sought to cultivate won him a wide and varied circle of friends and colleagues. When he passed through the streets of Sowcarpet, merchants and minions alike would salute him. Within three years of his arrival in Madras he had learnt enough Tamil to get around and it was not long before he could speak it as though to the manner born. He was by now more Tamil than Marwari and bridged the intellectual, cultural and professional worlds of the Mylapore Brahmin and rival Egmore Group and Sowcarpet, the city's financial hub. The combination was both heady and potent.

By a sale deed dated 28 March 1929, Ramnath and two others, K.N. Kotnis, manager of the Bombay Company, and Mahadev Kasheenath, accountant and auditor, purchased 844 acres along the coast, south of Elliot's Beach in Madras, for a consideration of Rs 60,500. These lands were later transferred to the Bombay Company, possibly during a period of financial difficulty when he had to struggle to retain his creditworthiness as a sahukar. But by now Ramnath was a man of property and was in the years ahead to purchase prime real estate in major cities all over the country. Real estate spelt security and time and again proved a hedge against political and commercial misfortune.

*

Within a decade of his arrival in Madras, quite a transformation had taken place. A confident Ramnath had metamorphosed into a Householder, Nationalist, Legislator, Businessman, Landlord and Social Worker. Enter Mr Ramnath Goenka, Ramnathji to some or RNG in the third person. The change in status notwithstanding, the man remained an uncut diamond.

RNG was by now a committed Gandhian worker, active on many fronts. He wore khadi but does not appear to have taken to the Gandhi cap. He headed the local Pinjrapole Committee, was honorary secretary of the Sri Sanathana Dharma Vidyalaya Association and a founder member of the Sri Venkatesh

Ousdhalaya, an Ayurvedic dispensary, and later funded a home for orphaned and destitute children. He supported local charities and patronized many temples around Sowcarpet, though a devotee of the great Shaivite Kapaleeshwar temple in Mylapore. In a letter to Jamnalal Bajaj he noted that the khadi cloth store was doing well, with demand exceeding available supplies. He worked zealously to propagate Hindi and take it down to the grassroots. The Indore Congregation of the Hindi Prachar Sabha elected Gandhi as its chairman. The Mahatma extolled the efforts being made to spread Hindi as a national language and remarked that 'the true soldiers and leaders of this group are Ramnath Goenka, Jamnalal Bajaj, Rajagopalachari, Pattabhi Sitaramaiya and Harihar Sharma'.

Once when Gandhi had come to Madras, insistent crowds gathered for darshan. A tired Bapu had retired. It was left to RNG to find a solution. This he did by persuading Gandhi to stand at the doorway in front of which he spread a large white cloth on which he said each person should place a donation to the Congress, each according to his or her ability. The stratagem worked! Darshan was granted and a goodly collection obtained.

These were years when RNG was growing a family. Bhagwandas went to school but was tutored at home by a young graduate, C.P. Seshadri. 'Masterji', as he was universally known, was later to serve the *Express* for all his working life. He first came to the Sowcarpet residence in 1933 to be met by an RNG brushing his teeth with a neem twig. 'Baggie,' he called out, Seshadri remembers, and a roly-poly eight year old breathlessly responded with a 'Yes, Bauji.' Masterji described Moongibai as matronly, austere and pious and constantly subject to her son's childish pranks.

As Masterji described it, RNG was a busy man and spent little time at home. The mornings would be spent with dalals (brokers) come to discuss market trends, with Reuter's commercial service delivered to him by a Bombay Company cycle peon. He would then leave for office. The evening routine was an early supper followed by visits to business colleagues and a late-night return. He was a racing enthusiast until about the time he resigned from the Bombay Company.

His nationalist urges marked out RNG for politics, but it was by invitation rather than choice that he first entered the legislature. He must obviously have spoken earlier, but one of his first notable interventions came some time in 1928 when the Council debated the forthcoming visit of the Simon Commission that was to sound out Indian opinion and recommend reforms conducive to greater representative government. He rose to support an amendment favouring a more balanced commission 'not as a politician but as a businessman, and all the same as an Indian'. He noted that the timing and manner of the commission's appointment

> . . . has resulted in a wild storm of protest in India and the movement for the boycott of the Simon Commission has received the support of every political party worth the name . . .
>
> Sir . . . I would like to state honestly and candidly that we have not the slightest confidence in the Simon Commission. (Mr Satyamurthi: Hear, hear.) We do not believe that they possess any knowledge of India or Indian conditions or have any sympathy for Indian aspirations. Sir John Simon may be the greatest constitutional lawyer and an able advocate. But, in my opinion, to have too clever a lawyer is always a dangerous thing. (Laughter.)
>
> Mr President, as I said once and I repeat it once again, there are only two sections, one the non-official and the other the so-called depressed classes who are against the boycott of the Commission. As a businessman, Sir, I must say that the non-official Europeans are the best and the most honest business people. They are most straightforward and, in business, I should prefer Europeans to Indians. But . . . Sir, may I ask them one simple question? Have they ever stood up for the Indian people against the British Government?
>
> Mr S. Satyamurthi: Hear, hear. That is their honesty.
>
> Mr Ramnath Goenka: I was only referring to their business honesty.

> Mr S. Satyamurthi: Parliamentary honesty.
>
> Mr Ramnath Goenka: I cannot recall one single instance, Sir, in which they have supported us in our quarrels with the Government except in one or two commercial matters in which it touched their pockets. (Laughter and Swarajists: Hear, hear.)

RNG recalled how non-official Europeans had opposed further reforms in 1919 during the Secretary of State for India, Mr Montagu's visit to India, and made appeals through the Anglo-Indian press for his boycott. It was clear that the Europeans did not want Indians to get control of the government:

> Therefore nothing is surprising in the attitude taken by the non-official Europeans in India. I for one do not care what they say or do, because we can very well afford to ignore them. (Swarajists: Hear, hear.)

That was strong stuff, straight from the shoulder. It revealed a mature parliamentarian attuned to the parry and thrust of debate.

A more emotional moment was to come some months later, on 9 October 1928. The occasion was an adjournment motion on the seizure by the police of copies of *Songs of Bharathi*. Subramania Bharathi, acclaimed as the Tamil poet laureate, had tragically died seven years ago after being hit by the swinging trunk of a temple elephant at Triplicane in Madras. Between interludes as a journalist with *Swadesamitran*, where he translated news stories appearing in English dailies into Tamil, Bharathi wrote poems of patriotism, social reform and devotion with a rare passion that won him renown. He discarded classical Tamil for a simple style, intelligible to the common man, writing of India and its glorious future, once rid of foreign rule. Having visited Banaras and gained entrance to Allahabad university, he had experience of the country's enormous diversity yet saw it as a single, united entity, writing thus of Mother India:

She has thirty crores of faces,
But her heart is one;
She speaks eighteen languages,
Yet her mind is one.

This was a poet after RNG's own heart and the ban on Bharathi stirred him to the core. He confessed that he was but an 'occasional speaker' but this was a motion on which he could not remain silent:

> Mr President Sir, . . . I am not a Tamil scholar; I do not know even the A, B, C of the Tamil language. From what I have already heard of Bharathi's songs and from what hon. members have said on this occasion, I would say that the Tamilians of this Province have every right to sing these songs. As a member of the Committee of the Hindi Prachar Sabha, I want to say that these books were published by that Sabha at their own cost, and whose workers (sic) beg from door to door to educate the people of Madras in Hindustani. They stand to lose to the extent of not less than Rs 2000.
>
> Yesterday, the Government brought forward a motion for the sanction of a sum of Rs 4000 for a book regarding South Indian birds. This sum of Rs 4000 has in my opinion been thrown into the Bay of Bengal. It was the duty of the Government to publish the songs of Bharathi and broadcast them; it was for them to distribute free copies to illiterate masses to read them. My hon. friends on the opposite benches said yesterday that those books would be useful to the agriculturists. I cannot really understand what agriculturists have got to do with those books. If the agriculturists have got to do with any songs they are Bharathi's songs and Bharathi's songs alone.
>
> . . . On the one hand the hon. Education Minister [Mr P. Subbarayan] says that he wants these books to be taught in the schools of Madras; on the other hand, the hon. Law Minister [Diwan Bahadur Krishnan Nayar] says that he does not want these books and that they contain seditious matter . . . The feeling in this House and outside is unanimous that the action of the Government is wrong.

Tongue-in-cheek, RNG continued in a manner reminiscent of later times when every proscription and assault on the *Indian Express* group of newspapers enhanced its circulation and prestige:

> . . . Mr President, I am pleased to see that by this motion and by this confiscation, the prestige of Bharathi's songs has increased. People who have not yet bought a copy will buy one now to see what it contains, and even I, who do not know Tamil, will ask one of my friends to buy one for me to see what is in that book. Like that, there will be more people who will buy a copy each. Therefore I say, as a matter of fact the hon. the Law Member and the hon. the Home Member have done a great service to the country and to the Madras Presidency . . .

RNG was far-sighted in his vision of India and was quick to recognize the importance of professional education. On one occasion when Satyamurthi, who was piloting the Annamalai University Bill, objected to the establishment of a faculty of commerce, he was instantly on his feet:

> Commerce and Industry are the only two things on which India can prosper, and it is not in imparting mere academic education that the growth of India lies.
>
> If we go into the history of India, we will see that the British people who are now here, came in the first instance only as commercial people and not as a Government. If there is anything most needed in India at present it is, in my opinion, a sound education in commerce and industry. Hence, Sir, I support the motion of Mr Venkataraman Ayyangar and oppose the views expressed by Mr Satyamurthi with all the emphasis I can command.

Dismissing the plea that many graduates were unemployed, he retorted:

> As a matter of fact, it would have been appropriate for a businessman like Sir Annamalai Chettiyar to start a University where commercial and industrial subjects alone would be taught . . .

Legislative activity had its limitations and the freedom struggle appeared to jump from one non-cooperation movement to another. In between, the nationalist discourse was somewhat confined to the political salons of the day, with occasional forays into the countryside and workplace. There was clearly need to reach out more effectively and take the nationalist message to the masses. What better medium than the newspapers. The Anglo-Indian press had seen steady growth since Hickey's short-lived *Gazette* stirred and scandalized high society and those that walked the corridors of power in Calcutta towards the close of the eighteenth century. However, the vernacular and nationalist English papers gained readership despite the influence of the Anglo-Indian press. The *Hindu* was established in 1878 in support of the appointment of the first Indian Justice of the Madras High Court and remained in competition with the *Madras Mail* (incorporating the *Madras Times*), the voice of the establishment. Both were evening papers.

One of the five founders of the *Hindu* then launched the more radical *Indian Patriot* in 1905. This waned against competition from the better-produced *New India* of Annie Besant, which campaigned for Home Rule. *New India*, however, lost ground when it opposed non-cooperation as a method in 1921. The breach was filled by *Swarajya*, which had been started by T. Prakasan in 1922. The breakdown of the Gandhi–Irwin pact in 1932 and Gandhi's call for another round of civil disobedience marked fresh efforts to give impetus to the nationalist press. The *Mail* was on the other side, *Swarajya* was languishing, and some felt the *Hindu* was a trifle too staid.

It was in these circumstances that an Ayurvedic doctor and Congressman, Varadarajulu Naidu, decided to close his paper, *Tamil Nadu*, originally a vernacular weekly but a daily since 1927, and launch the *Indian Express* in 1932. He poached an editor from the *Hindu* and declared his paper's credo in the first editorial:

> Owing no allegiance to any political party in the country, it will stand staunchly for freedom in all national spheres of activity. Non-communal in outlook, it will advocate justice to all communities in political, social and economic life with a view to welding all of them into a great Indian Nation.

Surveying the political scene, it noted the failure of the Second Round Table Conference and said the rising tide of Indian nationalism

> . . . had forced the British rulers to abandon their traditional method of governance of this great Dependency . . . We cannot condone the British Government (sic) in replacing the rule of law by the rule of Ordinance, not unattended with violence which, to the bureaucratic mind is apt to look like reason in disguise. Personal liberty has been curtailed (with the launching of civil disobedience), public activities not to the liking of the Powers that be have been paralysed and the Press has been effectively muzzled. It is hard to believe that it is the object of the Government to wipe the Congress out of existence by mustering the leaders and their followers behind the bars of the prison door. The Government ought to have the wisdom to know that is as hard to kill a national institution as it is to kill a popular idea, and the Congress is unquestionably a national institution.

The editorial went on to criticize the Communal Award as

> an arrangement that tends to keep the country distracted in diversity and perpetuates the communal idea and communal bickering.

At this critical juncture in the nation's history, the *Indian Express* demanded discernible movement towards Dominion Status for India.

The first issue of the *Indian Express* was dated 5 September 1932. It had an ornate masthead with a crest resembling a heraldic coat of arms inscribed with a Tamil motto. The front page was completely devoted to seven display advertisements. Sunlight soap and Evan's Limes and Glycerine offered good grooming. Sanatogen and Nestle's Malted Milk promised to 'banish weakness' and promote 'glorious health'. The West End 'Dost' pocket watch was part of the necessary accoutrement of a gentleman. And the United India Life Assurance and Reliance Assurance Co. guaranteed 'complete and absolute safety of investments and efficient and sympathetic service' and 'maximum benefit for small payments'. What more could the reader desire!

The paper was priced at one anna and published from the 'Tamil Naidu' Press at 41, 42 Mukker Nallamuthu Chetty Street, G.T. (George Town), Madras. The editor, K. Santhanam, was a protégé of Rajagopalachari.

Running a daily newspaper was no easy business and Varadarajulu Naidu was soon in financial difficulties. Within weeks he was ready to sell. S. Sadanand who, full of zeal, had started the Free Press Service as a nationalist news agency, was at hand and took over the paper. In 1933, the *Express* opened an office in Madurai and launched its Tamil sister paper, *D(h)inamani*, a year later, with RNG's support. Sadanand too soon found it hard going. RNG bailed him out by buying Rs 30,000 worth of debentures. But continuing financial difficulties forced Sadanand to turn to K.M. Mathullah, head of the City Bank in Madras, for advice. Mathullah saw a business prospect and thought he might buy out Sadanand and run the paper under new auspices under Pothan Joseph, a relative by marriage, assisted by his two younger brothers. The proposition was put to Pothan's elder brother, George Joseph, a barrister and well-known nationalist figure and friend of Sadanand, who firmly discouraged a family adventure with somebody else's money.[1] A bid by the Travancore Quilon Bank people, who had an association with what is now the *Malayala Manorama* Group, also proved abortive.

*Dinamani* had meanwhile caught the eye of the government. An official File No. 88/16/35 records a note from the Home Member seeking a security of Rs 2000 from it. An attached telegram from the Government of Madras to the Director of Public Information, Simla, dated 24 July 1935 reads:

> [*Dinamani*] is a Tamil daily . . . [that] purports to help Tamils in the struggle for independence . . . Tone [is] distinctly nationalist. Habitually publishes articles on communism. Published on June 19 a mischievous and venomous article on Quetta earthquake that damage to great extent was caused by [ammunition] exploding. Circulation about 500. Editor and Publisher and Printer is S.V. Swamy, [a] Hindu Brahmin aged 28.

*Dinamani* had urged that the Quetta Fund, for which a public appeal had been issued, should be used exclusively for relief and not to reconstruct the cantonment, which had suffered considerable damage. Political workers had been barred entry into Quetta, arousing suspicions.

Swamy was later succeeded jointly by Chokalingam and the redoubtable A.N. Srinivasan, the latter remaining as editor of *Dinamani* until 1984, though he continued as a trusted adviser and friend of RNG even thereafter.

In 1935 the Free Press Service collapsed. Sadanand was desperate. On 1 October 1936, Publicity Madras Ltd was floated with RNG as managing director holding 51 per cent of the shares and Sadanand the balance. It is ironic that Rajagopalachari initially warned against putting money in an English-language newspaper for which he saw little future as the British would soon depart. Now it was he who urged RNG to rescue and build the *Express*. However, Sadanand decided to fight to retain control. Matters went to court. There was unpleasantness. Blows were exchanged between some of the partisans, and relations were strained. Nevertheless, a steady turnaround was discernible in the affairs of the *Express*.

Sadanand, a considerable nationalist newspaper figure in his own right and later to found the *Free Press Journal*, had introduced several innovations. He made the *Express* a morning paper, carried news on the front page under multiple column headlines in one or more decks and reduced the cover price.

With the change of guard, Santhanam quit, much to Rajagopalachari's chagrin, and Khasa Subba Rao took temporary charge. Pothan Joseph had by now made a name for himself through his 'Over a Cup of Tea' column in the *Bombay Chronicle*, but felt increasingly uncomfortable as editor of the *Hindustan Times*, which he now edited. Devadas Gandhi was the rising star. Joseph resigned in 1936 and toured a Europe darkening with the menace of rising Nazi and Fascist power. The New Year saw him back home. RNG had begun to see publishing as his mission and decided he had discovered the editor he was looking for—Pothan Joseph.

Sadanand by now had developed other ideas. RNG needed Rs 25,000 to buy him out outright but was strapped for cash. Hence an urgent and revealing letter in May 1938 to Jamnalal Bajaj whom, he said, he regarded as a father like Rajagopalachari. After laying out his financial transactions, assets and liabilities in a concise statement that established his positive net worth, he said:

> My serious problem is that I cannot pay Rs 25,000 [at very short notice]. If I do not take it [*Express* and *Dinamani*], the only Congress Party paper will pass into the hands of the Justice party. They are willing to buy and Sadanand is not concerned. You must know how well these newspapers have served the Congress this past year. I do not want these papers to pass out of my hands now.

He believed that his own future was now bound with that of these newspapers. He was still working for the Bombay Company and earning about Rs 20,000 per annum in salary and bonus. But this job did not hold any interest for him and he intended to resign and set up a factory to make brass and copper utensils in which he saw good money. (He had sold a plantation company and still owned General Swadeshi Ltd, trading in handloom textiles.) However, the pressing problem was to get the money needed to buy Sadanand's stake in the *Express*. The letter continued:

> The ideas expressed above are a plan for a new chapter in my life. But nothing can be done without money and, come what may, I will not take a loan in Madras. Could you please yourself lend or introduce me to some friend. I am not asking for favours, only a business arrangement . . .

Jamnalal helped RNG, though it is not known in what manner. RNG later wrote and thanked him, stating 'this is the first time in my life when someone spoke to me frankly about my mistakes' committed in moments of 'excitement'. Jamnalal also told him that Rajagopalachari, then Premier of Madras, was unhappy with him. RNG replied that he had written a letter of apology to Rajagopalachari, which he enclosed, and told Jamnalal that misunderstandings had arisen between them over Santhanam's departure from the *Express*. More recently, Rajagopalachari had been stung by the *Express*'s criticism of his government, probably caused by tales carried to him by K. Srinivasan, editor of the *Hindu*, which 'does not want any nationalist paper, other than itself, in Madras'. Nevertheless, RNG assured Jamnalal that he had 'always put the interest of the nation over my own selfish interest'.

Writing to Rajagopalachari, RNG assured him of the most loyal support. In an interesting explanatory note he said:

> For the policy of either the 'Indian Express' or 'Dinamani', I am not personally responsible. Inevitably, these papers have to be run by persons over whom I have no strict control. Further, we always felt that you would welcome frank criticism by your admirers. Now I see we had not quite understood your mind.

RNG explained that Khasa, joint editor of the *Express*, honestly felt the present policy of the paper was in the best interest of the country and Congress. But, henceforth, Joseph and he would abide by Rajagopalachari's instructions if they knew his mind. However, Pothan and Khasa proved 'adamant' and Rajagopalachari was reported to be threatening action against the *Express*. If this is true, RNG told Jamnalal in another letter, 'we will fight [Rajagopalachari and his ministers] to the bitter end, because we believe that truth and justice are on our side'.

RNG would not normally permit anybody to browbeat his editors into following a particular line and would often palm off criticism of what appeared in his papers by protesting that his editors were a law unto themselves! Yet he was sufficiently close to Rajagopalachari at various times to seek to soothe his ruffled feathers. The *Express* had criticized his introduction of Hindi in classes six to eight while he was Premier of Madras in 1937, more so the government's use of the repugnant Criminal Laws Amendment Act to deal with Ramaswami Naicker and others agitating against this policy. This irked Rajagopalachari who chided Goenka. RNG was prepared to be rebuked up to a point, but then decided that enough was enough. He was not going to be pushed around.

The Lion wore khadi. But it could roar. In any event, a crisis was averted.

Goenka imparted drive to *Dinamani* as well as to the *Andhra Prabha* (1938) and, subsequently, *Kannada Prabha* (1967). He was to own a chain of newspapers read throughout Madras Presidency and the princely states of Travancore, Cochin and Mysore, encompassing all of South India.

*

When Pothan Joseph joined the *Express*, its circulation was no more than 2000. The new editor resumed his chatty and irreverent 'Over a Cup of Tea', hired Vasu as a political cartoonist and generally enlivened the paper. His wide contacts, independent stance, style and bonhomie left an imprint on the paper. RNG trusted his credentials and left him to hew his own path. Keeping the *Express* going was a daunting task for a nationalist paper that was starved of the kind of advertising support that the Anglo-Indian press enjoyed. Salaries were low and RNG on occasion was reduced to selling unsold copies as waste paper to augment the kitty. Srinivasa Iyengar, the distinguished corporate lawyer, was a pillar of moral and financial support. As a morning paper the *Express* scored over the *Hindu* and the *Mail*. Starting van editions also enabled RNG to reach mofussil (district) readers ahead of the rival papers that took the overnight train.

On one occasion, Joseph asked Khasa to write an editorial criticizing the Madras High Court's tendency to reverse acquittal orders by lower courts in murder cases. On reading the edit, RNG declared it would evoke contempt proceedings. Joseph argued that a charge of contempt would enhance the prestige of the paper and accordingly ran the piece. True enough, the *Express* was hauled up for contempt. Srinivasa Iyengar advised printing an apology to save the paper from further trouble. This was done but it had in addition to pay a fine of Rs 250. This was one of the rare occasions that the *Express* ever backed down in the face of contempt or privilege proceedings.

Campaigns were launched by the *Express* against the Travancore and Mysore durbars for their negative attitude towards local nationalist elements. The paper was banned for a while in both princely states. The Travancore ban was, curiously, levied under the provisions of the Sea Customs Act. The *Express* saw a loophole here and ingeniously moved its distribution centre to the then Madras and Southern Maratha Railway's Trivandrum railway station as that was nominally designated as part of British India! Sales were brisk.

The *Express* was the first paper in Madras to announce the outbreak of the Second World War. This it did in a special supplement on 1 September 1939, copies of which were rushed to the Beach where Subhas Chandra Bose was addressing a meeting. A copy was passed up to the rostrum. Bose read out the dispatch and then remarked that if the Congress had accepted his suggestion made earlier that year to issue a six-month ultimatum to Britain to quit, India would have been free that day.

The war aroused tremendous reader interest coupled with nationalist fervour with regard to Britain's war aims for India. Events were to follow in rapid succession. However on 9 February 1940, the *Express* office at Mukker Nallamuthu Street was partially gutted. R.A. Padmanabhan reconstructed the events later from a report in the *Hindu*.[2] The fire broke out in the premises of the *Express*, *Dinamani* and *Andhra Prabha* around 7.15 p.m. Four fire engines fought the blaze for an hour. By then it had consumed 'stores, including newsprint stocked in a large godown. The building itself suffered damage, but the fire was controlled fortunately before it spread to other portions where the machinery stood'. The fire was noticed by a passer-by, who sounded the alarm. A number of press workers who were meeting on the top floor of the building were able to rush out to safety. RNG, Joseph and Sivaraman reached the scene to see the building smouldering.

The Governor and others conveyed their sympathies and hoped that the paper would rise again 'like the Phoenix'. It did. K.R. Srinivasan, the *Hindu* editor, generously got the *Express* printed at the *Swadesamitran* press and thereafter invited the paper to take over its recently vacated premises and rotary press at 100 Mount Road. It had itself moved the previous year to a spanking new building at 2 Mount Road, where it is located to this day, and had installed new printing machinery. The transaction suited both sides and spoke of the cordial relationship that now prevailed between the two rivals.

The fire thus turned out to be a boon for the *Express*. It gained a fine building and a duplex rotary with a capacity of twenty-four pages and 30,000 copies an hour, in place of its old-fashioned flatbed press. This ensured a better deadline and a product of distinctly superior quality. Furthermore, the *Express* collected insurance. Uncharitable critics hinted that the fire was an inside job cleverly staged by RNG to overcome certain financial embarrassments. The fact is that none complained.

On 21 February, the *Express* appeared from its new premises, carrying a large notice announcing its new address and generous thanks to the *Hindu*. It also ran a special Aurobindo Supplement that had been prepared in the midst of the shifting, with RNG dragging a bemused Joseph to Pondicherry for darshan of Sri Aurobindo and the Mother.

Joseph had found a delectable topic for more than one 'Over a Cup of Tea' column. He wrote of fires through history—the burning of the Library of Alexandria, the Great Fire of London and the Reichstag fire. He told his readers that 'Earth, Fire, Air and Water comprised the early elements of Science. Whisky came much later from Scotland!'

Once ensconced at the new address at 100 Mount Road, Joseph reported that the *Express*, *Dinamani* and *Andhra Prabha*, 'the Three Musketeers' were all in fine trim 'despite the Ordeal by Fire, which they had survived in chaste vindication of their Right to Live'. It was pure whimsy.

> We apologise for our presumption in the past of dreaming that Mukker Nallamuthu is the Fleet Street of Madras. Under the admonition of Fire, we change our opinion and regard Mount Road as the demesne of distinction. A quarter of a century ago, 'The Mail' had been housed in the Port Trust area of George Town. 'The Madras Standard' used to be in Broadway, 'The Madras Times' in Mount Road with Mr Glyn Barlow, former Principal of Pachaiyappa's College functioning as its genial editor. 'Justice' came as an event of Mount Road vagrancy. But in George Town Mrs Besant had her 'New India' and Mr Prakasam his indomitable 'Swarajya'. 'The Indian Patriot' was a George Town phenomenon and it is in George Town that Mr G.A. Natesan showed that journalism in India need not be a Beggar's Opera. The tide of prosperity was, however, in the direction of Mount Road. They are all gone, the old, old familiar faces.

Tongue-in-cheek, Joseph described 100 Mount Road 'where "The Hindu" won its pre-eminence in the country as the Fatehpur Sikri of Indian journalism. The Tower of Victory—that is where we are.'

Under Pothan Joseph, the circulation of the *Express* soared to 20,000. Joseph demanded higher salaries for the staff, to little avail. His battle with Sir C.P. Ramaswamy Aiyar was undermined by the latter's offer to the *Express* to print a Travancore supplement. RNG, however, needed both circulation and revenue. Joseph demanded a doubling of his salary to Rs 1000 a month (his predecessor had got Rs 150) as the circulation of the paper had doubled during his tenure. He had long railed against what he considered the exploitation of working journalists by newspaper managements, and concluded his epistle with the line that he would quit if he did not receive satisfaction. Goenka replied that he could quit if he wished. The *Express* was by now well established and Khasa Subba Rao could take over as editor.

The parting of the ways had come. Joseph quit in January 1941, perhaps the first of a procession of Goenka's editors to do so. He went on to edit Jinnah's *Dawn* after a wayside halt with the Muslim League's *Star of India* in Calcutta. Khasa Subba Rao took charge of the *Express*. For Goenka, the newspapers truly became his business. Independence could not be far away and stirring times lay ahead.

# 2

# Getting Rooted in Madras

With the assumption of office by popular ministries under the 1935 Act, the government felt the need to keep close watch over the media. The home ministry had on its files a note on 'Tendencies in the Indian Press since the introduction of provincial autonomy' by J. Natarajan, deputy principal information officer, dated 8 October 1938. It read:

> There has been a distinct change in the attitude of newspapers in India in regard both to their sphere of interest and criticism. It was inevitable that, with the setting up of autonomous governments in the provinces, newspapers should devote greater attention to provincial problems. But it was not anticipated that newspapers generally regarded as 'pro-Congress' would take an independent attitude and criticise the popular provincial governments no less vehemently than they did the previous diarchic regime.
>
> Indian Nationalist Press: Well established papers in this class have been strongly critical of Congress governments' resort to 'repressive' measures—the enforcement of the Criminal Laws Amendment Act in Madras, and demanding of securities from newspapers in Bombay and in the CP.
>
> Congress Reaction: That Congress ministries and party leaders generally feel the effects of this criticism and need for

> a party press is evident from the fact that, within the last three months, two new papers have been started, namely, the National Herald from Lucknow and the Indian Express from Madras.
>
> The Indian Express . . . is well-controlled by the Madras premier, Mr C. Rajagopalachariar (sic), who has given short shrift to Congress socialists and anti-Hindustani agitators and has been described by them as a Nazi in his methods.

The *Express* began to consolidate its position after the move to Mount Road, with *Dinamani* bringing in the money. The 1939 Tripuri Congress rocked the Congress, with Subhas Bose's election as Congress president being virtually vetoed by Gandhi. The *Express* was strongly critical of the All-India Congress Committee (AICC) for the charade of electing nominal leaders by rotation on regional and community considerations when it would be more sensible and honest to make the Mahatma's de facto position de jure.

The Second World War intervened and brought with it stringent regulations under the Defence of India Ordinance. There was a good deal of interest in war news and the *Express* scored by subscribing to the Free Press Service whose sympathetic London correspondent, Margarita Barns, picked up news of Indian interest that Reuters ignored. But the curbs on the press were irksome. The Indian and Eastern Newspaper Society (IENS) had been started in 1937 to serve the business interests of the press. Now, with the invocation of regulations, the IENS resolved in November 1940 that there should be an advisory committee to assist the official chief press adviser. Thus the All-India Newspaper Editors' Conference (AINEC) came into being. The *Express* was represented in both the IENS and the AINEC, and no sooner had the latter been constituted than a controversy ensued regarding the 'assurances' allegedly given to the authorities on behalf of the press. The restrictions hurt and matters soon came to a head.

Meanwhile, the war was going badly for the Allies, particularly in the Eastern theatre. The sighting of a powerful

Japanese armada with several aircraft carriers off Port Blair and the bombing of Colombo proved disquieting. Blackouts and air raid drills were ordered in Madras. The 6 April 1942 issue of the *Express* reported the bombing of Vizagapatnam harbour and Cocanada (Kakinada). A nervous Presidency administration first warned of increased risk to Madras and then issued a communiqué on 11 April advising 'all those whose presence in the city is not essential, to leave within the next few days'. This was a signal for a general exodus, which gained momentum with the government evacuating its own departments to inland districts. The secretariat moved to Ooty, Madanpalle and Chittoor, the high court to Coimbatore and the M&SM Railway Headquarters to Hubli, Bellary and Guntakal! Banks and prominent business establishments scattered.

The *Express* criticized these hasty moves and forecast a breakdown in essential services that could render Madras something of a 'no-man's land'. It estimated that almost three-quarters of the city's inhabitants emptied out during that Frightened Fortnight. Nehru and Rajagopalachari appealed for calm and deprecated talk of an imminent invasion. The evacuation order was officially reversed on 25 April. However, in compliance with earlier instructions that dangerous animals be shot, the Madras zoo sadly lost its tigers, lions, panthers, bears and reptiles; only 'inoffensive' animals like elephants, giraffes and ostriches were spared. The *Express* reported on 26 April the city's cats were looking lean, while

> it almost seems that the city's dogs have evacuated to other places where they can get more food and there is happily a diminution in the number of bandicoots on the prowl in the streets during the nights. The crow population, however, is facing famine.

Alarums and excursions notwithstanding, the famous Coimbatore Krishna Iyer Hotel in Triplicane could boast, like London's naughty Windmill Theatre, 'We never closed'. Cinemas too had remained open. But for the faint-hearted, normalcy was truly restored on 28 April 1942 when the *Express* ran an advertisement promising 'Cheerful breakfast in the morning; Luxurious lunch in the afternoon. Nothing like Arya Bhavan'. That was reassuring.

However, more eventful days were ahead. The failure of the Cripps Mission in April 1942 led the Muslim League to demand separation from a united India. Rajagopalachari, a Congress Working Committee member, dropped a bombshell by proposing this demand be nominally conceded and a national government be formed by the Congress and League in order to stave off partition of the country. There was consternation in the nationalist ranks.

The *Express* trenchantly opposed this thesis in an editorial entitled 'Panicky Resolution' and subsequently attacked an adamant Rajagopalachari's explanations as 'politically unsound' and 'disastrous'. It said this 'Samson without his locks' was 'no longer competent to direct the Congress Legislature Party in Madras' and suggested forfeiture of his party membership. Gandhi anguished for some time and then proposed a 'drastic remedy': Britain must Quit India. The die was cast.

On 9 August 1942, Gandhi, Azad, Nehru, Patel and other leading Congress members were arrested. The government had decided to meet the challenge head on. There was a clampdown on the Press. The *Express* editorially recalled Gandhi's words at a recent AICC meeting that 'the Press should discharge its duties freely and fearlessly. Let it not allow itself to be cowed down or bribed by the Government'. It spelt out 'The Issues' and the 'Duty of the Press' on successive days. It mocked the AINEC for its pusillanimity in being 'willing to wound but afraid to strike'. It said the nationalist press could not be an official trumpet and it was incumbent on the AINEC president, its erstwhile benefactor, K. Srinivasan of the *Hindu*, to convene a meeting of editors and give a fitting reply to this attack on the Press.

On 15 August 1942 the *National Herald* suspended

publication. Within days the *Express* and, later, others, followed suit. An *Express* editorial captioned 'We Shall Wait for the Dawn' gave notice of closure from 19 August which day's issue carried one of the most powerful *Express* editorials of all time, entitled 'Heart-Strings and Purse-Strings'.

> . . . We do not want to detail to the public the gagging orders that we have received. Suffice it to say that we cannot publish news relating to our leaders, to the Congress movement, or relating to anything for that matter—indeed, not even facts which vitally affect the community—unless it is contained in a Government communiqué or in a report from a registered correspondent blessed by the District Magistrate. It would be nothing less than a fraud on the public for us to send out a paper containing just that and nothing more.
>
> Personal interest and the motives of gain, which, according to British economists, are the only things that influence the ordinary human being, dictate to us that we should carry on this paper under the only conditions under which we can carry it on, that is, obeying all the restrictive orders. But political economy fails in the face of impressions and events which we cannot forget if we are to live a thousand years. We cannot believe that the same desire for freedom does not exist in the minds of our people as we are told it does in the minds of the Icelanders and Laplanders. The human race is said to be fighting for its freedom; what avails it to us unless it includes the freedom of our country? Personal loss and inconvenience to us or to the public of the Presidency cannot count for anything in this crisis. The hard fact of the situation is that if we went on publishing, the *Indian Express* may be called a paper, but cannot be a newspaper.
>
> We have never pretended we are blessed with more wisdom than others . . . We too have seen the sun rise. We have no regret in suspending publication, because we firmly believe that the children of India will hear the voice of the Mother, telegraph or no telegraph, newspaper or no newspaper. Gandhiji has given his message to the people and it does not require further publication. His message lives and will regenerate itself in the hearts of every Indian . . .

The message was unequivocal and deeply moving. The only solution the *Express* saw was for the government to release the Mahatma and concede the national demand.

Soon thereafter, RNG presided over a 'Suspended Newspaper Editors' Conference' in Bombay. Some fifty nationalist editors attended. The *Express* remained suspended for three months and carried blank editorials over several days. An open split within the AINEC was only averted because the body was compelled to take a more forceful stand against continuing press restrictions. The AINEC in fact called for a national newspaper hartal on 6 January 1943 in protest against a blatant pre-censorship order in a bid to hide the disgraceful Chirmur and Ashti massacres in the Central Provinces. The nationalist papers shut down countrywide. It was an impressive demonstration.

Many nationalist figures had gone underground to escape the police dragnet, notable among them members of the youthful Congress Socialist group. Jayaprakash Narayan came to Madras after escaping from Hazaribagh jail. The authorities got scent of his movements and a friendly police contact told RNG he 'smelt' something and would like to search his house and when would it be convenient to do so? RNG invited him over at 5 p.m., but had JP booked to travel by train with a Tamil lady as man and wife, and had him immediately put on a train to Bombay from an adjacent station. RNG played a dual role, publishing his newspapers even as he churned out subversive literature and supplied arms, safe haven and a contact point for the Congress underground.

At least five staff members of the *Express* Group in Madras actively participated in the nationalist movement. Chokalingam, editor of *Dinamani*, performed individual satyagraha and was imprisoned for some time in 1941. Sivaraman, assistant editor, went underground the following year to report on the nature and intensity of public sentiments. Other staff members were leading accused in the Sirkali bomb conspiracy case. The *Express* had become a nursery for revolutionaries.

Narrating his past in the affidavit he filed before the post-Emergency Shah Commission in 1977, RNG was to say:

> In 1942, I was put in charge of the 'Quit India' movement in South India and . . . came into contact with all the leaders who were underground. Most . . . including Jayaprakash Narayan, were under my shelter.
>
> In accordance with the wishes of Mr Phillips, the then Personal Representative of President Roosevelt, I surreptitiously edited and published a book called 'India Ravaged' giving details of all the atrocities committed by the British Government in the 1942 movement. This book was banned by the Government but was in great demand as an underground document . . . I was also an author of a proscribed book captioned 'Quit India' which created a sensation all over the world.

Devadas Gandhi, Sucheta Kripalani and others had helped collect material for *India Ravaged*, which RNG got printed almost overnight. It purported to give an account of 'atrocities committed under British aegis over the whole sub-continent of India in the latter part of 1942'. It estimated 25,000 persons were killed, though the official figure placed the number at 2000. Dedicated as 'a Trust to You, Dear Reader', it said:

> Please realise that this book will be no suitable ornament at present for mahogany drawing room tables or ivory bookshelves—no doubt its rightful place. The despoilers and oppressors of India want to hunt it out of view. They cannot stand its fierce light. Whether, therefore, you are an Indian or a Foreigner temporarily in India, we entrust this and subsequent volumes to you for safe custody, by all the ingenious means one employs to save a treasure from theft or robbery, and for as many people to read as you can personally arrange.

The preface made three apologies. The narrative was incomplete; it was unauthorized; and it was 'not of de luxe standard' as it was 'printed in a roving press under impossible conditions which cannot be disclosed lest . . .'

*India Ravaged* narrated stories of severe repression in Chirmur and Ashti in the Central Provinces, hitherto suppressed, and of the terrible sufferings experienced in the wake of the great Midnapore cyclone, where police action precluded proper relief operations. Shyama Prasad Mookerjee, then a Bengal minister, resigned in protest. His resignation letter and speeches delivered by K.C. Neogy, N.M. Joshi, the labour leader, and others in the Central Assembly were censored but published in the volume.

Aruna Asaf Ali, Achyut Patwardhan and R.R. Diwakar were among the leading nationalists whom RNG shepherded from one safe house to another. If K. Kamaraj sent anybody to him, he would put him in funds or buy him a railway ticket to a safe destination.

C. Subramaniam recalls directing the Coimbatore district Congress underground cadres in 1942, many of them textile workers, who were actively engaged in sabotage. A train was derailed and a military airfield attacked. The saboteurs then had to be secreted away in their villages and kept in funds. Knowing of RNG's association with the movement in Madras, Subramaniam went to seek his assistance at the *Express* office in Mount Road. There, to his astonishment, he was led to some basement cupboards stacked with proscribed literature, crude bombs, explosives, fuses and other incendiary wherewithal.[1]

Earlier, before Quit India, Sardar Patel had taunted RNG for his failure to make Madras too hot for the British. How should he do that, RNG inquired? By poisoning wells, the Sardar replied. Shocked by this advocacy of violence, RNG asked whether the Sardar had Gandhi's clearance. Not satisfied with his affirmation, a troubled RNG thought he should check this directly with the Mahatma. So he travelled to Wardha and posed the problem to Bapu, who replied enigmatically, 'If you believe in non-violence you would not have come to me.' Interpreting the statement as a go-head signal, RNG returned home. During the ensuing 1942 movement, RNG supplied the necessary chemicals to Aruna Asaf Ali and others to poison some water sources. The amateur conspirators mixed the deadly ingredients with poultry feed and gave it to some unsuspecting chicken to test its efficacy only to discover, somewhat sheepishly, that the birds enjoyed the repast!

Gandhi was later to say that the violence that accompanied the Quit India movement was wrong. RNG confronted the Sardar with this reprimand and charged him with practising a cruel deception. Years later, Arun Shourie recounted RNG retailing the Sardar's retort: 'Ramnath, don't you think a general has the right to sacrifice his men for the cause?' The moral he drew was that Publisher-General Ramnath Goenka reserved to himself a similar right.

Despite their occasional differences, Rajagopalachari showed marked affection and respect for RNG. Asked about this, Rajaji is said to have replied that few knew the extent of RNG's services to the country. During the difficult days of the Quit India movement, thousands of ordinary Congressmen went to jail, leaving their families in dire need. Moved by their plight, Rajagopalachari summoned RNG and told him he must do something to relieve their distress. RNG did so. He collected funds and sent regular money orders or delivered donations to a large number of workers throughout the Presidency. This kept the wolf from the door of impoverished families, lists of whom would be sent to him with addresses. It took courage, compassion and patriotism to shoulder a task that could so easily invite trouble. Rajaji was to say it saved both Congressmen and the Congress.

*

There were pressures on the *Express*. By 1941, Joseph had left and, though Khasa remained, RNG himself took a hand in editorial work. On 15 August 1942, RNG, managing editor of the *Express*, and C. Cunchitapatham, manager, were fined

Rs 100 on a charge of publishing an allegedly obscene advertisement that others had also carried without attracting similar attention. The prosecution was launched on the basis of undisclosed 'correspondence from the Government'. The defence counsel pleaded that the fine be raised to Rs 201 so that an appeal might be filed. This was refused. The *Express* wrote a critical editorial and was almost had up for contempt. But a warning shot had been fired.

RNG was pushing his luck. Two years later, in 1944, the *Express* carried a news item to which the British police commissioner issued a correction. It was not published. On the third day, the apprentice sub-editor on duty, K.R. Sundar Rajan, kept receiving calls from this officer later and later into the night for confirmation that the correction was being published. Sundar Rajan was evasive but finally decided that he must consult RNG as the chief sub-editor was taking a break. So he called him at 1.30 a.m. and told him the problem. RNG's response was that 'if the man calls again, just tell him to shut up'. When he did call again, Sundar Rajan said that Mr Goenka had not replied to his query and hung up. Nothing further was heard.

On another occasion, a protest speech in the Bengal legislature against a government ordinance was locally censored. None dared publish it. RNG showed the news item to A.N. Sivaraman, his friend and confidant in *Dinamani*, who counselled caution. RNG's reaction was to publish it in the dak edition where it would not be noticed until too late. The press could have been sealed under wartime regulations. Fortunately all was well.

Earlier, profits had come from *Dinamani* and *Andhra Prabha*, where Narla Venkata Rao was to take managerial and then editorial command in slow stages. By 1944 the *Express* started making modest profits. Circulation was up. The paper was dynamic, in the forefront of the freedom movement in the South and particularly appealing to young people. But internal differences had arisen. H.Y. Sharada Prasad had recently joined the *Express* and was later to recall the day in 1945 when RNG and Khasa summoned the entire editorial staff to a meeting to discuss the issues involved. 'At one point, Goenka raised his voice and Khasa coolly got up and walked out saying, "Goodbye, gentlemen."' Years later, RNG was to visit Khasa when he was admitted to the Madras General Hospital with a stroke. Sharada Prasad happened to be present and reports RNG greeting Khasa breezily with a 'There can be only one Khasa and no second. And there can be only one Goenka and no second!'

The Gandhian G. Ramachandran was appointed editor for a while but RNG remained editorially active. Anandilal Goenka, an old family friend, visited Madras and stayed with him around that time. A very early riser, he saw RNG at work with sheets of paper strewn on the floor. When he asked if RNG had been up the whole night, the latter replied: 'Anandilalji, I get up at three o'clock. To run this paper I have to write too. I write one draft. If I don't like it, I tear it up and throw it away. I write one thing ten times before I feel I have expressed my thoughts well.' He would send off the article in time for the morning edition. Thereafter he would take a bath, breakfast on idli-dosa and rush to the office, returning for a quick lunch, then reappearing only late in the evening after meeting his contacts, finally to retire at 11 p.m.

With the approach of Independence, European interests began to hedge their bets in India. RNG had a nose for property and early in 1946 clinched a deal to purchase the magnificent premises of the Madras Club off Mount Road, including the Club House and Hick's Bungalow, set in 23 acres of land, for Rs 14.85 lakh. He got it for a song. The necessary loans were arranged to make this bargain purchase. Immediately thereafter a Rs 10 lakh scheme was planned to develop the property as a residential, commercial and press complex. Unfortunately, this was stalled as the government launched acquisition proceedings in October 1947 to take over part of the estate. Ultimately the *Express* did construct some buildings and renovated certain existing structures at a cost of a little over Rs 20 lakh. Some of the new premises were let out to corporate houses and the Andhra government for an annual rental of Rs 1.09 lakh.

The *Express* moved into Express Estates (as it came to be known) in 1949. Years later the government made another bid to acquire part of the property under the Urban Ceiling Act, 1978. The *Express*, however, pleaded that after allowing for appurtenant lands, peripheral areas, mandated setbacks, bonus lands for expansion, pavement areas, etc., there was actually no ceiling surplus land. Finally, exemption was granted on grounds of expanding press requirements. The Urban Ceiling Act was annulled some time later. A similar assault on the Express properties in Bangalore was repelled on the plea that an adjacent police station had infringed the newspaper's expansion rights which would have precluded any 'surplus' land, and that the beautiful Express guest house grounds had become a conservation area for several 100-year-old trees. RNG had an argument for every occasion and was fiercely protective of his expanding properties!

The well-known architect Charles Correa was later invited to prepare a blueprint for developing Express Estates. He did work on it but no progress could be made thereafter on account of urban land ceiling problems. Long after RNG's death, the main Madras Club Building, which should have qualified as a heritage structure, was, alas, torn down.

*

Kamaraj, a rising Congress star in the Madras firmament, owed much to RNG, who cultivated him and introduced him to the elites of Mylapore and kept him in funds. RNG was induced by the Marwari community to stand for the Madras Corporation from Sowcarpet against Balasundaram, a Scheduled Caste candidate, in 1938, but there is no evidence that he actually contested the poll. However, Kamaraj used his influence to get RNG nominated to the Constituent Assembly in 1946, where he supported an amendment placing 'taxes on sale or purchase of newspapers and on advertisements published therein' in the Union List. This was adopted and incorporated as Entry 92 in the Seventh Schedule. He had formally graduated to national politics. His signature is recorded on the last page of the ornate, 'illuminated' copy of the Constitution of India that was signed by all Members on 26 November 1949, along with those of Feroze Gandhi, Harekrushna Mahtab, Jerome D'Souza s.j, and Sunder Lall. The cover bore the new national emblem, the Lion Capitol from Sarnath with the Dharma Chakra embossed at its base. Below that was the national motto, 'Satyameve Jayate', Let Truth Prevail, a maxim that RNG adopted for the *Express*.

Though the transfer of power ending colonial rule was a remarkably orderly affair, there were some strains and tensions. In 1946 an incident occurred in Madras, in which RNG was called upon to intervene. The car of a British High Court judge, Byers, was pelted with stones by some agitators while driving down the street. Unnerved, the judge pulled out a firearm and fired in the direction of a youth. This caused a commotion and some persons approached RNG to take up the matter. He did so by writing a confidential letter to the Chief Secretary, Ramunni Menon, suggesting that 'in the present atmosphere the Hon. Mr Justice Byers should not be entrusted with judicial work'. The advice was apparently heeded and Byers soon retired and sailed for England. Goenka had thought it best to avoid undue publicity and have the matter disposed of quietly.

Independence dawned on 15 August 1947. The *Express* editorial said the historic day 'marks the close of an old era and the beginning of a new age. For Asia, it gives a new leader, a new outlook. For the world, it gives a new idea and a new method.' After paying tribute to the Father of the Nation, it called for unity, peace and service . . . 'Every Indian must live for India just as India must live for all. To adapt great words for a great occasion, India expects every man to do his duty.' A special *Express* supplement carried Nehru's message, 'A New Star Rises in the East', echoing the moving 'Tryst with Destiny' oration that he delivered as prime minister in the new Parliament of India the previous night at the stroke of the midnight hour.

Madras rejoiced, as did all of India. RNG himself led a procession through George Town organized by the Madras Jewellers and Diamond Merchants Association, which culminated in a huge rally. T. Prakasam hoisted the national flag and RNG addressed the assembled gathering. The *Express* reported the event on 17 August under a two-deck caption, 'Vindication of Trust and Non-Violence; Mr Goenka on Significance of Independence Day'. This was perhaps the first and last time that RNG allowed his newspapers to treat any of his activities as news (or carry his photograph) except in respect of parliamentary proceedings or if he was acting in a representative capacity. That was to be a strict code. Otherwise, when RNG spoke, it was through editorials, signed articles and statements, though he would give interviews to other journals.

A couple of days later, RNG visited Delhi and was persuaded by his ICS friends to celebrate the end of the Raj. 'For the first and last time,' he confessed, 'I had drinks with them at India Gate.' This, however, was not the least or the last of his 'sins'.

India was to become a Republic on 26 January 1950. The question arose as to who should become the country's first President. Rajagopalachari, as the first Indian Governor General, was a logical choice and favoured by Nehru. Others saw Rajendra Prasad, who had presided over the Constituent Assembly, as the appropriate candidate. Nehru was troubled and wrote to Patel on 15 September 1949:

> I am told that active and vigorous canvassing has taken place on this subject and there is a large majority who favour Rajendra Babu. The Biharis, of course, are in it, the Andhras, and a good number of the Tamils. Then generally the protagonists of Hindi favour Rajendra Babu. I was a little surprised to learn that Shyama Prasad Mookerjee also favours him.
>
> This is not merely a question of favouring Rajendra Babu, but rather of deliberately keeping Rajaji out. One of the most active agents in this business is Goenka.[2]

RNG thought Rajendra Prasad was more of a mass leader and Rajagopalachari had rocked the boat in 1942. In the event, Prasad was elected.

Rajagopalachari was given a grand send off to Madras but scarcely had he settled down when Nehru summoned him back. Elections for the Congress Presidency were due and the conservative Purushottam Das Tandon appeared to have an edge over others. Nehru asked if Rajagopalachari would care to step into the ring, but on his declining J.B. Kripalani was fielded—only to lose. Soon after, the Sardar passed away and, at Nehru's insistence, Rajagopalachari returned to replace Patel as home minister.[3]

It was in this capacity that it fell to the home minister to pilot the Constitution (First Amendment) Bill, 1951, qualifying rights to free speech and property. Article 19(1)(a) guaranteeing freedom of speech and expression was made subject to 'reasonable restrictions' on grounds listed in Article 19(2). This followed the ban on *Crossroads*, the Communist weekly edited by Romesh Thapar in Bombay, within the territories of the Madras Presidency.

RNG was up in arms. He thundered against the Bill and brought out a tract entitled 'Freedom Fettered' under his own name, 'Ramnath Goenka, M.P.', which was widely distributed. The preface said:

> Freedom of the Press in India has been fettered. Eighteen months after adoption of the Constitution guaranteeing to all

> Citizens of the Republic liberty of thought and expression, that vital right has been taken away.
>
> . . . Pandit Nehru himself addressing the AINEC in December 1950 said, 'I would rather have a completely free Press with all the dangers involved in the wrong use of that freedom than a suppressed and regulated Press'. But on May 12, 1951, Pandit Nehru's Government introduced in Parliament an amendment to the Constitution empowering the imposition of 'reasonable restrictions' on freedom of speech and expression 'in the interests of security of the State, friendly relations with foreign states, public order . . .' Protests were of no avail. The Bill was rushed through Parliament and passed within three weeks.
>
> . . . The Press in India is now virtually free to publish only what the party in power wishes to be published.

Thirty pages of close analysis followed and each phrase like 'public order' and 'security' was minutely examined. Indian Press opinion was cited to indicate widespread opposition to the measure as well as the London *Daily Express*'s gleeful comment that 'One by one, Nehru is losing his Western pen-pals'.

RNG's criticism was, in a real sense, mistaken. The amendment liberated the Press from arbitrary restraints. The insertion of the qualification 'reasonable restrictions' in Article 19(2) implied a bar on unreasonableness and made any restriction justiciable.

Given constitutional powers under the First Amendment, the government went on to introduce the Press (Objectionable Matter) Bill, 1951. Rajagopalachari explained that in the light of certain recent Court rulings, the purpose was to introduce a more liberal measure than the Press (Emergency Powers) Act, 1931 that it replaced. It was intended to curb incitement to offence, scurrility and obscenity. Goenka and Deshbandhu Gupta of *Tej* were among the most persistent critics in the House through all stages of the Bill. Rajagopalachari gave every assurance against misuse and argued that freedom of the Press was not in danger; it was 'the freedom of irresponsibility' that the Bill sought to check.

G.N.S. Raghavan was in 1951 with the *Indian News Chronicle* in Delhi, then jointly owned by Deshbandhu Gupta and Goenka. RNG would often drop into the paper's office at Mori Gate and commandeer Raghavan's services to draft his marathon speeches against the Constitution Amendment Bill.

The weekly *Dinamani Kadir* was launched in July 1950 and was an instant success, attaining a circulation of 128,000 within a year. The Madurai edition of *Dinamani* was started in 1951 at the behest of Kamaraj who wanted to reach the southern districts with the Congress message in the run up to the forthcoming general elections. Sivaraman established great rapport with readers by polling them on the features they would like to see regularly.

The first general elections were held in 1952. Nehru apparently asked RNG if he would contest. Kamaraj, then Tamil Nadu Congress president, offered him Tindivanam, a weak constituency in South Arcot, which RNG somewhat grudgingly accepted as he had determined to contest the poll, and was fed with assurances of victory if he would only organize funds, posters and vehicles. His principal opponent was Tirukural Muniswamy of the Tamilnadu Toilers Party, the forerunner of today's Vanniyar-dominated PMK. C.A. Narayan, an *Express* manager, was pressed into service. A helicopter was hired and copies of *Dinamani* and *Express* were showered from the air on a bemused electorate. Nothing worked. Muniswamy described RNG as a Marwari and 'a northerner by upbringing, culture, civilisation, habits, language, life, situation, food, dress, everything . . .' He was promising to spend lakhs for the development of the district, Muniswamy said, but whose money was it if not that of the toilers? The anti-Hindi agitation was gathering momentum and the *Liberator*, an English-language paper edited by Dr A. Krishnaswami, harped on Dravida linguistic and regional prejudice. Both RNG and his Assembly running mate were defeated. RNG privately blamed the 'tin gods of the Congress'[4] and, sensing the outcome on polling day, retired from the counting booth shortly after noon, leaving Narayan to watch over the remaining formalities.

Later, Kamaraj urged RNG to start some industry in the state. RNG said he had his hands full with his newspapers. Nevertheless, he bought a licence issued to the TVS Group and passed it on to his sambandhi (son's father-in-law), Shreyans Prasad Jain. That is how Dharangadhra Chemicals came up in Tirunelveli district. RNG had not quite forgotten his election promises while contesting the Tindivanam seat.

RNG was disheartened by his poll defeat, but greatly relieved that he had not travelled to Delhi and on to Calcutta for a special AINEC meeting as earlier planned. And thereby hangs a tale, narrated at the end of this chapter. Nor was he persuaded to contest a by-election soon after from the Arupokottai constituency as urged by some.

What alarmed him was the Congress's electoral debacle in the Madras Presidency. The party had won only 152 out of the 375 seats. The Communists got sixty-one and nine other parties made smaller gains. There were sixty-six independents. In current parlance, that was a truly hung Assembly. Prakasam brought 166 members together under the banner of his United Democratic Front. The Governor was in a dilemma over whom to call upon to form a ministry. RNG saw a Red peril. It simultaneously occurred to Sivaraman, C. Subramaniam and a few others that the only sane course would be to place Rajagopalachari in the saddle. Would he agree? RNG worked indirectly behind the scenes so as not to offend Rajagopalachari or alert the opposition. Nehru was sounded and personally welcomed the idea. Rajagopalachari was reluctant, then hesitant and finally asked to know Nehru's mind. Nehru did not wish to influence the Madras Congress Legislature party but, gauging the tide of opinion, expressed his approval. This was communicated over the *Express* and *Hindu* teleprinter lines.

Rajagopalachari finally agreed, but declined to contest an election at his age. Moreover, he had until recently occupied the highest post in the land as Governor General. The answer lay in finding him a place in the Upper House as a nominated member. RNG was delighted. The *Express* Group warmly endorsed the solution. Bitterness was forgotten. An old friendship was revived.

Rajagopalachari was soon to turn to RNG for help. Having stabilized the government, he was anxious to show results. For this he needed funds and accordingly decided to float a public issue. The Reserve Bank had advised a loan of Rs 3 crore but Rajagopalachari felt he needed to do better and floated a Rs 5 crore loan. RNG sent an urgent and confidential teleprinter message to Lala Sri Ram, a doyen of Indian industry in his time. He pleaded that Rajaji had faced all onslaughts and created an era of hope and confidence. Failure of the loan would set the clock back. He continued:

> He has sent you a personal letter, which I am sending you through my office air packet . . . I wonder if you cannot influence your friends like Sir Purshotamdas Thakurdas and others whose institutions can afford to invest a decent amount. I suggested that Rajaji write a letter to J.R.D. Tata also, but he is afraid that his letter may fall into the hands of a paper like 'Blitz' who [sic] are likely to misuse it.
>
> . . . I need hardly remind you that Rajaji has been solely responsible not only for putting down the Communists in this State but also for preventing them from spreading all over India . . . He richly deserves your support not only with your friends but . . . [those] in the Reserve Bank of India who [sic] can take a good portion of it [the loan].

Lala Sri Ram replied a few days later to say that he had written to Purshotamdas Thakurdas, the New India Assurance Company manager, and to Rama Rau, the Reserve Bank Governor. He had addressed no one in Calcutta, knowing RNG would have alerted Shanti Prasad Jain, who had influential friends there.

The year 1953 saw unprecedented floods in Madras. Mount Road was ankle deep in water and even the Cooum River was in spate. There was a power failure and AIR went off the air. By then, RNG had established a foothold in Bombay and Delhi by acquisition. The *Express* boasted that it was on the march.

On leaving the *Express*, Khasa had joined *Swarajya* (which was revived after a period of closure). In a passionate reminiscence, he tore at Goenka's *Express*:

> 'The *Indian Express* was started in 1932 and soon filled the void created by the unfortunate cessation of *Swarajya*' says the *Indian Express* in an editorial styled 'Ourselves', patting itself on the back 'with pardonable pride' on the occasion of 'its first simultaneous appearance at Delhi, Bombay and Madras', as a 'not unimportant provincial paper' aspiring to blossom now into an 'all-India organ of public opinion with a nation-wide circulation'. Whether different provincial newspapers falling under a single ownership, deprived of their old names and rechristened afresh with a single name common to all of them, can thereby be lifted out of their provincial status to a pinnacle of all-India importance, is a problem of journalistic alchemy which does not seem to me as simple as it apparently does to Sri Ramnath Goenka . . . One state added to another and then another, becomes three states and not a nation . . . These towering ambitions of . . . expansion, putting as it were Northcliffe himself in his grave to shame, never crossed the brain of poor Sri Prakasam. That is why he could create *Swarajya* though he could not maintain it for more than a dozen years. That is also why the *Indian Express* is the *Indian Express* as *Swarajya* was *Swarajya*, and the one cannot take the place of the other, or fill the void left by it. For all the commercial attractions of such a myth to Sri Goenka, especially on the eve of the advent of the Andhra State, the void created by the 'unfortunate cessation of *Swarajya*' still remains, and it will certainly not be filled by Sri Goenka, whatever the number of the papers acquired by him. Quantity is no substitute for Quality. Even the miraculous feat of turning a black dog into white may some day be performed, but the millionaire collector has little chance,

> ever, of stepping into the shoes of a man of no property whose strength lay in his non-possession of goods, and who served the humanity of his neighbourhood with abandon and detachment that unpropertied heroism alone can command. How many Birlas will make a Mahatma? So many and more of Goenkas will not make a Prakasam . . .

*Swarajya* and the *Indian Express*, wrote Khasa, 'belong to different hemispheres'. The 'proprietorial spirit was conspicuous by its absence in *Swarajya* . . .'

> Sri Goenka has perfected all the formal outward forms of newspaper get-up . . . and the *Indian Express* has overtaken the finest products of newspaper enterprise in the country. But his acquisitive orgies have been oppressive in their effects, and the hurt caused by them to the soul of journalism stamps him a rank outsider . . . For all his flaunting of valiant recklessness, everything is commerce to Sri Goenka. Even patriotism is a matter of commerce. His occasional enchanting generosities are in essence masterpieces of commercial calculation. The primordial rule in commerce is that everything in the world has its price, and Sri Goenka has been relentless in his pursuit of talent and influence to adorn and decorate his papers. What money cannot buy is just what he has missed, and that was exactly the source of the charm and strength of *Swarajya* . . .
>
> If today, the greatest of our newspapers have become prone to issue special supplements in the name of private firms in return for a few pages of advertisements, it must be said to be due not a little to the example . . . set by the *Indian Express* . . . It is a measure of its failure that its opinions do not count for much, and nobody takes them seriously. It has failed to establish a sense of oneness in the public mind with its purposes, and on account of the different voices in which the various units of the group have spoken on occasions, it has not been able to establish a renown for integrity.[5]

That was a stinging rebuke from someone who had been a close associate. Was it deserved? There is little doubt that RNG kept his eye on the main chance. But are special supplements altogether sinful and is plant modernization wicked? And if different papers in the group sometimes spoke in different voices, did it connote editorial freedom or pandering to the mob?

The agitation for a separate Telugu-speaking Andhra State in 1953 was a precursor to the larger reorganization of states to follow some years later. Three regionally powerful organs of the *Express* took different stands. The Telugu *Andhra Prabha*, under Narla, was a strong advocate of the new state. The Tamil *Dinamani*, under Sivaraman, conceded Andhra in principle but differed on details; the *Express* took a via media. The future of Madras city and the sharing of river waters were among the principal bones of contention. Narla was willing to surrender Madras for Vishal Andhra (not a hyphenated Andhra-Telengana as suggested by some) but pleaded that Guntur be the capital rather than Kurnool, which was ultimately selected. However, he opposed the proposed Krishna-Pennar link and urged construction of the Nagarjunasagar project instead. RNG felt each paper should speak for the communities it served and left it to his editors to determine the line they followed.

B. Gopala Reddy, the first chief minister of Andhra, found it fit to write to RNG thanking him for his electoral support and pleading for the *Express* Group's guidance and help in the tasks ahead.

Much controversy followed the States Reorganisation Commission's Report, especially with regard to the break up of the composite State of Hyderabad. RNG thought the answer lay in forming a larger Dakshina Pradesh. He had set his heart on it. Indeed, he had 'quarrelled with all the local politicians' and felt 'miserable' when the idea was discarded, as he wrote to Lala Sri Ram, his friend and confidant.

That *Express* salaries were poor was also undoubtedly true. RNG tended to look on workers as malingerers and those inclined to trade unionism or socialism as 'communists', a totally degenerate species! Pothan Joseph had long inveighed against the rapacity of newspaper proprietors as a genre and labelled managing editors as 'damaging editors'. Sivaraman, himself an ascetic, notes that he stagnated on the same salary for years together until RNG remembered that perhaps prices had gone up and he deserved something more! Sivaraman's own view of RNG was that there was 'really no limit to his meanness or generosity'.

The *Express* was closely monitored and records of the daily editorial conference notes indicate that RNG kept himself posted with the minutiae of whatever was going on. The group's circulations in the South were rising and on that basis advertisement rates had also been adjusted. It was at this juncture that the Audit Bureau of Circulation did a sample re-audit on which basis the circulation figures of *Dinamani* and *Dinamani Kadir* were scaled down. The *Express* challenged this before the Madras High Court in 1954 and finally secured an out of court settlement that vindicated its position.

The Avadi Congress of 1955 was a major event and resolved in favour of a 'socialistic pattern of society'. The Yugoslav Communist leader Tito was a special invitee. RNG was made a principal organizer. He set up the Satyamurti Nagar venue and supervised the logistics. The session over, he angrily refused to submit any accounts to Kamaraj. However, he used savings from the public collections gathered for the occasion to build the Teynampet property for the Congress in Madras.

*

A major crisis confronted RNG in 1959. Visiting Khasa in hospital he exclaimed that he had decided to close the *Express* in Madras. Why, an amazed Khasa ventured to ask. RNG replied that there were only three reasons to run a newspaper, namely, profit, prestige and patriotic service, and none of these inducements held good now.[6] Labour unrest was delaying the printing and dispatch of the papers, affecting circulation and revenues. Wages were in dispute in the wake of the Wage Board award. A strike ensued, led by Chittaranjan, an employee, and Mohan Kumaramangalam, the union lawyer, both communists. In the case of another local newspaper closure, the workers had decided to set up a cooperative. The Madras labour minister, R. Venkataraman, himself a labour leader, was not disposed to intervene and appeared to favour the cooperative idea.

A desperate RNG decided on drastic action. He declared a lockout, closed his three Madras papers and relocated the *Express* and *Dinamani* just across the border in Chittoor, an hour's drive away from Madras, and the *Andhra Prabha* in Vijayawada. The workers were compensated. The union was stunned. Some new hands were recruited as trainee sub-editors. P. Tharayan, a raw graduate, recalls being offered a salary of Rs 105 and told, 'If you do well, you are bound to come up in life. Look at me!' The *Dinamani* later launched another *Andhra Prabha* edition from Bangalore to serve interior areas of that state. The *Express* and *Dinamani* were not to return to Madras until 1965.

The inauguration of the Chittoor edition was not without an element of drama. The Andhra power grid failed the day the paper was to commence publication. RNG immediately got down to work and was able to persuade the Orissa chief minister, Harekrushna Mahtab, to release sufficient power to Andhra from the Machkund hydro-electric station. As a result, the Chittoor edition appeared as scheduled.

Years later, in 1970, RNG presided over the fiftieth anniversary celebrations of the Dakshina Bharat Hindi Prachar Sabha in Madras that had actually been founded by Gandhi in 1918.

Rajendra Prasad, Lal Bahadur Shastri and Indira Gandhi had been its presidents after the Mahatma. It had by then taught Hindi to over 10 million people and had trained 12,000 pracharaks who were teaching in more than 2000 centres. It had published learning material of different levels of comprehension for Hindi learners and self-instruction booklets for those wishing to learn South Indian languages through the Hindi medium.

Despite his love of Hindi and his zeal for national unity through a common medium of expression, RNG was no Hindi bigot. During the 1965 anti-Hindi agitation in Madras, which turned violent, he agreed with Rajagopalachari that Hindi should not be made compulsory as that would reduce Tamilians and others to second-grade citizens. Both *Dinamani* and the *Express* took this line editorially and gave wide coverage to the agitation. Yet he was disturbed by the excesses committed. He suggested that Frank Moraes, the *Express* editor, editorially seek Rajagopalachari's resignation. Moraes counselled against this as it would further inflame passions. RNG did not concur with this view but left it to Moraes to decide. He was also critical of both the Centre and the state government for not having done enough over the past fifteen years to prepare the people of the state for the proposed linguistic change. Two years later, in 1967, the Dravida Munnettra Kazhagam (DMK) swept to power on a wave of linguistic resurgence.

The Tindivanam election of 1952 had given RNG his first intimation of rising Dravida power. Yet, he counted his electoral defeat on that occasion as a blessing. Nehru had proposed amending press laws in the wake of strong objections to the Press (Objectionable Matter) Act and wished to sound out media opinion. To this end, Deshbandhu Gupta summoned an important meeting of the Indian and Eastern Newspaper Society in Calcutta. RNG had planned to go to Delhi from Madras and thereafter accompany Deshbandhu to Calcutta, but abandoned the idea in view of the Tindivanam election, which was taxing all his energies. It turned out that Deshbandhu could not get a booking on the Delhi night air mail flight to Calcutta on the appointed day. Learning of this, RNG surrendered his own confirmed seat to his friend and colleague. And so it was that

Deshbandhu took the ill-fated flight that crashed shortly before landing in Calcutta. RNG was later to say that he lost Tindivanam but saved his life. Deshbandhu tragically perished instead.

*

During his Madras years, RNG was busy developing his newspaper interests, gaining more than a foothold in provincial and national politics, and raising a family. He was essentially not a family man, being the adopted son of an adopted son, but not oblivious of familial responsibilities. He had bequeathed his ancestral properties in Bihar to his elder brother, who resided in Janakpur in Nepal, and was later to care for the latter's four sons whom he helped educate in Madras and then set up in business.

The Goenkas' was a traditional home. RNG would read the Ramayana, do Shiva puja, practise yoga and go for a daily walk. He would worship daily in one or another temple, going frequently to Tirupati and Kanchi. Moongibai would tell him that as long as she was alive 'Lakshmi will be there in this house'. Bhagwandas (BD) went to the Hindu Theological High School in Sowcarpet and then to Presidency College, Madras. He thereafter worked as an apprentice in the *Express*, moving systematically from one department to another, going later to the United States to train in printing technology in which he took an interest. The two daughters, Krishna and Radha, were some years younger.

RNG was always busy and found little time for the children who grew up under Moongibai's care. When at home, there were many visitors and guests at meals and correspondingly less family privacy and time for togetherness. RNG arranged BD's marriage to Saroj, the thirteen-year-old daughter of Shreyans Prasad Jain of the Sahu–Jain group, in 1944. This was an alliance he keenly sought and the wedding was celebrated with éclat in Dalmianagar. RNG was immensely pleased and proud for this, he said, was the first wedding of a natural son in his family after two generations. A special train was arranged and all the relatives and family elders mustered strong. *Express* workers in Madras received a bonus.

Even in the 1950s Lala Sri Ram would urge RNG to spend time with his children, maybe over meals, and talk to them and encourage them to share their lives with him and his with theirs, thereby lighting up his own 'dull and dry life'. One letter (November 1955) read:

> It is all very well to serve the country, economically, politically and otherwise, but certainly it is your sacred duty to educate these children and make their lives complete—not only their life but your own, which is devoid of affection and real happiness. You are running after mirages.

But there was little time for family and home as RNG was involved with the great and the mighty in Madras. They were his friends and associates and he would play rummy and bridge with them while they joked, discussed current events and affairs of state, not unmixed with juicy gossip.

Even after his grandchildren arrived, family relations remained relatively formal, even distant. He was more feared than loved, a presence rather than a parent. Believing in traditional values, he argued that his eldest granddaughter, Arati, should not go to college as 'women should stay at home, do daily worship and look after the house'. But the two younger siblings, Ritu and Kavita, managed to cross this bar. However, being a bundle of contradictions, RNG also said that 'there cannot be educated men without educated women'. He founded the Moongibai Girls School in 1949 and, in a message to it in 1986, hoped it would 'continue to supply to our nation a stream of girls of culture, character and courage'. In 1985 the Moongibai Goenka Educational Trust morphed into the Bhagwandas Goenka Educational Institution, a company charged with converting the school into a college. That objective remains to be realized. Obviously, RNG was a conservative at home and a radical abroad.

Unhappiness dogged RNG through a series of family tragedies. BD and Saroj had their differences. Radha suffered from a disability, to RNG's great distress, and lost her husband, Shyam Sunder Sonthalia, from kidney failure in 1965, despite unsparing medical care at CMC Hospital at Vellore and the import of a dialysis machine and doctor from the United States. The machine was subsequently donated by RNG to the CMC, thus laying the foundations of nephrology in India. He looked on his elder son-in-law, Ajay Mohan Khaitan, Krishna's husband, as his 'second son' and brought him into the *Express*. Unfortunately, Krishna and Ajay suffered a broken marriage. RNG would not countenance a divorce, as family prestige could not be sacrificed. This rigid stand estranged his daughter. But he was affectionate towards her son, Vivek Khaitan, whom he adopted at the end of his life, as well as to Manoj Sonthalia, Radha's son.

RNG nursed Moongibai tenderly when she was stricken with cancer and was distraught when she finally succumbed in 1966. He himself experienced bouts of ill health, partly the product of a hectic and irregular routine. He was fond of his family but did not know how to show affection. His work increasingly took him away from Madras and when he returned there later in life, especially after BD's death, which dealt him a shattering blow, he felt the loneliness here more than anywhere else. For it was from Madras that he had advanced on to the national stage, becoming itinerant, virtually, and losing something of happiness on the way.

# 3

# Taking Wing to Bombay

The closing stages of the Second World War brought winds of change and, with it, renewed stirrings of independence. Bombay was in many ways the political capital of nationalist India and it was to that city that RNG now turned his attention. None knew that Independence was quite so near. The war over, members of the Congress Working Committee were released from prison and decided to start a chain of English and vernacular newspapers to wage the next round of the freedom struggle. Sardar Patel raised Rs 1 crore to float two separate companies, Akhil Bharat Printers Ltd and Hindustan Newspapers Ltd, to take care of the infrastructure and run the newspapers respectively so that if any one was ever seized by the government the other might survive—a tactic RNG was later to employ. The printing company had leading industrialists on its board under K.M. Munshi and the publishing house men like Patel, Nehru and Kripalani.

The English daily *Bharat* and the *Nav Bharat* were established in Bombay. RNG had ordered a modern rotary machine from the United States and this was on the high seas bound for Madras. Learning of this, the Sardar contacted RNG and asked if he would consider diverting his machine to Bombay and take subsequent delivery of a comparable unit on order. RNG replied, 'The Nation's need is greater than mine,' and complied. Meanwhile, Ramakrishna Dalmia, then one of the biggest names in Indian industry, made a bid to buy Bennett Coleman and Company, convinced that 'without establishing some big newspaper, I could not serve India effectively'. A deal was struck within twenty-four hours. He got the *Times of India* for a little less than Rs 2 crore.

RNG possibly knew of Dalmia's ambition through the family network (Dalmia's son-in-law Shanti Prasad Jain was the brother of his sambandhi Shreyans Prasad Jain). Be that as it may, he too had surveyed the Bombay media landscape. An Irishman, N.J. Hamilton, had quit the *Illustrated Weekly of India* and started the *Morning Standard* and *Sunday Standard* just before the outbreak of the Second World War. The paper did well and earned good profits for a while, but then ran into financial difficulties, compelling Hamilton to let out part of the Sassoon Dock premises, Newspaper House, to a Gujarati newspaper, whose owner soon bought the entire building. Hamilton moved his editorial offices to Mubarak Manzil in the Fort area and had the paper printed at a commercial press. He converted the *Morning Standard* into a tabloid under Russi Karanjia, to no avail. Losses mounted. Further troubles threatened liquidation. Hamilton was desperate. It was this pioneering venture, fallen on bad days, that RNG now eyed. Let Hamilton tell the story:

> When Ramnath Goenka of Madras approached me in 1946, with a proposal to purchase both newspapers, I was not averse to it, particularly since he wished me to continue the management. Accordingly, I disposed of my proprietorial rights . . .
>
> Goenka's son was dispatched from Madras to work under me and 'learn the business'. Bubbling with enthusiasm and with a strong physique, Bhagwan was a most likeable person. Unfortunately, we crossed swords over the question of 'free

distribution'. I was having copies delivered to a selected list of possible subscribers, when one day, I found to my consternation, that without informing me, Bhagwan had stopped this distribution. This annoyed me intensely and I told Goenka Sr. about this interference. He sent a telex to Bhagwan asking him to return to Madras. About four weeks later Bhagwan came back to Bombay.

He took off his shirt and showed me several weals on his back and said, 'For God's sake, Norman, if I ever do anything again, unwittingly and without your knowledge, let me know at once. Don't tell father, he'll be furious as these weals, which are his handiwork, will show. He will not stand for disobedience'. I was shocked. Thereafter, Bhagwan was a model understudy, exuding confidence and displaying the most extraordinary interest in every phase of newspaper administration. I predicted a brilliant future for him.

. . . Mr Goenka, unlike most Indian newspaper proprietors, spent lavishly and engaged the very best contributors, covering every aspect of editorial interest. He did not look for an immediate return, twofold, as most others expect. He was content to build with an eye on the future . . . Personally, I could not have found a better person to work with than Ramnath Goenka. Agreeable, courteous and ever keen to adopt anything that might help the papers prosper, he was, to my mind, an ideal proprietor.

Having taken control of the *Morning Standard*, RNG repurchased Newspaper House and decided to move back to the more spacious Sassoon Dock. A Mr Kapadia was in charge of the *Sunday Standard* editorial section when RNG dropped in one Saturday evening as the pages were being locked up. He inquired of the boss if publication would be suspended for a few days until the office and equipment were shifted back to Sassoon Dock. 'No,' he replied. 'It's going to be like D-Day. We will shift everything in one sweep and make a landing in Newspaper House.' And that is precisely what happened.

Around the time of the Naval mutiny in 1944 there was an explosion in the Bombay docks and a newsprint godown caught fire. The owners were distraught but RNG had the presence of mind to realize that the tightly bound newsprint reels would not suffer any great damage. So he quickly purchased the consignment for virtually nothing from the unsuspecting owners, to huge advantage to himself. His common sense and ability to take instant decisions were unfailing.

He was to undertake another blitzkrieg in Madras some years later when he moved into Express Estates. Newsprint was in short supply and worth its weight in gold. RNG had out of the blue discovered, negotiated and purchased a consignment on the high seas for delivery in Madras in just over a fortnight. Secure storage space was required but just not available. All right then, he said, we'll build a godown. He had steel moved in special wagons attached to express trains from Jamshedpur, got labour at double the daily wage rate to fell 100 trees from a forest, commandeered lorries to transport the logs to the site, and then scoured paddy mills in the districts to spread husk on the yet-to-dry floor of the huge, newly constructed godown, so that the newsprint reels should not spoil. The job was done in record time and he was for long to boast of this achievement.

A year after takeover of the *Standard*, Hamilton asked to be relieved of his management contract. RNG agreed. Bhagwandas and his understudy, Krishnan, were ready to step in.[1] There is a sequel to this story. Before setting up shop at Sassoon Dock, Hamilton had got a nice plot opposite Churchgate Station for his press. He had had to deposit Rs 19,000 on an auction price of Rs 35,000. However, he could not occupy it because it contained a Rehabilitation Hut, which he could not get removed. Much later he sold this lease to RNG for the deposit value of Rs 19,000. 'In a wink, the new owners had the hut removed and a building erected.' The plot was now worth Rs 35 lakh. Hamilton cursed his luck. RNG must have had a laugh.

Goenka was raring to go. A Marathi paper, *Loksatta*, was launched in 1948. A teleprinter circuit was installed and colour comics introduced in the *Sunday Standard* with a film magazine,

*Screen*, to follow. The *Morning Standard* had been renamed the *National Standard* on its takeover, and in 1953 became the *Indian Express*.

A few years earlier, Pothan Joseph had left *Dawn* to become principal information officer to the Government of India, only to quit before long. He had punched George Abell, the Viceroy Lord Wavell's political aide, for making a racist remark, and returned to Madras to contemplate his next step. There he met RNG who by now had many irons in the fire and was in need of editorial reinforcement. Knowing of Joseph's itinerant ways, RNG proposed his return as editor in Madras in all but name, with the paper's imprint continuing to carry the legend 'Edited, printed, published by Ramnath Goenka'.

Joseph agreed, and *Express* readers once more started their mornings with his lively column, 'Over a Cup of Tea'. RNG had begun to toy with the idea of starting a magazine and therefore readily accepted an invitation from *Collier's Magazine*, which was hosting a World Magazine Conference in Baltimore in 1946 and also exploring the possibility of entering the Indian market in association with the *Express*. RNG persuaded Joseph to accompany him and, along with two secretaries, flew to New York via London. He had himself fitted out with business suits and endeavoured to polish up his English. They stayed at the Waldorf Hotel in New York, visited the *New York Times* and then travelled by Pullman to Baltimore. Negotiations with Collier's proved infructuous. When he returned to India two months later, friends were struck by his Americanisms. Gee, he'd had a swell time! Even years later, RNG would many a time pull somebody up short with a 'Don't teach your grandmother to suck eggs'!

In 1947 RNG decided to get Joseph to move to Bombay from Madras. Joseph left Madras without settling his terms and conditions of service, and got Hamilton to negotiate on his behalf. But Goenka was grudging. Joseph had succeeded Kuppuswami 'Stalin' Srinivasan and now seemed ill at ease with the creeping crassness he saw entering journalism and public life after Independence. His colleagues included the legendary sports writer A.F.S. Talyarkhan and the budding Sharada Prasad, who had also moved from Madras as news editor. A major innovation that occurred at this time was the induction of Shanta Rungachary into the newspaper, initially working directly under Joseph. She was possibly the first woman to break into mainstream journalism.

It was a poignant moment on the evening of 30 January 1948 when news came of Gandhi's assassination at his prayer meeting in Delhi. The newsroom staff were stunned and disoriented. There was no time to lose if the edition was not to be delayed. Joseph quietly gathered the news flashes pouring over the ticker and retired to his cabin, emerging some time later with a polished and moving editorial that the paper carried:

> On his way to commune with his God, the hand of violence was raised against Mahatma Gandhi, and the illustrious apostle of non-violence passed immediately into his final communion with the infinite . . .
>
> . . . What is in store for us we cannot foresee, but Mahatma Gandhi has set for us the compass by which India must steer her course in the future.

To RNG, Gandhi was the quintessential nationalist leader—fearless, principled, resolute and visionary. It was the Mahatma who had called him to service, to work to unite India through the spread of Hindi and khadi, which Nehru called the livery of freedom; and then set the nation on the road to swaraj, with the Dandi salt march and the Quit India movement as milestones on the way. RNG felt personally bereaved. He had lost his greatest mentor to whom he had vowed to abstain from tobacco, liquor and meat, wear khadi and to do nothing against the interests of the nation.

Joseph had left his family behind in Madras and by 1948 was tired, even disillusioned. He resigned—only to start yet another new venture, the *Deccan Herald* in Bangalore. V.B. Kulkarni succeeded him as editor in Bombay to be followed in quick succession by Frank Moraes—who was marking time to get back his berth in his former paper, the *Times of India*—and then by Claude Scott. J.W. Ewing further consolidated the paper, which had in 1953 been renamed the *Indian Express*, until Moraes returned in 1957 to put his stamp on the paper, first in Bombay and then in Delhi. RNG would describe Frank as his Dilip Kumar, the reigning box office star in Indian cinema. This was in a way to return the compliment paid RNG by Sivaraman of *Dinamani*, long his alter ego, to the effect that Rajagopalachari, Kamaraj and others once strode the stage in Madras, but it was Goenka, the 'playback singer', who voiced the songs they sang that held the public in thrall!

*

V. Ranganathan, one of RNG's most trusted employees whom he moved from Madras, narrated the early history of the *Express* in Bombay. He arrived at a strike-bound *National Standard* in 1946, to take charge as circulation manager. RNG always put circulation above advertising, the latter being consequent on the first. At that time the paper sold fewer than 4000 copies, with British military personnel being major subscribers. With demobilization, circulation declined. The *National Standard* ranked fourth in Bombay after the *Times of India*, *Bombay Chronicle* and *Free Press Journal*.

There were two problems. The vintage Hoe rotary took over ninety minutes to print 4000 copies. This implied an early deadline, on the principle that a bad paper is better than a late paper. But if an important late news item was missed and was there in the competition, there would be the devil to pay, for RNG, sitting in Madras, would get a daily report on which paper had carried what in Bombay. The other handicap was that the paper's sole selling agent would dispatch the *Times* and

*Free Press* first and then saunter up to the *Standard* along with bundles of the *Free Press* group's *Navashakti* that was printed later on a slow flatbed press.

So Ranganathan decided to use the *Standard*'s sole van and gradually establish a new distribution system through direct supplies to numerous subagents, areawise and stallwise, instead of only through the sole agent. This worked, but left untouched the matter of mofussil distribution. The books showed that most agents had huge payment arrears and new agents, hard to come by in any case, were reluctant to take many copies for fear of being left with unsolds. Repeated queries through correspondence revealed that many agents simply did not receive their paper parcels. The next task was to track parcels from the office to the railway station. Soon enough, Ranganathan caught a packer outside Victoria Terminus loping away with a parcel that had ostensibly been dispatched to Poona. Thefts en route were also detected. The leakage was plugged. But it was hard work. Later, the *Standard/Express* was to appoint its own agents who gradually built themselves commanding positions as kings among newsagents in Bombay.

Once the *National Standard* had found its feet, RNG began to plan a Marathi daily. This fructified with *Loksatta*'s inauguration on 14 January 1948, with some of the credit for this new venture and for *Screen* going to B.D. Goenka. The Mahatma's assassination a fortnight later gave the new paper a boost in circulation. A Sunday edition was added in July, which rapidly gained in popularity under N.G. Jog, when squareword puzzles with prizes were introduced, first in the Sunday *Loksatta* and subsequently in the *Sunday Standard*. Jog's Sunday column, 'Viewpoint', ran for years and developed a wide following. By 1955 the circulations of the daily *Loksatta* and Sunday *Loksatta* stood at 85,532 and 65,549 respectively, that is, almost three times that of the *Express* and double that of the *Sunday Standard*.

T.V. Parvate and S.K. Pendse were editors of *Loksatta* in quick succession and were followed by H.R. Mahajani who built up the paper over the next twenty years. The States Reorganisation Commission's recommendation favouring retention of a bilingual Bombay incensed Maharashtrian opinion. The Samyukta Maharashtra Samiti launched a powerful agitation that turned violent. The *Express* favoured the status quo, a major issue being the future of the cosmopolitan Bombay city in what was feared may become a rather parochial Maharashtra. On the other hand, *Loksatta* upheld the cause but objected to the methods employed as well as to a united front with strong communist influence. The paper's editorial line resulted in a drop in circulation. RNG, however, supported his editor. He too was trying to construct a Dakshina Pradesh to avert the break-up of Hyderabad; nor did he take kindly to the communists. A new daily, *Maratha*, the organ of the Samyukta Maharashtra Samiti, fanned popular sentiments in favour of the agitation. The closure of the *Loksatta* squarewords competition in 1956 also ate into circulation. The outlook seemed bleak. But the *Loksatta*'s objective news coverage and basic support for the cause staved off a crisis. The closure of *Lokmanya*, a competitor, in 1958 boosted sales, and the decision in 1960 to end bilingualism and carve out Maharashtra and Gujarat as two separate states restored *Loksatta*'s primacy. By 1962 it was the largest selling Marathi newspaper, despite the launching of the *Maharashtra Times* by the powerful Bennett Coleman Group.

In 1957, Express Newspapers Ltd completed the construction of a six-storey office building at Churchgate, on the plot bought from Hamilton. The lease was for ninety-nine years. Built for under Rs 7 lakh, the building was rented out for a net income, less corporation tax, of Rs 2 lakh.

In 1957, too, Frank Moraes had joined as executive editor of the *Express* after leaving the *Times of India*. RNG, still managing editor of the group, wrote to him from Madras about plans for a new office:

> I am glad that you have raised the question of a new building for Bombay. This was in my mind for quite a long time, but the site at Churchgate on which we have put up the building was so small that it would not have accommodated our office, even if we had used all the flats. The total area in our present building [Sassoon Docks] is about 40,000 sq. ft., as against about 25,000 sq. ft. in the new building. If I had thought that I could accommodate conveniently our establishment in the new building, I would certainly have done so.
>
> If you can manage to get a site from the Government of India in the Backbay Reclamation area, I shall certainly put up a building to suit our requirements, in the course of the next year or two. The Government of Bombay allotted a site to the 'Hindu' who eventually did not start a newspaper there, but used the place for rental purposes. Why should they not give us a place?

In 1965 RNG's persistence paid off—a plot on Nariman Point was allotted by the then chief minister, Y.B. Chavan, and the twenty-five-floor Express Towers was occupied in June 1970. It had been RNG's ambition to have the tallest building in Bombay. Alas, Air-India put up a building next door. It was a floor higher and obstructed some of the view. Even so, the *Express* had a proud address, and a real nest egg from the rentals for twenty-two floors. The penthouse, to which Goenka later moved, was arguably to become India's most celebrated political salon.

Frank Moraes gave the *Express* a stamp it did not have in Bombay earlier, what with his high reputation, access and affable ways. He was a stylist and his political columns and more chatty 'Men, Matters, Memories' enjoyed a devoted readership. He was impatient with Congress socialism and began to mock at Nehru's trust in China. He felt Krishna Menon's influence on foreign policy was baleful. Events in Tibet and tensions along the Himalayan marches reinforced this view. The liberation of Goa was welcomed but the Sino-Indian conflict and the 1962 debacle had the *Express* Group gunning for Menon.

That same year saw RNG and the *Express* actively involved in an election campaign in Bombay. In the 1962 general election, there was a historic contest between Krishna Menon and Kripalani for the North Bombay parliamentary seat. Menon was Nehru's candidate, the Acharya the combined Opposition's, with Gandhian and clandestine anti-Nehru Congress support. RNG virtually took charge of Kripalani's campaign—a trial run for future Grand Alliance and Janata front politics—and made Shreyans Prasad Jain's Carmichael Road residence his headquarters. The *Express* was fully involved. Its press churned out leaflets and other election material. C.A. Narayan and Ranganathan, both *Express* personnel, were given charge of suburbs along the Western and Central Railway respectively. The South-Indian-dominated areas like Dharavi, Chembur, Deonar and other pockets were systematically wooed by RNG personally. He set up canvassing booths and would address audiences in Tamil, remaining on the campaign trail till late evening. He would then return to headquarters, review reports on the day's campaign and plan the next day's strategy. He was indefatigable. Copies of the *Express* were publicly burnt in Bombay by irate Congress and Left supporters. In the event, Kripalani lost by a huge margin, but RNG had fought the good fight and, though bruised, was unbowed.

Just before the 1962 general elections, RNG had established the *Indian Express* in Delhi. Moraes had been getting restive in Bombay, partly on account of the personal trauma of having to look after his once vivacious but now tragically ill wife, Beryl, and accordingly sought a move to Delhi. Goenka agreed as he felt it would be appropriate to fly the *Express* flag in the national capital, and not treat Delhi as a subordinate office. Accordingly, in 1961, Moraes went to Delhi as editor-in-chief of the *Indian Express* . . . He took Nandan Kagal of the *Times* with him, and D.R. Mankekar, also formerly of the *Times*, was transferred to Bombay as resident editor. He was forced out by RNG some years later, to be replaced by V.K. Narasimhan as resident editor.

Moraes was to be in Delhi until 1972, when he left for London. He had an apartment in Bombay in the prized Mafatlal Park on the sea face along Warden Road that RNG coveted. The latter hoped that when Moraes left for London, this enviable piece of real estate would come his way. However, Moraes had an understanding that he would return the flat to Mafatlal's, the promoters, should he ever vacate it. Honour bound, Moraes surrendered the apartment as promised. RNG was greatly annoyed and felt cheated.

Meanwhile, the *Indian Express* in Bombay continued to gain in circulation. The landmark stories in Bombay during Moraes's tenure included the famous Nanavati case involving a dashing naval officer and the murder of his wife's alleged paramour; the trial of Mundhra, a stockbroker and speculator; and Pope Paul VI's visit to the city for the Eucharistic Congress. The circulation of the *Express* surpassed that of the *Free Press* while *Loksatta* topped among all Marathi papers. RNG exulted that one of his papers should surge ahead of all others and remain the front runner in a vernacular language and major news centre. Mahajani, a Sanskrit scholar, Royist and social worker, was succeeded by another Royist, Latey, who was at the helm of *Loksatta* for the next decade, to be succeeded by Vidyadhar Gokhale, a dramatist and literary figure though ideologically on the political right; and then by Madhav Gadkari. Govind Talwalkar, later to become editor of the *Maharashtra Times*, cut his teeth in the *Loksatta*, which he joined in 1948 and served for two decades.

The 1950s and 1960s were thus years of expansion for the *Express* Group. *Screen* continued doing well, selling over 100,000 copies from Bombay and Madras, though the Hindi *Screen* was discontinued in 1955. The Madurai edition of the *Express* was started in 1957. The following year saw the launching of the *Express Echo* in Madras. This was a short-lived venture that folded within six months. The *Financial Express* appeared in 1961, to be followed by *Express* editions in Bangalore (1965) and Ahmedabad (1968). In between, the *Kannada Prabha* was also launched in Bangalore, and the *Andhra Prabha* shifted there from Madras. RNG was here, there, everywhere, planning, goading, modernizing, fighting rearguard actions against wage boards, unions and anybody else who crossed his path, and reorganizing his growing empire. The group was now well connected through an all-India teleprinter network, linking all capitals to the publication centres from which feeder lines reached down to the districts. In addition, there was a regular air-container service between Madras, Bombay and Delhi to relieve pressure on the teleprinter circuit which had to carry both news and advertisements.

*

By the late 1950s, with his empire expanding and a highly able professional, Frank Moraes, on board as his editor, RNG also set to work to redefine editorial and work practices. Early in 1958, he wrote to Moraes:

> A word about our stand on major questions of policy. Despite certain points on which we have to differ from the present Congress governments, we have by tradition and in practice been what might be generally called a Congress paper. This means in effect that we have to justify to ourselves first every deviation from the Congress stand before we reveal it to the public. In recent years, we have tried to form and express definite and consistent views on national and international issues, political and economic. If we have to depart therefrom, we should do all to avoid the impression that there is a sudden and steep change in policy. I should like your comments.

RNG was particular that the paper should not be Delhi- or Bombay-centric and that regional and, especially, South Indian news should appear. This should also apply to editorial comment and readers' views. He pointed out that large numbers of South

Indians now lived in Bombay and Delhi and they would want news from their native regions. Local editorials should also be encouraged when circumstances warranted.

He concurred with Moraes's view that there should be resident editors in the major regional editions to facilitate local direction and supervision of regional newsletters. He said he was doing his best to improve equipment and the quality of newsprint to avoid reel breakages and ensure better printing.

Special arrangements were made for foreign coverage, with regular newsletters from Pakistan, Ceylon, London, Washington and Nairobi. A standard pagination was agreed upon by subject matter and editors were encouraged to take their own regional correspondents' reports on the front page and the Op-Ed page, so as to give the paper a distinctive look. Stress was laid on sport, particularly racing, and Court news, including income tax related matters. Cross translation and publication of special reports from the *Express* and its vernacular counterparts was enjoined. The Late News box on Page 1 was mandatory, with the New York cotton quotation alongside. Good writers were commissioned, Aneuran 'Nye' Bevan, the British Labour leader, among them.

Editorials on economic topics were in the main to be written in Madras; while Bombay, and to a lesser extent, Calcutta, were made responsible for daily Commercial Notes and market and industrial trends and reactions. There is a famous *Express* anecdote that old-timers recall. When Finance Minister T.T. Krishnamachari presented a soak-the-rich budget, Professor K. Swaminathan, the Madras editor, pondering over what he should write, thought fit to consult RNG, a close friend of the finance minister. Came the tart reply: 'Swami, you write . . . you write what will increase the circulation of the paper. I will take care of myself!' This was akin to a British paper's crisp message to a photographer who was sent to cover a war but cabled back that he could not find it: 'You send pictures. We'll supply the war!' (This celebrated remark gave the English author Evelyn Waugh the idea for his novel *Scoop*.)

By 1970, having built the Express Towers at Nariman Point, RNG lost no time on letting out space. IBM was interested. Kanwar Rajinder Singh, representing that multinational, went to meet RNG and a deal was struck. IBM took three floors. Meanwhile, Singh got to know and admire RNG. Came the Emergency in 1975, and the government put the squeeze on the *Express*. Banks would not loan money and newsprint had to be purchased immediately to keep the paper going. Aware of a looming crisis, Singh offered advance rentals for IBM's Express Tower offices and repeated this three or four times. The total advances ran to about Rs 30 lakh. Then there would be no money to pay salaries at the end of the month and Ved Prakash, an *Express* manager, would again plead for advance rentals.

RNG was immensely grateful and was later to repay the debt he felt he owed Singh. When the Janata government took office, George Fernandes, as industry minister, sent IBM and Coca-Cola packing. Singh left IBM and subsequently took over the *Daily* in Bombay from R.K. (Russi) Karanjia, the owner-editor. Not having any knowledge of the newspaper business, Singh approached RNG for help. Notwithstanding the *Daily* being a nominal rival, with Russi Karanjia, a hardened *Express* critic, continuing as editor, RNG offered his blessings and instructed Ranganathan, his trusted lieutenant, to render Singh all assistance. Some years later, Singh wanted to sell the *Daily* and offered the title to RNG at a highly concessional price. RNG was ill and the matter was not pursued.

*

With the bifurcation of bilingual Bombay state into the new states of Maharashtra and Gujarat in 1960 RNG had begun to think of expanding into Gujarat. *Western Times* was the only English daily in the state and there was surely scope for another. The *Times of India* had the same idea. Hitendra Desai, the chief minister, presided over the inauguration of the Ahmedabad *Express* in 1968. Arrangements were made for its printing at the Sandesh press until the *Express* had set up its own plant.

The Gujarati *Jansatta* and *Loksatta* were registered in 1952 and commenced publication from Ahmedabad and Baroda respectively. *Jansatta* was later to start an edition from Rajkot as well. The Marathi magazine *Lokprabha* also made its debut in Bombay. During this period, anti-reservation riots broke out in Gujarat and the chief minister, Madhav Sinh Solanki, came in for strong criticism. A mob attacked the *Express*'s Ahmedabad office. RNG visited the city and, sensing that a certain staff member was possibly being unduly influenced by the chief minister, sent for Hiranmay Karlekar, senior editor in Delhi, to oversee matters during this critical period.

With so many irons in the fire and losses mounting on his investments in jute and iron and steel, RNG was constantly facing financial problems. He had invited company deposits in Ahmedabad, but at the time of maturity in 1972 found himself unable to redeem the debt. Ranganathan, the business manager, was frantic. He kept telephoning RNG at various centres but realized that RNG was obviously trying to avoid him. Suddenly, getting word that Goenka had left Delhi that morning by the hopping flight for Bombay, Ranganathan sought to waylay him at the transit lounge at Ahmedabad airport. Not seeing him there, he inveigled himself into the aircraft to find RNG pacing up and down the aisle. Rattled at being discovered, and at being told that the Ahmedabad depositors were agitated, RNG exclaimed that he had no money and if Ranganathan could not procure the necessary funds by collecting arrears or from fresh borrowing, he could sell the unit. 'I have burnt my fingers in Ahmedabad,' he snapped. The plane departed. The money was somehow managed and disaster averted.

A decade earlier, in the early 1960s, RNG had tried to get

the Nizam of Hyderabad to invest in *Express* shares. Prior to that he had got round Sanjiva Reddy, the Andhra chief minister, to reverse an order of the state's chief town planner and permit the *Express* to build an office in Chittoor in what was a designated residential area. This he did, but not before making some rather uncomplimentary remarks about RNG. A Mr Taraporevala was at that time financial adviser to the nizam and RNG sent a member of the staff, S.N. Shastry, as his emissary to see if the nizam's fortune could be tapped. Taraporevala was responsive as the *Express* was now publishing from Bombay. He said he would consider taking a 51 per cent stake in the paper together with an interest in the management. Some time later, RNG visited Hyderabad and was closeted with Taraporevala. The meeting over, Shastry inquired what had happened. RNG remarked that Taraporevala was a shrewd Parsi who wanted his pound of flesh. 'He seeks an interest in the management, but find out from him how much of that he wants.' Taraporevala in turn told Shastry, 'Your man is a shrewd Marwari. He wants my money and no interference. My reports are that he is very volatile and changes his mind from time to time . . . Can he guarantee a return on the money?' Shastry thereupon suggested that preference shares would be the answer.

The deal fell through. But RNG was later to give Shastry what he thought was a delicious line: 'A newspaper is a peculiar amalgam of public service and public patronage. It is not a business and has its own special economics.' It was heads I win, tails you lose!

*

Back in Bombay, around 1979, RNG felt the urge to streamline editorial operations. R.V. Pandit, publisher of *Imprint*, was engaged as a consultant and N.J. Nanporia, former editor of the *Times of India*, was also brought in. Eyebrows rose.

S.K. Krishnamoorthy, the resident editor, went on leave. Vegetable prices and other items of consumer and family interest began to appear on the front page. An editorial announced that the *Express* in Bombay intended to move from 'politicking' to reporting news that matters to ordinary individuals. This was to be an exercise in 'relevant journalism'. Protests followed, both from within the organization and from readers who felt the paper was being dumbed down at the cost of what they considered to be serious and important news. The arrangement did not last. RNG could be mercurial.

Another time he invited Dom Moraes, Frank's son, to join the *Express*, dangling the carrot of a new magazine he planned to launch. Earlier, RNG had met Dom in London and asked for his assistance in hiring bright British journalists to improve the standard of English in his paper. Dom hosted a lunch attended by several promising English reporters. By the end of the lunch a few were recruited on fancy terms. Few actually got to India. Moraes Sr., then the *Express* editor, knew nothing about this and was furious. However, now Dom joined as editor of the Sunday paper. Inviting him to lunch at the penthouse, RNG wanted him to sack Darryl D'Monte, his cousin and resident editor of the *Express*, as he was a 'communist'. Dom laughed this away. Then, according to him, RNG said, 'You think you are being a gentleman. Gentlemen never become rich. I have only seen one bigger bloody fool than your father, and that is you!' Dom was amused. But he was soon ready to quit as the promised new magazine never materialized. Dom believed that, having just written a biography of Indira Gandhi, Goenka felt he might be useful in seeking a reconciliation with her. This was unlikely. As Dom said later, Mrs Gandhi never read the book. She accused Dom of misrepresenting her.

Strikes were not uncommon in the *Express* and kept recurring, aggravated by poor labour relations. George Fernandes was the rising trade union leader in Bombay. He had won the loyalty of the transport and taxi workers and, with Madhu

Limaye, organized the first Bombay bandh in 1958. He turned next to organize the newspaper workers and began with the *Indian Express* workers at Sassoon Dock. A clash with RNG was inevitable, following which they met and struck up an instant rapport. Fernandes recalls that he and Limaye would meet with editors and leading journalists before launching on any major political or union activity. In this process, he also met RNG and found that for any cause on which they had a reasonable point of view they could count on his support.

Many years later, Datta Samant followed the same trajectory of unionizing various firms and industries, becoming a labour don through strong-arm methods employed by his Maharashtra Kamgar Sangh. In the middle of 1981, Datta Samant announced that he enjoyed majority support among *Express* workers and not the recognized union from whom a section of workers had indeed turned away. Goenka had just gone ahead and implemented the Palekar Wage Board Award, the first major newspaper group to do so, when Samant demanded that the *Express* pay 20 per cent bonus, plus make a 10 per cent ex gratia payment over and above a further Rs 200 a month flat increase in the emoluments of all employees. This was by any standards a preposterous demand and RNG countered that he was only able to cope because of the rentals received from his properties.

The chief minister, A.R. Antulay, who was smarting from a recent *Express* exposure of an alleged cement scandal that had greatly embarrassed him, wanted to see Goenka cut to size. Rajni Patel, the Bombay Congress leader, sought to plead the workers' cause while Ram Jethmalani stepped in to reason with Samant to drop his extreme demands. Samant agreed to abide by the verdict of an independent audit of the *Express* books of account, to establish whether or not there was a capacity to pay, only to prevaricate and finally back off from that understanding.

Samant then threatened dire consequences and initiated a

go-slow. Workers refused to do overtime. The *Express* Group's printing schedules were totally disrupted even as editorial work was organized elsewhere. RNG threatened a lockout and some days later announced a three-month lockout to be followed by permanent closure if matters did not improve. The Maharashtra government came out with an ordinance prohibiting closure of any plant employing over 2000 workers, against which the *Express* filed a writ. Loss of wages began to tell on the idle workers and after some weeks a third of the employees signed an undertaking dissociating themselves from Samant and agreeing to return to work.

Arun Shourie, then executive editor, had been summoned to Bombay from Delhi by RNG to assist Hiranmay Karlekar, then the resident editor, in dealing with Samant. S. Gurumurthy, RNG's financial adviser, meanwhile persuaded Dattopant Thengdi, leader of the Bharatiya Mazdoor Sangh (BMS), the trade union formation of the Rashtriya Swayamsewak Sangh (RSS), to intervene. Dr J.K. Jain, a surgeon and friend of RNG, had meanwhile spoken to the RSS leadership, which was in session in Bangalore. BMS strongmen together with Shourie and Karlekar then entered the *Express* premises, breaking through a cordon of strikers, at the head of loyalist workers. A coordination committee of *Express* workers and readers had been formed to build support against Samant's bullying tactics. Public sympathy gradually turned in favour of the *Express* and Samant discovered that he had lost out. The *Express* resumed publication. The strike was over.

There were two interesting sidelights to the lockout that say something about RNG's fabled parsimony. RNG came to Bombay during the strike but decided that it would be best to stay in the shadows as otherwise he would be besieged by importuning workers and busybodies. He was booked at the Taj but as word leaked out he asked to move to a suburban hotel. Ranganathan, his Man Friday, thought Hotel Searock in Bandra would be suitable. The hotel manager was delighted and promised to do his best. That meant a suite with a view. For such an honoured guest he put prestige before price. RNG arrived. Delay in opening the suite brought on some initial irritation. When he saw the luxurious apartment he immediately asked the tariff. When told it was Rs 2500 a night, he exploded and, turning on the hapless Ranganathan, said, 'So this is the way you waste my money! I do not have enough to pay my staff . . . No, get me an ordinary double room, that will do, although I cannot afford even that.' The double room cost Rs 650 a night.

The *Express* management had taken rooms at a modest establishment, the West End Hotel, to set up an emergency office. As soon as the lockout was lifted, RNG turned to Ranganathan and said, 'This is enough. You have all lived in luxury in the hotel. Now let us be back to work in the office. I have no money to waste.' This, Ranganathan reminisced, was RNG's usual cost-consciousness spiel: 'He knew very well that his team had stood by him throughout the ordeal. But he never once acknowledged this or gave anybody any credit. On the contrary, he would like to make one feel guilty, however hard we worked, and we knew that. That was his way of showing approval. For him, disapproval meant being sacked!'

*

RNG was declining in health through the latter part of the 1980s. Yet in 1990, the *Express* bought up the Sterling Group of Publications, including *Gentleman* magazine and a clutch of specialized journals, from Minhaz Merchant. RNG's grandson Vivek struck the deal. What the *Express* got in addition was the Sterling premises at Nariman Point, 1500 square feet of covered area, valued at about Rs 70 lakh. For RNG, real estate always mattered. Ultimately, it was earnings from his properties that sustained the *Express* Group.

One last cameo from the penthouse in Express Towers,

RNG's home in Bombay and the headquarters of the *Express* Group. In 1984 there had been a change of guard in Delhi. Rajiv Gandhi was prime minister. A year later, the centenary of the Indian National Congress was being celebrated at the Oval grounds in Bombay . . . Ramnath Goenka was down with a bad chest condition and alone in the penthouse with his secretary, Prema Parthasarathy. A grand laser show depicting the freedom struggle had been programmed for that evening. RNG had been invited but chose not to go. He had broken with the Congress after the 1969 split and his battles with Indira Gandhi had not healed the wound, though he now placed great hopes on her son, Rajiv.

Yet, old loyalties tugged. He walked out on to the terrace to see the light show being beamed from atop the adjacent Air-India building. Desirous of a better view, he got a trembling and anxious Prema to escort him twenty steps up a service ladder to the cooling towers. Then, clutching the railing, he crawled on all fours to a vantage point and ordered a chair on which he sat to watch the show. It was sunset and there was a particularly glorious view. Waves of nostalgia and pride must have washed over him during the next half hour. Then he said, 'Let's go down. But don't tell anybody.' It was 28 December 1985.

# 4

# A Capital Move

Even as he was busy establishing himself in Bombay, RNG began to cast his net wider. Right from the time he had teamed up with Sadanand in Madras in 1936 he had begun to share the latter's vision of a truly national news service. Although the two of them parted company over control of the *Indian Express* in Madras, they remained close friends and had mutual regard for one another. RNG's tenure as a member of the Constituent Assembly must also have opened his eyes to media possibilities in the national capital.

In 1945, Sadanand and Ramnath Goenka presented the Indian and Eastern Newspaper Society a memorandum with regard to organizing an Indian news agency that would gather and disseminate both domestic and international news. The IENS unanimously endorsed the concept of a news service cooperatively owned by the newspapers of India, and resolved to set up a committee consisting of K. Srinivasan of the *Hindu* and the president of the IENS, an Englishman, to frame concrete proposals. This done, a company called the Press Trust of India (PTI) was incorporated in Madras on 27 August 1947.

Reuters had come to India in 1878 soon after the inauguration of a submarine cable between London and Bombay. To fill the domestic news vacuum, K.C. Roy and Usha Nath Sen set up the Associated Press of India (API) in 1908, essentially a small but effective news pool. Reuters absorbed this as its Indian limb in 1919, but registered it as a private Indian company in 1945. Sadanand had set up the Free Press of India News Agency in 1927 but this faced closure when the nationalist-oriented United Press of India (UPI) came into being in 1933 with Dr B.C. Roy as a promoter. UPI lacked resources while Reuters-API had a European bias. PTI was designed to be the corrective.

With Independence approaching, Sardar Patel decided to recall Reuters' Indian telegraph licence. Reading the writing on the wall, Reuters sought negotiations, and a three-year partnership agreement was worked out whereby PTI would take over Reuters' Indian operations and be responsible for international coverage from Cairo to Singapore. PTI set up an India desk in London. Pakistani objections intruded and there were differences over coverage of the Kashmir question, UN proceedings and news from the Communist bloc. With the partnership agreement due to expire, further negotiations were opened in 1952. Neither RNG nor Sadanand had been particularly enamoured of a partnership with Reuters. They were minority members of the Indian delegation under K. Srinivasan that negotiated the deal. They preferred an arrangement with the Associated Press of America. In fact RNG thought an agreement with the French agency Agence France-Presse (AFP) might be even better.

RNG had succeeded Kasturi Srinivasan as chairman of PTI in 1953 and assumed the burden of steering the negotiations. Reuters put a price tag of £40,000 for bulk purchase of its services. RNG beat this down to £30,000, adding to the pressure by dropping hints of an AFP alternative. It had been hard going. But then RNG was nothing if not a tough negotiator.[1] One of the factors that spurred RNG was the snide comment of an English critic who had in a book entitled *The Price of Truth* scoffed at the notion that Indians would be able to run a truly objective news agency. The sneer hurt. This was a challenge that had to be met.

However, in 1954, the first Press Commission under Justice G.S. Rajadhyaksha referred to certain undesirable features of Indian newspaper ownership such as giving undue publicity to proprietors and showing bias in favour of their business interests. This criticism was extended to PTI, cooperatively owned by some of these same business magnates. Improper management and nepotism were alleged and reference was made to complaints that where certain business interests were concerned PTI 'has shown willingness to accommodate them by not covering news which might affect them adversely . . . or which might publicise certain private interests'. The commission therefore recommended transfer of PTI by Act of Parliament to a public corporation.

Devadas Gandhi, PTI's chairman at the time, issued a rejoinder, 'Press Commission and PTI, A Caveat'. This repelled the criticism and argued that the issues raised related to the initial transition period and that things had changed:

> The Board of Directors took effective charge from early 1953 when the old order changed. Before that date, conditions were in the very nature of things irremediable. As soon as the new administration came into being, the new Chairman, Mr Ramnath Goenka, devoted himself almost exclusively for several months correcting past errors and making a new start . . .

*The Times* of London carried a dispatch from its Delhi correspondent stating 'the inadequacies of Indian agencies for which foreigners cannot be blamed is recognised by the Commission'. The remark was rebutted by Devadas Gandhi, who added that 'the Board of Directors must always function—and clearly appear to function—in the interest of the Press as a whole and not in the special interest of a few'. Two members representing small newspapers were added to the board. The concept of a public corporation divorced from newspaper ownership was firmly opposed. Much later, public interest directors were also included, persons like P.N. Haksar and Justice H.R. Khanna among them. None could now say that PTI was a monopoly or operated by a cabal.

In his presidential speech at PTI's annual general meeting in December 1953, RNG said:

> Although we represent here our own newspapers, in a wider sense we are also representatives of the public itself, I should add trustees charged with the duty of running an efficient national news service. We are the eyes and ears of the people and on the service we render them through PTI depends to a large extent their knowledge of and relations internally as well as with the rest of the world.

He denied that any large newspaper house dominated PTI.

> The maximum shareholding is limited to Rs 25,000, carrying five votes, while on the other hand, five small newspapers, each owning a Rs 100 share, can claim the same number of votes. In other words, viewed as a whole, the balance of voting strength is in the hands of smaller newspapers against the bigger ones. The number of votes in PTI is 214, distributed among 127 shareholders . . . The newspapers and the Government should cease to think of PTI as a private venture or a limited company. It should be treated as a non-party, non-political, non-profit making and non-controversial national service and asset.

RNG was to continue to take a paternal interest in PTI and its Hindi counterpart, Bhasha. He was zealous in guarding their independence and promoting PTI's viability, expansion at home and abroad, and modernization. In 1954, PTI appointed a committee to rationalize its subscriptions. RNG was a member. Its chairman, Parulekar, later reported that the principle of 'one paper, one subscription' with a surcharge at higher slabs was adopted. Despite being the most adversely affected, Goenka 'willingly accepted, and today has to pay Rs 18,500 a month instead of Rs 3500 which in earlier days would have been a single subscription for all the [*Express*] group'.

Years later, in 1986, as chairman of PTI, RNG signed an agreement with the Madhya Pradesh State Electronics Development Corporation to set up a joint venture, Information Technologies Ltd, to make computers, news terminals, facsimile equipment, multiplexers and other data communication products. PTI's own R&D department developed some of these.

Even while immersed in IENS and PTI work, RNG was busy elsewhere. As a member of the All India Newspaper Editors' Conference he had visited the United States and Canada in 1945 with Devadas Gandhi, on a special mission to procure supplies of newsprint for the Indian press. His own establishment too was poised for expansion. The *National Call* had been started by J.N. Sahni and K.D. Kohli in Delhi in 1932 but then sold to Ramakrishna Dalmia who thought that if G.D. Birla owned a newspaper, he too should have one! At that time the government had put an embargo on new newspapers as it was in no position to supply newsprint. Dalmia renamed his paper the *News Chronicle* but soon acquired the prestigious *Times of India* in Bombay. With the lifting of the ban on new newspapers in 1948 he thought fit to launch a Delhi edition of the *Times* and dispose of the *Chronicle*. Deshbandhu Gupta, owner of the Tej group, purchased the *Chronicle* in 1948, but on running into a loss got RNG, a friend and AINEC/IENS colleague, to partner him. The paper, located in Mori Gate, was renamed the *Indian News Chronicle*.

As fate would have it, Deshbandhu Gupta was killed in an air crash in Calcutta in November 1951 (see Chapter 2, pp.59-60). He had been in debt and Lala Sri Ram, who had been very supportive, was now greatly concerned about what would happen. He wrote to RNG, who helped clear Deshbandhu's dues. The correspondence shows that he wrote off a sum of

Rs 40,000 that Deshbandhu Gupta owed him and made a further contribution of Rs 25,000 to the bereaved family. Vishwabandhu Gupta, Deshbandhu's son, says that RNG virtually became his guardian and guide. Since the *Tej* group could no longer manage the *Chronicle*, RNG took it over, getting a plot belonging to *Tej* on Bahadur Shah Zafar Marg as part of the deal.

RNG brought in 'Stalin' Srinivasan as editor of the *Indian News Chronicle*. He was followed by Kotamaraju Ramarao (who was tragically killed when he accidentally fell off a train), with G.N.S. Raghavan as news editor. Later, Claude Scott, the *Express* editor in Bombay, would keep an eye on the *Chronicle*, which was renamed the *Delhi Express* and finally became the *Indian Express* in 1953. As always, the mother edition, Madras, was called upon to nurture the new addition to what was now a uniformly named *Express* family. And as always, everywhere, A.N. Sivaraman, RNG's 'best man', led the team. P.D. Sharma joined as news bureau chief, to be followed by K. Subbarayan. But in 1954, the year following the renaming of the *Delhi Express* as the *Indian Express*, when Lala Sri Ram wrote to congratulate RNG on becoming a grandfather, Goenka was in despair and narrated a tale of woe.

The Delhi edition was not doing well. Soon after taking over what was then called the *Delhi Express*, Claude Scott wrote to RNG in February 1952 to say that the paper was losing Rs 50,000 a month. Every economy had been made but improving the paper would raise expenses further. Scott felt that one solution would be to start a Hindi paper, which the circulation people thought might initially sell 10,000 copies with a low cover price and a crossword competition. He warned of initial losses but hoped that if the *Express* got in on the ground floor, benefits would follow. RNG was enthused and believed the Hindi paper might even boost sales of the English edition. He went ahead and appointed the litterateur Indra Vidyavachaspati as editor and asked Scott to launch the new venture by July at the latest.

Vidyavachaspati suggested that the new paper be called 'Prabhat' with or without 'Samachar' as a suffix. 'Aalok' was another option. Scott thought this too highbrow and feared that a Sanskritized paper would not sell. RNG agreed and said he had told Vidyavachaspati that the language used should be simple Hindi mixed with Urdu words. 'Delhi Samachar' now led the field among names. The circulation manager, however, won the day with *Jansatta*, in keeping with *Loksatta*, omitting 'Delhi' in any title so as to avoid localism. A publicity drive was launched. Dummies were prepared. Everything was ready when on 19 June 1952 Vidyavachaspati wrote to Goenka that, even as the great day was about to dawn, RNG had forgotten to mention the editor's terms. 'I think,' Vidyavachaspati added plaintively, 'this is necessary!'

A month after the launch, sales were around 6350 copies. RNG was worried about the Sanskritized language. Vidyavachaspati was more concerned over the management style of the new general manager, Feroze Gandhi. He had been hired from the *National Herald* in Lucknow so that he and Indira, now the prime minister's official hostess in Delhi, might be together. RNG reminded Vidyavachaspati that they had agreed that *Jansatta* would be a pro-Congress paper, anti-communal and intelligible to the common man. Since the editor had replied defending his writings, RNG thought it best that they part company. V.N. Tewari took over. Circulation through the second half of 1953 averaged over 11,000 copies. RNG's target was 20,000.

However, losses were mounting. In consultation with Rafi Ahmed Kidwai, RNG decided to close *Jansatta* with effect from the end of May 1954. Entreaties by the editor and members of the staff that he visit Delhi and meet them fetched the stock reply that he was already heavily committed and that he should be spared the pain of seeing 'scores of colleagues and co-workers going into the wilderness', something he had never previously experienced. He had offered three months' severance pay to all workers plus encashment of any accumulated leave. Beyond that, he held out the assurance that should advertisements pick up and earnings improve from other publications, *Jansatta* would hopefully be restarted. Some workers suggested a cut in pay, others that RNG allow the employees or others to start a cooperative with his goodwill. The Delhi Union of Journalists (DUJ) reminded him that in the case of the *Bharat* in Bombay, the Court had ordered a severance pay of six months. It cited the closure of *Bharat*, the *Times of India* in Calcutta and the *Indian News Chronicle* in Delhi as 'symptoms of the same evil of unplanned and uncontrolled expansion . . . Enlargement of opportunities has proved illusory; it has raised false hopes, and has in fact produced unemployment and distress in a larger measure than before . . .' The DUJ appealed to the Press Commission to take note of these trends.

Vidyavachaspati had the last word. In an article titled 'Hindi Journalism: Prospect and Retrospect' in the *Organiser* dated 15 August 1954 he wrote:

> Hindi journalism today presents the alarming prospect of the rising sun being sought to be blacked out by encircling clouds . . . With the entry of capitalists in the field of journalism . . . the editor is no longer his own master. He is now the paid agent of one who thought primarily in terms of profit and loss . . . The editor's pen is now in bondage.

He saw two other dangers, namely, the tendency of capitalists to concentrate in one centre, leading to cut-throat competition, and the fact that press barons had reduced Hindi papers to carbon copies of their English counterparts which enjoyed preference in every respect.

It was in the run-up to this denouement that RNG had unburdened himself to Lala Sri Ram some months earlier:

> You know the circumstances in which I got involved in my Delhi newspaper venture. I knew it was an impossible job for a person who cannot be on the spot practically all the 24 hours. You will be shocked to hear that this has cost me

> already Rs 25 lakhs and I have now come to the end of my resources. Delhi still continues to lose Rs 80,000 a month . . . If I have not been able to reduce losses it is because of the absence of advertisements . . . The simultaneous publication of the *Indian Express* in Madras, Bombay and Delhi will doubtless help me in this respect.

The *Express* Group was at that time the largest chain of newspapers in the country.

The first Press Commission was appointed in September 1952 as the government felt that a review of the status and working of the print media was needed, in view of new developments and changing circumstances after Independence. There is an apocryphal story that while tendering evidence before it, RNG startled that august body with the statement that he had committed every crime in the Indian Penal Code, excepting murder, but even that should not be excluded in future! The echoes of the *Jansatta*'s closure had scarcely died down when the commission submitted its report. RNG did not like what he read. Lala Sri Ram queried him on rumours that the *Express* might close. He replied that this could happen 'in case the Government is foolish enough to accept the recommendations of the Press Commission presided over by Justice G.S. Rajadhyaksha where nobody who knew anything about the economy of newspaper production was there'.

The Press Commission had recommended a price-page schedule, to protect smaller papers from what it considered unfair competition, as well as a wage board to determine scales of pay for working journalists in various categories of press establishments. In consideration of the first issue, the IENS met and adopted a scheme that it commended to the authorities. RNG (who had quit the IENS) denounced the suggested schedule which he said gave weightage to larger newspapers and would 'make the rich richer, and the poor poorer'. He insisted that any price-page schedule would be ultra vires of the Constitution as 'restrictions on the volume of expression is not one of the [reasonable] restrictions permitted to be imposed by legislation'. He argued that about half the advertisement revenue in the country was being garnered by half a dozen newspapers, including the Big Five, namely, the *Times of India*, *Hindustan Times*, *Hindu*, *Statesman* and *Amrita Bazar Patrika*. He said at least part of this revenue must be forced to trickle down to the smaller papers. He therefore proposed a voluntary ceiling of eight pages for all newspapers and a ceiling of one-third on their advertisement content. Moreover, should newspaper prices be raised, this would exclude less affluent readers. 'Past experience has shown that, especially in the case of Indian language newspapers, whenever the price has been raised from one anna to one and a half annas, the circulation has dropped by a third to 40 per cent'.

A copy of this letter was forwarded to the minister for information and broadcasting, B.V. Keskar, on whom the IENS delegation had waited. RNG showed how the Press Commission's proposed price-page formula would harm small papers as well as the *Express*.

An ordinance promulgated by the government in regard to wage fixation of working journalists also invited RNG's wrath as another violation of press freedom. In an internal office memo, he said: 'The Government had demanded power to fix the wage of journalists under the ordinance. This will mean that it is the Government who will be their masters and not the newspapers concerned. They naturally will look to Government for favours rather than to the newspapers they serve.' This would spell the end of democracy. He suggested that the matter be brought to the attention of the Commonwealth Press Union and that Moraes write on this editorially and Mankekar take up the issue with the AINEC.

G.L. Mehta, the well-known public figure, wryly commented that the country could now boast of 'Working Journalists, Lurking Journalists and Shirking Journalists'!

*

Delhi had in 1958 become the *Express* headquarters, with Moraes as editor-in-chief.

A building had been constructed on Bahadur Shah Zafar Marg and RNG was on the lookout for tenants. He persuaded Moraes to use his good offices with Ellsworth Bunker, the American ambassador, to get the United States Information Service to occupy two floors in the building as its existing premises in Connaught Place were inadequate. Bunker was interested but Washington denied the funds.

Goenka agreed on the need for a block-making department and library in Delhi, and for standardized types. There were discussions on a cartoonist and cartographer. Abu Abraham was to join later but K.B. Kumar was given space to set up what was probably the first cartographic news service in the country. On the quality of newsprint and flongs, he pleaded import restrictions. Quite some years later, he approached the industries minister, T.T. Krishnamachari, with a scheme to set up a public limited company to produce newsprint with Canadian or American technical collaboration in view of the acute newsprint shortage. He sought approval for himself and his associates to hold a 'substantial interest' in a 72,000-tonne-per-annum capacity unit, and to reserve 18,000 tonnes for self-consumption with a 10 per cent increase annually for his own expanding requirements. Nothing came of it.

He worked out another plan to establish an Indian News Service Ltd, initially in collaboration with the *Times of India* group. This was incorporated in 1959 with a share capital of Rs 5 lakh. He and Moraes were shown as the two promoters. This closed in 1961 by when the *Express* teleprinter circuit was fully established.

Turning to the editorial side, RNG felt need for 'zoning' of editorial comment, so that state editions had a regional content, and wrote to Moraes and Mankekar on this score. Mankekar replied, opposing the use of smaller eight-point type to accommodate longer editorials, which he saw as a South Indian weakness. RNG took out his foot rule and, after making careful comparative measurements of editorial lengths over a week as against the *Hindu*, proved him wrong!

More seriously, Mankekar commented that the real problem with *Express* editorials was that the lower-middle-class clerical community was increasingly seeing them as too rightist, reactionary and intemperate. This segment of the population made up the bulk of the *Express* readership and they were, by inclination, more radical in outlook.

This appreciation brought a considered response from RNG, ensconced in Madras. He said Mankekar was partly right, but this policy was the culmination of many factors. He went on:

> The Government . . . are going towards the extreme left without weighing the ultimate pros and cons of their policies. No responsible government, particularly in a country where the mass of the people are ignorant, can be carried away by sheer emotion and enthusiasm . . . In our country, it is only the consciousness of privileges and not of responsibility that reigns supreme. This is true not only of the masses but also of our political leaders, who are more for catching votes than educating the masses and improving the calibre of their thinking and sense of responsibility.
>
> . . . No government can be run for any length of time on slogans and shibboleths, which is what the Congress governments are trying to do . . . In fact there is no leader in the country. All of them are the led . . .
>
> We have now got to tread the path of unpopularity, the road to educate the people in making them think that here is an alternative to socialism and communism . . . We may pay for it for the time being, but there is a chance that in the final event, a strong section of the people will appreciate our line. There is, of course, the other alternative. That is the way, which is adopted very successfully by papers like 'The Hindu', that is neither fish nor fowl . . . My misfortune is that I have always taken a strong line . . . We cannot ignore the manner in which . . . Pandit Nehru is flouting intelligent public opinion and is practically acting as a dictator . . .

> On one matter I will readily agree—that our language should be more temperate. Strong language does not always pay dividends. And, if we use strong language too often, it will lose its value and meaning . . .

RNG's Congress moorings were beginning to weaken.

*

RNG was no stranger to Delhi or to its political elite when the *Express* came to the capital in 1958, and his opinion often carried weight with the powers-that-be. He knew Jawaharlal Nehru and readily gifted a press worth about Rs 1.75 lakh to the Associated Press Ltd (*National Herald* Group) in Lucknow, with which Nehru was associated. He thereafter gave Feroze Gandhi a managerial appointment at the *Express* in Delhi. Feroze would come for half a day and later combined his duties at the paper with his role as a newly elected Member of Parliament. His newspaper experience probably stood him in good stead in securing the enactment of a Private Members' Bill protecting newspapers from breach of privilege for bona fide publication of parliamentary proceedings.

Feroze Gandhi investigated the operations of insurance companies and spoke eloquently on the subject in the course of the Insurance Amendment Bill. Dalmia's Bharat Insurance was in the dock as a result of official investigations into that magnate's business affairs. Later, in 1957, Feroze took a leading role in the Mundhra exposure, which brought him into conflict with T.T. Krishamachari, a great friend of Goenka. Mundhra was a businessman who had acquired a controlling interest in a number of companies whose share values, among others, started tumbling following Krishnamachari's socialist budget of 1957. In order to stabilize the market, the finance ministry, with Krishnamachari's approval, got the Life Insurance Corporation to buy into 'blue chip' companies, and a special bail-out package of a kind was negotiated for Mundhra who was in distress. This in turn gave rise to suspicions that Mundhra had been favoured. A 'scam' that was not, snowballed sensationally as the minister distanced himself from some of his key officials who had acted in good faith and were ultimately exonerated.

Years later, in 1964, RNG wrote to TTK reminding him that 'because of the attitude adopted by Feroze Gandhi to you, I sacked him with serious consequences to myself'. Some felt that Feroze was actually eased out by RNG in order to avoid further embarrassment to Nehru, while others contended that this was done at the instance of Indira Gandhi. But now, in his 1964 letter to TTK, RNG recalled his sacking of Feroze Gandhi in the context of another matter—the government's appointment of two directors on the board of Bennett Coleman following a charge of financial irregularities, as a prelude to ousting Shanti Prasad Jain, its chairman and owner. The fallout of that episode was to create lasting enmity between RNG and Shanti Prasad. Yet, he now appealed to TTK not to push things too far. RNG advised that in case some drastic remedy was necessary, the *Times of India* should be placed in independent hands for, say, five years and not left to the mercy of the 'turncoats' within the *Times* that the government favoured.

RNG said he knew for a fact that the charge of embezzlement against Bennett Coleman arose when 'private money had to be given to politicians, particularly Congressmen, for election or other purposes'. He could prove this. Some Rs 10–12 lakh were involved, he asserted—the larger sums being bruited about were make-believe.

Earlier, in 1954, when the Birlas were interested in setting up a steel plant with American collaboration, TTK as minister of commerce and industry had backed this but was blocked. This so incensed him that he submitted his resignation to Nehru and left for Madras. M.O. Mathai, the prime minister's personal private secretary, records that he subsequently sent a message to RNG over the *Express* teleprinter asking him to request TTK not to create problems and return to Delhi. There was a hint that TTK might get the steel ministry, for which he hankered, in a reorganization of portfolios that was under consideration.[2] TTK did get the steel portfolio as an additional charge when this ministry was created in 1955.

RNG played a significant role in another cabinet appointment. His personal staff in Madras recall Goenka phoning Nehru in Delhi and recommending C. Subramaniam for inclusion in the Union Cabinet, possibly as finance minister, in the reshuffle that followed implementation of the Kamaraj Plan in 1958. A little later, Nehru called back asking RNG to request Subramaniam to go up to Delhi. He did so and was inducted into the Cabinet. RNG was to tell friends that he too had been previously sounded for a ministerial berth but had declined. He preferred to remain behind the scenes.

Nehru was a broken man after the Sino-Indian conflict and passed away in 1964. He was succeeded by Lal Bahadur Shastri, who himself died of a heart attack in Tashkent eighteen months later. Morarji Desai was a strong contender for the top position, but Kamaraj had other ideas. Much has been said about RNG informing Kamaraj of Shastri's demise, and of the two of them travelling to Delhi the following morning and discussing the succession en route. RNG suggested Indira Gandhi's name and Kamaraj reportedly welcomed the idea, provided she was now willing (which she was not in 1964). He believed, like others in the Congress 'Syndicate', that they would be able to manage her, but not Morarji. Kamaraj announced a party consensus in her favour and she was duly elected prime minister. Gulzarilal Nanda, a second-time acting prime minister, was overlooked. Is this the real story?

On 11 March 1966, RNG wrote to Nanda from Madras apologizing for the article 'Bring in Morarji' which had appeared in the *Express* the previous day. He continued:

> May I assure you that it does not reflect my opinion. Indeed, I was shocked to see it and I have written to Mr Frank

> Moraes expressing my feelings. A copy of my letter to him is enclosed . . .
>
> In the last two years, family worries have prevented my paying personal attention to affairs in *The Indian Express* and the present lapse is a result of that. I hope such instances will not be repeated.

This was not to be the last time that RNG dissociated himself from one or another member of his staff as the occasion warranted. His temper tantrums sometimes served this very purpose. He would operate on several tracks.

A year later, on hearing from Shreyans Prasad Jain that Morarji was angry with him, he sent the latter, now deputy prime minister, a long letter of explanation. This was dated Delhi, 25 April 1967.

> I should have called on you to let you know where I stand. The reason why I have not done this so far is because I have been terribly upset by one thing. The regard and respect I have for you as the only living statesman in the Congress, is matched only by my distaste and dislike for Kamaraj . . . I simply cannot reconcile my respect and regard for you with, let me put it plainly, my hatred for Kamaraj.
>
> Perhaps I should tell you why I cannot have any regard and respect for Kamaraj. Even before the Congress debacle in the last general election I had come to the conclusion that Kamaraj was not serving the best interests of the Congress Party. His association in Tamilnad with E.V. Ramaswami Naicker, who has wounded the religious sentiments of the people, was bound to boomerang. I had, in fact, warned Jawaharlalji about this some years ago . . . As I see it, Kamaraj has become a menace to the Congress Party. He is, in fact, presiding over the liquidation of the Party . . . even if unwittingly . . .
>
> Kamaraj's decision to work with people like Atulyababu and Patil has done a lot of harm . . . in Bengal . . . [Other instances of mishandling are cited from Bihar, Kerala and Orissa.] It is not a question of Kamaraj's personal integrity. The real question is whether what is good for Kamaraj is good for the Congress or good for the country.

> Kamaraj's capacity for mischief has been very great for several years . . . He first contrived to make Shastriji the Prime Minister and he later contrived to give the succession to Indiraji. In both instances, his motive appears to have been the same—to have as Prime Minister a person whom, he thought, he could manipulate from his position in the Party . . .

There was more in the same vein in this astonishing letter. Morarji replied the very next day. He said he had no anger against Goenka and no hatred for Kamaraj. Nor had there been a rapprochement with the latter. He chastised RNG, saying, 'When you have made up your mind, I know your passions and prejudices [leave] no place for reason or argument.'

*

Always on the lookout for talent to strengthen the *Express* stable, RNG brought in veteran journalist Prem Bhatia, as political correspondent and then resident editor in Delhi in the 1960s. RNG suggested campaigns against three former Congress chief ministers, Pratap Singh Kairon of Punjab, Bakshi Ghulam Mohammad of Jammu and Kashmir and Biju Patnaik of Orissa, on charges of corruption. Bhatia records being asked by RNG to launch a news and editorial campaign against all three.[3]

The Congress split in 1969 found RNG firmly on the side of the 'Syndicate'. He now saw Indira Gandhi as the real enemy of the Congress and thoroughly disapproved of Morarji's ouster and the party's lurch to the left with bank nationalization. He canvassed for the Opposition candidate, Sanjiva Reddy, for the office of President that same year. But Reddy could not prevail against Mrs Gandhi's nominee, V.V. Giri. Soon after, the vote on the Bill to abolish the privy purses of former princes was adopted by the Lok Sabha in the teeth of fierce opposition to reneging on a constitutional contract. The focus then shifted to the Rajya Sabha. Every vote counted. RNG spoke to S.K. Poddar, a Congress MP and friend from Calcutta, and 'ordered' him to vote against the measure. Poddar agreed but, like other Members, remained under heavy pressure to follow the Congress (I) whip. RNG kept ringing him up so that he should not falter. He insisted that Poddar not just abstain, but vote against. He did so. The Bill was defeated by a single vote. Indira Gandhi was, however, able to secure her objective with the passage of the Constitution (26th) Amendment Act after her re-election in 1971.

The 1971 elections were hotly contested. The *Express* knew which side it was on and, with RNG's full backing, led the electoral charge with a series of signed front-page articles by Moraes titled 'Myth and Reality'. These took up various aspects of Mrs Gandhi's promises and programmes and sought to puncture them. But the Congress slogan of Garibi Hatao carried the day and the Congress (I) was returned with a substantial majority. The *National Herald* exulted in the result with the quip 'Moraes Myth, Indira Reality', which Frank took in good spirit! RNG personally entered the fray in this election, openly breaking with the Congress, to stand as an Independent from Vidisha in Madhya Pradesh with the blessings of the Rajmata of Gwalior, Vijaya Raje Scindia, whose electoral fiefdom this was, and the full support of the Jana Sangh (JS) of which she was an important functionary. He won handsomely, as expected. This was to be the beginning of his more open association with the JS and RSS, a trend influenced by the rajmata and by RNG's growing friendship with Nanaji Deshmukh, a leading RSS personage.

On the eve of the poll Moraes had called on the people to 'Vote for India'. In its aftermath he endorsed 'The People's Verdict' but said that Mrs Gandhi should now focus on restoring law and order and curbing corruption. 'Authority should not make the Prime Minister authoritarian.' But that, alas, was the direction in which things were moving. With the victory over Pakistan in Bangladesh, the London *Economist* proclaimed Mrs Gandhi 'Empress of India'. But, like Joan of Arc, she had started hearing voices—of conspiracy and a foreign hand.

Moraes retired in 1972 to be an *Express* pensioner in London until his death in 1974. The *Express* mourned his loss in a glowing editorial. Nandan Kagal, his deputy, who might well have succeeded him, unfortunately died in harness when only forty-six. It was S. Mulgaokar who took over in December 1972. For RNG, this was to be beginning of another long *Express* partnership.

*

Back in Parliament after twenty years, RNG joined with others in the Opposition to forge a united front against Indira Gandhi. He was now more often in Delhi and this was soon to become his operational base, with his suite in the Express Building on Bahadur Shah Zafar Marg and, later, the Express Guest House at 130 Sundar Nagar becoming a political hub and convivial rendezvous for people of every description.

Among those deeply concerned with political and social trends in the country was Jayaprakash Narayan. A somewhat lonely figure who until now had devoted himself to gramdan, he seemed to voice the nation's anguish against growing evidence of moral rot. He first sought to build a national consensus on an agenda of reform but, unable to make much headway, assumed leadership of the fight against such ills as corruption. The Nav Nirman agitation in Gujarat in 1974 awakened him to the power of youth, and it was to the people, and especially the youth of Bihar, that he turned. He called on them to renounce their studies for a year to work with him for national regeneration. The Chhatra Yuva Sangharsh Vahini spearheaded the struggle that ensued. It was met with repression.

JP had known RNG from Quit India times but had turned away from him on being led to believe that Goenka wanted unscrupulously to 'grab' Indian Iron and Steel from Biren Mukherjee (see Chapter 5, pp.125-26), whom JP rated as a most honest man. But it was to JP that RNG now turned as a messiah. Before long, JP changed his mind and rediscovered in RNG a dynamic and faithful warrior in a common cause. Thereafter RNG took over, becoming the mainstay of the Bihar movement and JP's campaign. He decided that JP's voice needed amplification and reach, and what better medium for this than the press. In 1973 JP was assisted to start *Everyman's*, an independent sixteen-page tabloid without any advertising, together with a Hindi counterpart, *Prajaniti*, in the Gandhi Peace Foundation. Vatsyayan, the distinguished writer, was editor and had Prabhash Joshi to assist him. The paper was, however, printed at the *Express*. This not being a very practical arrangement, *Everyman's* editorial department was then transferred to the *Express*, with Irfan Habib and later Ajit Bhattacharjea as editor. JP, Ganga Sharan Sinha, a well-known politician, Radhakrishna, head of the Gandhi Peace Foundation, and Mulgaokar were members of the editorial board. Ashwini Sarin was a roving correspondent and Prabhash Joshi, Punyapriya Dasgupta and H.K. Dua wrote for it. When *Prajaniti* was censored, it was replaced by *Aas Paas*, a sport and film journal. All these were printed and published by R.K. Mishra for the Lok Niti Parishad at the Chronicle Press, Bahadur Shah Zafar Marg. But for all practical purposes they were *Express* publications.

Leafing through *Everyman's* headlines provides a glimpse of what it offered.

20 July 1974: Time for Struggle, not for Studies. Corruption has crossed all bounds.

3 August: The day will come when I will ask policemen and others not to obey their officers but to obey the leader of the movement. I am not saying so now. Today I say to them what Gandhiji said: 'Do your duty but do not act against your conscience. Do not obey illegal orders.'

21 September: Dilli chalo.

6 October: During the Bihar bandh, JP said the Bihar Government must go. If not the P.M. should go.

November 1974 saw JP lathi charged at a rally in Patna. Indira Gandhi retorted that she would not bow to demands from the streets. The government accused JP of being a tool in the hands of the Jana Sangh and Anand Marg.

The Pokhran nuclear explosion in May 1974 had been followed by a Congress conclave at Narora to fashion a strategy to counter JP.

*Everyman's* headlines continued:

8 December 1974: Plan for Electoral Reform by V.M. Tarkunde, M.R. Masani, A.G. Noorani, P.G. Mavlankar and Eric da Costa.

JP recalled Indira Gandhi's dismissal of the EMS government in Kerala in 1957 when she was Congress president in order to justify the Bihar government's current demand for removal of her government.

2 March 1975: Call for a million-strong demonstration before Parliament on 6 March to press demands for an end to corruption, electoral reform, removal of unemployment, institutional changes, revocation of the external Emergency (imposed in 1971), and repeal of MISA.

9 March: Mohan Dharia, Minister of State, dismissed for seeking dialogue with JP. Chandra Shekhar, Krishan Kant and other Young Turks restive.

6 April: Pistol shown in Allahabad High Court and grenade attack on Chief Justice of India in Delhi.

4 May: Ashwini Sarin's story from Banda: '1500 Harijan girls sold every year'.

11 May: JP's manifesto for a new Bihar with the establishment of Janata sewaks from the village upwards.

Gujarat polls were announced for June 1975 with a Janata Front opposing the Congress as the culmination of the Gujarat movement.

The last issue of *Everyman's* appeared on 22 June 1975. The lead story was headlined: 'Congress going Fascist to retain Mrs Gandhi' after the Allahabad Court ruling.

RNG had sensed a looming national crisis and JP as the one man who might save India. He turned to him, as he had to Gandhi at the time of the freedom struggle. It is far from certain that he agreed entirely with JP's philosophy or manner of struggle or really understood or believed in Total Revolution, an inchoate concept to his practical mind. But this was war and not the time to ask questions, but to do or die. The *Express* teleprinter network enabled JP to keep in touch with his lieutenants and monitor trends and events.

It was not long before Indira Gandhi hit back. In a public address in Bhubaneshwar on 1 April 1974, she said 'those taking money from the rich have no right to talk about corruption'. This was a jibe against JP's enjoying RNG's support and hospitality, about which the CPI was blunt and scathing. It was rumoured that a harried prime minister might call a snap election. This diverted attention from Bihar and Total Revolution to an Opposition bid to form a united front, which some hoped JP might lead. A national coordination council was indeed formed. In any event the battle had been joined.[4]

Meanwhile, another scandal surfaced in 1974 with regard to the activities of a Congress MP, Tulmohan Ram, who was found to have committed forgery to secure import licences for some Pondicherry businessmen. L.N. Mishra, minister for railways, and until then one of Indira Gandhi's trusted lieutenants, was also under pressure for his alleged part in this murky business. Stormy debates followed in Parliament and the government was hauled over the coals day after day. Indira Gandhi was charged with protecting Tulmohan Ram and generally shielding corruption. Gujarat remained tense and the JP movement was gathering momentum. The government was reeling under the onslaught and an agitated prime minister arraigned party MPs for not coming to her aid by aggressively turning the heat on the Opposition.

K.P. Unnikrishnan, a Congress MP from Kerala, whose family was well known to RNG, had gone to see her when she started talking about JP, Goenka and the *Indian Express* teaming up against her. Unnikrishnan took the hint but said he would have to get evidence on the basis of which he could go on the offensive. The material was provided. It came from the CBI, the finance ministry, the company law department and other sources. Since this was confidential material and could have attracted attention under the Official Secrets Act, Unnikrishnan passed on some of it to the *Patriot*, which ran a sensational front-page story on 4 December 1974. The wire services and other newspapers immediately picked up the story. The mechanism for the counteroffensive against Goenka and JP, whose names were linked to a conspiracy against democracy and stability, was a privilege motion in the Lok Sabha. Congress and Leftist members led the assault.

The story is told in the official parliamentary record. The *Patriot* had alleged that Goenka, his son, BD, and the latter's wife, Saroj, and two *Express* employees 'are to stand trial for cheating, forgery and criminal conspiracy in Madras'. The gravamen of the charge was that the *Express* had cooked its accounts and records to show non-existent newsprint stocks based on documents from a fictitious Calcutta firm, Radha and Co., which it had hypothecated to the Punjab National Bank to get excess cash credit facilities. An alleged report of the chief cost accountant of the finance ministry about malfeasance by the *Express* was also cited. The events were said to have transpired in 1968 but had been brought to light only in 1974 after due investigation. It was further stated on the floor of the House that some of the funds so obtained had been improperly used for share dealings. RNG's connections with the National Jute Company, Calcutta and the Indian Iron and Steel Company were mentioned, as also JP's association with RNG and

*Everyman's*. No holds were barred. The argument was that if in the Tulmohan Ram case a privilege motion was filed and access to official documents provided, the same must follow here.

Unnikrishnan used harsh language. He described Goenka as 'a habitual offender, Seth Golmal of the Indian business world, a Natwarlal [con man], one who has poisoned the wells of public opinion'. He and his family were also accused of misusing trust funds of the Sri Venkateswara Temple in Tirupati 'to commit the same crimes any number of times'. Here was an Ivan Krueger, 'less his positive qualities'. The *Express* Group, Unnikrishnan said, undergoes metamorphosis: it was a private limited company in 1959, a public limited company in February 1961 and again a private limited company in 1968, and indulged in 420 (fraudulent) activities in between. Another MP, Bhogendra Jha said that the House was not discussing Tulmohan Ram, whose guilt could be measured, but 'atulmohan', something immeasurable. Although RNG's original culpability dated back to 1968, he had misused his position as an MP to block investigations into his criminality. The indictment was total and the language unrestrained.

RNG heard out his traducers over two days of tumultuous proceedings in December 1974, and then rose to reply. He said that the wild allegations levelled against him did not pertain to a period when he was an MP nor did they relate to the conduct of a Member of Parliament. The motions moved against him were therefore patently untenable and unsustainable and were clearly 'part of a campaign of calumny and vilification against me which is entirely politically motivated'. Moreover, the motions were based on only one ground, namely, that a prima facie case had been established against him in the Court of the Metropolitan Magistrate, Madras. This claim, however, had absolutely no foundation. In fact, the Court had rejected the prosecution's plea for committal. Both the *Patriot* and the CBI, on whose press release it had relied, were 'guilty of *suppressio veri* and *suggestio falsi*'.

On the charge of cheating the Punjab National Bank of Rs 40 lakh in 1968, it was noteworthy that neither the bank in question nor the Reserve Bank of India had made any complaint. Indeed, the *Express* remained a valuable client of the Punjab National Bank. No charges based on any report of the chief cost accountant of the finance ministry had ever been referred to him. As regards swindling the Tirupati Devasthanam Board, this was an old chestnut. It had been inquired into by the law minister at the request of the then Speaker and it was certified that no misuse had been found. RNG accused the CBI, the government and some of its other agencies of going out of their way to harass him. Their hands were not clean. In conclusion he affirmed that there could be no privilege without responsibility, but that several members had shown utter irresponsibility. He knew he had become persona non grata after the Congress split and things had got worse ever since Jayaprakash Narayan started his movement. He was content to let justice take its course and had the fullest confidence in the judiciary. About Radha and Company, he said he would answer in Court. The reply was forthright and stinging.

The following day, the Lok Sabha took up a privilege motion by RNG against All India Radio. He charged it with motivated coverage of and commentary on the preceding debate in repeated news bulletins, including citations from expunged material. This constituted a breach of privilege. He chastised AIR for being an official trumpet and advocated that it be converted into a truly autonomous corporation as recommended by the Chanda Committee. The information and broadcasting minister, I.K. Gujral, made light of RNG's objections and said he was welcome to have his views on freedom of the press of which he was a 'personified negation'.

The Speaker finally gave his ruling, rejecting both privilege motions. Regarding AIR, however, he opined that it was improper to broadcast or print observations that did not form part of the official record of the House. But he condoned the lapse on this occasion as his expunction orders may not have been heard clearly by everybody in the Press gallery on account of the hubbub on the floor of the House. RNG had won the day.

There was a sequel to this episode. Some years later Unnikrishnan got married and sent RNG an invitation card along with a letter. RNG did not attend but wrote to the bride, a Rajasthani, extending her his sympathies along with a beautiful saree as a wedding gift! She was furious. Unnikrishnan was amused.

Indira Gandhi had tried to influence RNG through C.P.N. Singh, a public figure from Bihar, who hinted that the cases against him might be dropped if he took a more moderate line. When RNG criticized such efforts, Mrs Gandhi had it conveyed to him that C.P.N. Singh had spoken out of turn and had not consulted her before talking to him. But, B.N. Tandon, Joint Secretary to the Prime Minister, notes that C.P.N. Singh had told him that he was talking to RNG expressly at her behest. He also writes that the CBI director, Devendra Sen, had confessed to him that the CBI had not been very fair or scrupulous in investigating RNG. Sen had submitted a note on Goenka's affairs to her and she had thereafter called him for a discussion. 'The CBI got the banks to harass Goenka, which is very improper.'[5]

Matters were coming to a head. L.N. Mishra died on 3 January 1975 from injuries sustained in a grenade attack on him at Samastipur railway station in Bihar the previous day. Mrs Gandhi immediately charged JP, railway workers and the Anand Marg with responsibility. Many thought otherwise. Mishra was a man who knew too much. He had for years been a principal slush fund collector for the Congress but was seen as a liability after the Tulmohan Ram licence scandal, leaving him both resentful and fearful. His wife was to say later that he had a premonition of danger to his life four or five months before his murder. He thought his phone was being tapped and that the CBI might raid him at any moment. Many suspicious circumstances came to notice, not least the manner in which the inquiry into L.N. Mishra's assassination was abandoned. Apart from its contemporary reportage, the *Express* subsequently published a pamphlet indicting the government for Mishra's murder.[6] The author, 'A.S.', presumably Ashwini Sarin, an *Express* correspondent.

The nation was polarized. Then on 12 June 1975 came the judgement of Justice Jag Mohan Lal Sinha in the Allahabad High Court on Raj Narain's election petition against Indira Gandhi. The petition was allowed. Mrs Gandhi stood disenfranchised for six years. There was pandemonium in the Court and stunned disbelief in the country. Sanjay Gandhi rallied his storm troopers to demonstrate in favour of Mrs Gandhi. An appeal was filed and in an interim ruling on 23 June Justice Krishna Iyer, vacation judge of the Supreme Court, granted Indira Gandhi a conditional stay until final disposal of her case. She was permitted to retain the office of prime minister and her seat in Parliament but was debarred from voting. The Congress president, Dev Kant Barooah, declared, 'Indira is India and India is Indira.' The die was cast. Two days later, on 25 June 1975, JP addressed a massive rally at the Ram Lila Grounds in Delhi. That same night, as India slept, Mrs Gandhi declared an internal Emergency. Opposition leaders were arrested and the Press muzzled. When 26 June dawned, the country found itself gagged and shackled.

# 5

# Business Bubbles in Calcutta

Ramnath Goenka used to say that newspapers were his business. This was true. The jewel in his crown was undoubtedly the *Express* Group, which brought him power and influence. But to sustain his newspapers without having to bow and scrape he invested in real estate. This was to prove an invaluable hedge against enforced losses on account of political pressures as much as the normal vicissitudes of business. Express Estates, Madras, the Express Towers in Bombay, the Express Building in Delhi and sundry other office and residential properties throughout the country underpinned the solvency of his ever-expanding newspaper empire. As Russi Karanjia would say, in this case admiringly, RNG's Fourth Estate was founded on Real Estate.

This was for the most part an indissoluble marriage. He would seldom part with any acquisition, though he did so selectively for strategic gain. His last illness, which was to prove fatal, was in pursuit of purchase of land for new offices in Calicut and Trivandrum. An apocryphal story attributed to G.D. Birla was that even were RNG laid to rest, somebody need only refer to a good piece of real estate for his soul to manifest itself to close the deal!

RNG rose from relatively humble circumstances but readily gave away his modest inheritance of house, fields, orchard and dharamsala in Janakpur in Nepal to his elder brother. Then, unencumbered by anything more than his wits, the young lad went to seek his fortune in Calcutta, a home from home and the proving ground of aspiring Marwaris. Though he lived in Calcutta but briefly before going to Madras, he was to return again and again. He had a deep familial sentiment for the city and a house on Ashok Road in Alipur. Many family marriages were celebrated there. Calcutta, like Madras, was home. Bombay and Delhi were his political stage.

His early career as a dubash for Walker and Co. and then the Bombay Company came to a close around 1936 when he had to end what was becoming a conflict of interest between his work with this European concern and his own business and political interests. He entered into a share-broking partnership with J.R. Pilani in 1936, dealing also in bullion. A firm of his called Vishnu Laxmi Depot traded in brass sheets. These were partly turned into zip fasteners by R.S. Jhaver, who also had a small pharma company called Tablets India, in both of which RNG had an interest. He supplied sugar machinery through the Bombay Company to one V.S. Thyagaraja Mudaliar in Tanjore and once had occasion to go and live with him for three months in order to stabilize the operation of the sugar factory.

RNG traded in hessian well before he entered jute manufacturing. There could be a delay of anything up to two to three months between delivery of hessian bales for export and shipment. This uncertainty led to speculation on the price at which 'pucca delivery' would be made, this being the day when the bales were actually loaded on to the vessel. Profits were earned on the margin between the initial delivery and the so-called PD price, these transactions being something in the nature of futures trading. RNG had a gambler's instinct and delighted in speculation. He loved making money, but was perfectly willing to bear losses. A relative would say of him that the more money he made the more he wanted. Some called this greed. He saw it as insurance against a rainy day and a bulwark against having to bend his knee before insolent might.

A media presence in Calcutta seemed appropriate on the eve of Independence. He started the *Nationalist* in 1944 in collaboration with Shyama Prasad Mookerjee, who was declared editor. Disagreements soon surfaced. Mookerjee belonged to the Hindu Mahasabha and felt that its ideology represented the 'nationalist' ethos. Goenka thought otherwise. The two parted company amicably and RNG was to remark that 'no politician can run a newspaper'. A sister Bengali paper, *Bharat*, edited by the anarchist and revolutionary Makhanlal Sen, was also passed on by RNG to Shyama Prasad. Neither survived for long.

In 1945 RNG decided to launch a paper on his own. The *Eastern Express* was located in a huge mansion on Lower Circular Road, the residence of C.S. Rangaswamy, a financial journalist and owner of the Dorchester Printing Works, where a hall was added to house a rotary. The staff was mainly from Madras, C.A. Narayan, Krishna and Gopi, a cartoonist, among them, with P.R. Srinivas as editor and RNG as managing editor. Harold Laski, Wickham Steed and H.N. Brailsford contributed to the paper. A.N. Srinivasan covered the charter meeting of the United Nations in San Francisco. Despite these offerings, as well as the Jane strip cartoon, this venture too did not last and was sold to the Jain Trust in 1946.

Goenka was generous in helping others in business. Thus it was that he bought some tea gardens in Assam in partnership with Krishnakumar and Radhakrishna Dalmia, share brokers and relatives from his mother's side. These were managed by them on his behalf but were finally gifted to that family. He would deal in jute and steel shares but his bid to gain a dominant interest in those industries was to come later. A survey conducted in the 1980s by the Indian Institute of Public Administration on the business connections of newspaper companies revealed RNG's interests in aluminium, cement, chemicals and castings.

The spread of communism in Bengal in the 1960s alarmed industry. The industrialist Ramakrishna Bajaj and others worried about communist penetration into the newsrooms of leading papers and the resultant bias they saw creeping into business reporting and commentary. A group of concerned industrialists hosted a meeting in Calcutta to which some newspaper barons were invited. RNG was present and, while agreeing with some of what had been said, fobbed them off, pleading the proprietors' inability to do very much because journalists were protected by the Working Journalists' Act and could not be easily removed.

This was to be a familiar ploy whenever it suited him. Rules did not necessarily apply in all circumstances. Once when C.R. Irani of the *Statesman* told him of the problems he was facing putting up a new building in Delhi, RNG cut him short with a 'You cannot do business if you are a saint. What will you do? You will make a plan. You will go to the New Delhi Municipal Corporation?' He must have chuckled before adding, 'If you want a building, just build it!' This was the philosophy that was to guide Goenka in his bid to become the country's greatest jute and steel magnate.

*

Why Calcutta? Why at all? Calcutta was 'home'. It was also the Marwari capital of India and, in the early 1960s, the country's largest industrial hub and port. RNG had gone Tamil, and though scarcely a typical Marwari, he knew that deep inside he was 'Made in Marwar'. Be that as it may, he had to prove that he was better than the rest, even the best. He would show them. But there was probably a deeper reason too. Hitherto, he had taken the problems of friends in Bengal and elsewhere to Delhi and there sorted these out for them through his wide ministerial and bureaucratic contacts.

Now, there was a deeper malaise, a cancer that threatened Bengal. The communist inroads were most disturbing. Labour unions were holding the state to ransom. Naxalite violence threatened order. More police powers bred corruption. Unemployment was on the rise. Frequent electricity breakdowns were slowing production and there were signs of disinvestment. Bengal seemed on the verge of collapse. For RNG, all this appeared as writing on the wall. He was to confide in Bholanath Sen, a one-time minister in the state, that 'if Bengal goes, everything goes'. It was therefore vital to save Bengal in order to save India. Consequently, if share prices were falling, this was a time to buy and revive the market.

Eugene Black, president of the World Bank, visited South Asia in 1960 on the occasion of the signing of the Indus Treaty that the Bank had brokered between India and Pakistan. The ceremonies over, Black visited Calcutta where RNG happened to meet him. Black commented on the depressed state of the share market and wondered how India could grow without a buoyant stock market. Then, using Indian Iron and Steel's balance sheet as an illustration, he commented that a share price of Rs 16 was shocking. Anywhere else in the world it would be Rs 80–100 or more. Investors did not invest for charity but for dividends and capital appreciation. RNG was an absorbed listener. Black's logic seemed unassailable.

That was the time when steel was the cornerstone of the arch of what some now call the old economy, the yardstick of a nation's economic strength. It spelt industrial power and prosperity. Three new integrated iron and steel plants were under construction in the public sector at Bhilai, Rourkela and Durgapur. Jamshedpur gave Tata's pride of place in the private sector. And here was IISCO, a blue-chip company, faltering though boasting the only Indian scrip to be quoted on the London Stock Exchange. Goenka's imagination was fired. He had already taken over the National Jute Mill and had a growing newspaper chain. Add IISCO, and he would have outdone both Tata and Birla. The idea was not born instantly. It grew over time, helped along by happenstance.

He started with jute, crossing the divide and moving from jute trading to jute manufacture. His intimacy with the Sahu-Jain Group, his sambandhis or relatives by marriage, and other jute barons served as an introduction. He systematically learnt about the jute industry through discussion, observation, technical study and intensive reading. Sensing an opportunity, he purchased the National (Jute) Mill, a medium-small unit of 50–60-tonne capacity in 1959 from Andrew Yule, an old British managing agency house. His aim was to make it the largest jute mill in Asia. To do this, he had to break a long-time production-price cartel that had restricted expansion to prevent newcomers or the rise of a dominant producer. He refused to compromise and succeeded in getting this informal arrangement annulled.

Expansion required a new manufacturing shed. He immediately set to work. The monsoon had commenced. He procured labour to fill a pond in the mill compound and then a road roller with which to compact the soil. He would sit on a stool, under an umbrella in pouring rain. With eight weeks of day and night effort, the superstructure was up and the plant installed and running. Old hands were stunned. They had never experienced anything like this before. His manager, Hari Bose, asked if he was satisfied. No, he replied, 'I'm not satisfied and never will be, even on death's bed. You must never forget you are fighting a mad dog!' There was indeed a mad doggedness about his drive. Everything happened overnight, on an impulse. However, Mill No. 2 was up. The market was down and losses were being incurred, yet Mill No. 3 followed in 1969 only to meet with a mishap and so never became fully operational. The roof collapsed and twenty people were killed.

RNG did not live in Calcutta but spent time there periodically, otherwise leaving things in the hands of managers, some of them birds of passage—Alok Jain, Chiranjilal Bajoria, Bhagwandas, his son, Shyam Sunder Sonthalia, his son-in-law, Sampat Nahata, Pradeep Ganeriwal, his grandson-in-law, and others—whom he would instruct on the phone from Madras, even while taking advice from elders in the industry. An absentee CMD was not the recipe for long-term success. Delegated power was no substitute, especially with a mercurial employer. But things went well at first with expansion and modernization. Mill capacity was expanded fourfold; productivity rose. The labour force correspondingly grew to over 22,000 personnel. By the early 1970s, the National Jute Company had become the largest single jute mill in Asia.

The National Company was a challenge. RNG would stand tall in Calcutta. If he lost, he always felt he could make it up again—later. The banks stopped lending at one time. Difficulties arose. He was conscious of the power of technology and wanted the latest and best. Technology too would enable him to cut down on labour. He would tell his managers that they should convince him or accept what he said. When they pleaded that he was perhaps right in theory but the situation would not permit that kind of action, he would respond by saying he had to run an industry. It was the 'situation' that must be corrected.

Initial success came with RNG's decision to introduce broadlooms for the manufacture of carpet backing, for which there was a growing demand in America. Broadlooms were not entirely new to India. He, however, went to the United States, inspected the machinery, familiarized himself with its operation, studied how carpet backing sales were organized and appointed selling agents there. Just then he had a stroke of fortune in the form of Peter Ganz.

RNG also had clout. The story is told of his being informed that processing of an application for import of some machinery would take ten days. RNG told his man to meet the jute commissioner and just tell him that Mr Goenka wanted the licence by that very evening. The commissioner later called back to say it would reach the National Company's office by 5.30 p.m. He must have known of RNG's influence with his superiors in Delhi.

Peter Ganz, a young American, had come to Bombay in 1960 to sort out some problem his small company had had with a mica exporter. He also had considered making caffeine from Indian tea waste and mentioned this casually to a visiting correspondent of the *Financial Times*, London, who in turn met Goenka at Shanti Prasad Jain's place. Goenka pricked up his ears and next morning arrived at the Taj Mahal Hotel, accosted Ganz and said, 'You have to come with me to Delhi to meet the Government, as we have to put up a caffeine plant in India!' Ganz protested that he was tied up with his own business but promised to put RNG in touch with some other people on his return home. This he did. He heard nothing further for some time and then suddenly got a message from London to be at the Waldorf Astoria at three o'clock the next day to meet Goenka.

They met. Ganz recounts what followed. RNG was with Bhagwandas and boasted about his newspaper empire, incidentally remarking, 'I've just bought a jute mill for my son in Calcutta.' Ganz said, 'That's funny. I've got a friend, Henry Wolfe, who is in the jute business.' 'That's the man I'm looking for,' said RNG. 'He is representing my worst enemies [the Jains]!' Ganz then decided to be tutored by Wolfe in the jute carpet backing business and to represent the National Company. RNG took him on. That was the beginning of a mutually profitable and occasionally stormy partnership.

Ganz soon discovered that Wolfe was undercutting him and promptly decided to learn the trade himself. RNG agreed, guaranteeing Ganz business worth $3 million per annum. In the second year, Ganz sold $13 million worth of carpet backing or more than what the National Company could supply. As sales volumes increased, RNG would cut the commission, leading to big fights. Finally, when sales overshot the National Company's expanded capacity, RNG formed a small consortium of mills to feed the booming American market. Export volumes grew to $35 million.

RNG began to dictate terms and could do so on account of foreign exchange and other controls in India. Ganz later turned the tables by commencing trade with Bangladesh too so that he could no longer be unilaterally pressured. His business peaked at $65 million per annum. By then synthetics had begun to enter the market and soon killed carpet backing. But even during this period, RNG had begun buying into Indian Iron and Steel. He pumped out money from National Jute and lost it speculating on Indian Iron. 'So the National Company . . . went way down . . . It was a crazy time.' Ganz's view was that 'He [RNG] lost National Jute because he screwed it up . . . . He couldn't do anything wrong in his mind. And he overpowered all other people.'

A huge fire in the mill in the early 1970s dealt him a hard blow. But he had begun to bleed the company and some jute dealers cheated him. The government was after him politically, but struck at his industries. He would say that if he was fighting the powers that be, he must have his hands clean. And so he would ostensibly keep his books in order, often on a tip-off of a raid. Around 1971, the National Company was raided for the third time. The authorities were certain that they would find all manner of irregularities. They went away sheepish, empty-handed. Everything was in good order.

One of his senior managers resigned four times. He was uncomfortable with the pace of expansion and disapproved of the siphoning of National Company funds for buying Indian Iron shares. He was repeatedly hypnotized into remaining. But RNG had lost the Midas touch, and his subordinates could not grow under a banyan tree. In the final analysis, it was a one-man show. This same manager said, the word compromise was not part of RNG's lexicon. People would carry tales to him. 'He should have had four eyes. But he had four pairs of ears instead.'

The National Jute Company may not have gone under but for RNG's Indian Iron caper. Profits from the company were used to speculate in IISCO shares, always in the hope that the money would be recouped. Meanwhile, the books were deftly written. But there was also considerable leakage in the purchase of jute as well as over-invoicing and under-invoicing of imported machinery and supplies, a lot of it from Thailand. One National Company buyer was caught red-handed by the customs authorities while returning from Bangkok and arraigned under the Foreign Exchange Regulation Act. In part, RNG's repeated demands for more money for speculative purchases in Indian Iron, phatka and other questionable deals engendered such transactions. By the time an internal auditor was appointed and a finance controller arrived thereafter from the State Bank of India, the company had been heavily milked. The bubble burst when profits fell below what was being siphoned out.

Things came to a pass when jute supplies and machine parts were purchased on udhar through promissory notes. Dealers knew that the National Company was sinking but RNG would assure them that all purchases were backed by his personal guarantee and that there was no need to fear default. If necessary, he personally would repay their dues. There was a storm in Parliament. RNG, then an MP, was hauled over the coals but defended himself gamely. The entire issue had been politicized, with the government trying to get at Jayaprakash Narayan through RNG. When the management of National Jute was taken over by the government on 30 July 1976, the company owed some fifty to sixty jute suppliers a total of around Rs 1.8 crore.

As RNG was unable to repay these amounts immediately, the jute creditors were promised repayment in due course under a formal agreement entered into on 30 January 1973. As these payments too did not materialize, the creditors formed a panchayat under Chauthmal Taparia and four others and negotiated a mortgage on the Express Building in Delhi until a full and final settlement. Simultaneously, the National Jute Company resolved that should any liability fall on the *Indian*

*Express*, it would reimburse the amount involved to the *Express* at 10 per cent interest.

The outstandings were repaid in instalments as the mill's fortunes registered some improvement. Since only four or five creditors remained to be repaid by 1976, RNG pleaded that he be released from the mortgage. The panchayat agreed even as it again supplied over Rs 1.5 crore of machinery parts to the National Company on credit against his personal guarantee. Soon thereafter, the government took over the management of the National Jute Company. Further repayment to the jute creditors was frozen.

After the Emergency was lifted, RNG wrote to the industries minister, George Fernandes, on what he said was a matter of his honour. Developments in the National Company flowed from the previous government's displeasure with him. The taking over of the National Company's management in July 1976 was vindictive, illegal, wholly unjustified and without a show cause notice or written authority. Baseless charges made against the mill remained unproven. After the Emergency, the new government had offered to restore the former management. He refused that offer as the government's mismanagement had meanwhile resulted in a loss of Rs 5 crore, a liability that he was not prepared to shoulder. The official managing committee was thereupon reconstituted and under its auspices the mill was able to break even. Further improvement was premised on institutional finance. This was promised but not forthcoming. A committee appointed to look into the affairs of the mill pronounced it viable. But the government suggested that RNG hand over 51 per cent of the shares to it before institutional finance was made available. He refused this 'immoral' suggestion. Yet he hoped that if the mill worked satisfactorily he would some day be able 'to take back the Company and discharge my moral responsibility'.

That day was not to come. Later in 1977, RNG forwarded a copy of his letter to the prime minister, Morarji Desai, with a covering note that said:

> I take the liberty of drawing your attention to the matter because it is a typical instance of the manner in which the present Government is perpetuating, and even compounding, the excesses of the Emergency instead of remedying them.

A Company Law Board inspection of the National Company in 1970 had led to several allegations of malfeasance but the subsequent CBI investigation uncovered no wrong. The matter was dragged through Parliament with much publicity to harass RNG, but nothing came of that either. Yet in October 1977, the Janata government petitioned the Supreme Court for permission to proceed with the prosecution. RNG was incensed.

The National Jute Company was taken over without compensation after Mrs Gandhi's second coming. The 1980s was not a good period for RNG. When he passed away in 1991, his debts to certain jute suppliers were still unredeemed.

*

If for RNG the National Company was an investment, his bid to take over Indian Iron and Steel turned out to be an adventure. What he had heard from Eugene Black kept ringing in his ears. Here was a gold mine that spelt industrial power. T.T. Krishnamachari and other friends advised him to desist from such speculation. But he was adamant.

Indian Iron and Steel was merged with the Steel Corporation of Bengal in 1952 to become more than ever before the flagship of Martin Burn, a leading British managing agency with multifarious interests in railway and electricity companies, engineering, coal and much else, making it the country's third largest industrial house. However, by the 1960s, Martin Burn was in decline. Two or three takeover bids were foiled, though Haridas Mundhra almost got away with it before Feroze Gandhi raised a hue and cry in Parliament in 1957 that aborted the move. A sharp fall in IISCO's share price whetted RNG's appetite and he rapidly enlarged his hitherto modest holdings with resources drawn from the then flourishing National Jute Company. Share values soared.

Many of his purchases were proxy or benami transactions through brokers who were glad to service an important buyer ready to play the market, buying and selling in accordance with market sentiments that he influenced through his interventions. He was once asked how he came by this kind of money. RNG explained that he had *Express* bank accounts in Delhi and Bombay and National Jute Co. bank accounts in Calcutta. So he would, say, issue a cheque on a Calcutta bank in Delhi (or vice versa) and then request the bank to give him a margin of some days before encashing it. Meanwhile, he would buy some more (IISCO) shares and deposit these with his Calcutta bank as collateral, against which he would draw money to honour his Delhi cheque when it came through clearing for settlement.

Came a day when the Calcutta bank apparently wrote and told RNG that unless his short-term credit was redeemed within a week, it would sell the shares he had deposited. Concerned that this would depress share prices and cause him a loss, he sought legal advice about restraining the bank from such a sale. He also advised his lawyer to purchase 50,000 shares. When the lawyer said he did not have the funds, RNG said he did not actually have to pay for the shares. If he could get an injunction against the bank, the share value could rise by maybe a rupee whereupon he could sell the securities the following day and walk away with a cool profit. The lawyer had no stomach for such a gamble. But RNG did win a twelve-day injunction against immediate sale by the bank of his securities. Word had spread. The courthouse was packed to capacity. He had, however, insured by telephoning Puttaparthi indirectly to consult Satya Sai Baba in whom he had great faith. But being a realist he also informed his lawyer friend that before risking anything you must know the right people in the right place at the right time. He was able to gauge the sentiments of ministers, bureaucrats and judges and act accordingly. Such was the audacity of the man and his amazing instinct for cold calculation! His actions were perhaps not strictly illegal, but certainly amoral. The laws and regulations with regard to such transactions have since undergone amendment.

IISCO was ailing though it was not until August 1971 that its shares dipped below par. Fearing that any large benami unloading would unduly depress share values, RNG felt it necessary to prop up the market through continuous buying. In a letter to Morarji Desai, finance minister, in July 1968 RNG denied trying to corner IISCO shares and said his purchases had stabilized the stock market 'when prophets of doom were thinking in terms of collapse of the economy'. He had honoured all his commitments scrupulously but was being 'hounded' by the Reserve Bank, the income tax authorities and by banks demanding immediate repayment of loans.

> I have borrowed approximately Rs 5 crores against part of my purchases both directly from the banks and through brokers and others against adequate security . . . I assure you . . . that I shall not buy any additional shares of Indian Iron but will endeavour to reduce my holding as and when suitable opportunities occur.

He linked this undertaking to the government's accepting a five-year loan repayment scheme that he proposed. He further said that he had no intention of ousting the present IISCO management (under Sir Biren Mookerjee).

In their annual report for the year ending March 1968, IISCO's directors announced their decision not to declare a dividend. Goenka was shaken. He foresaw a sharp fall in share prices and decided to stop the rot by making a bid to get himself elected chairman in place of Biren Mookerjee. For this he needed the neutrality, if not the support, of the LIC, the banks and other financial institutions that held a substantial block of shares in the company. He again wrote to Morarji

Desai, impugning the competence and conduct of the management in masking its appropriation of the Steel Corporation of India's shares in a so-called Investment Realisation Account in order to control a large block of voting rights—subsequently enhanced through the issue of rights shares—in favour of itself.

> From what has been summarised above, it is clear that about Rs 5 crores of the Company's funds remain invested in its own shares; that the Management had adopted colourable legal procedures to make IISCO hold its own shares, which is contrary to the basic concept of a private limited company under the Indian Companies Act; that the whole transaction is to the detriment of the shareholders outside the Management; that the Management fully attempts to benefit by this transaction; and, lastly, that the failure to declare a dividend this year after an unbroken record of dividends for 30 years, and the enormous delay likely to be caused and only now disclosed in putting through the Colliery Project, prima-facie raise serious doubts about the sincerity of the Management in conducting the affairs of the Company.

He appealed for an official inquiry into the affairs of IISCO.

The battle for the IISCO board was joined. Biren Mookerjee was a well-loved and greatly respected pillar of Bengal, who was being challenged on his home ground by a rank outsider. The bhadralok or Bengali gentry were outraged. A Marwari syndicate was organized, the Birla's quietly participating. It mustered 36 per cent of the equity (including *Indian Express* votes) and appeared to enjoy the support of another 6 per cent of the shareholders. The management group under Sir Biren was assured of 22 per cent of the equity vote. The LIC and banks owned 23 per cent of the shares, the balance being with miscellaneous shareholders.

It was at this point that disaster struck. Indira Gandhi nationalized fourteen major banks in 1969. A little later, the Reserve Bank froze the voting rights of all IISCO shares pledged with commercial banks and instructed that they be cast in favour of the management. Knowing which way the wind was blowing, RNG quietly dropped the idea of contesting the office of chairman. But a poll on the accounts that he called for showed a leakage of 9 per cent of his votes, presumably relating to refusals of proxies for the badla shares, with the banks. In 1970 the LIC and UTI bought a very large number of IISCO shares under instructions, to place the company beyond the reach of any raider. But IISCO was in trouble after the dividend fiasco. Further, the Bombay and Calcutta stock exchanges introduced certain restrictions encouraging bear sales and discouraging buyers. Share values tumbled to something of an all-time low. The LIC unloaded some more shares. Many brokers in Bombay, Calcutta and Delhi were badly hit. Goenka personally lost upwards of Rs 6 crore.[1]

V.K. Narasimhan, then editor of the *Financial Express*, was on the LIC board and a member of its investment committee. He was later to recount that at a certain stage, RNG's brokers found it unprofitable to keep RNG's IISCO badla shares. So they purchased shares from the LIC at Rs 17 and insisted that RNG take these at a time when he wanted the LIC to buy his shares at Rs 15 to offset his losses. This incident upset him greatly but he never spoke a word to Narasimhan, who had come on the LIC board as a representative of policyholders' interests and was determined to do his duty by them.

However, RNG got a friend to write a Letter to the Editor arguing that the LIC should not become a dealer in shares and depress the market, but play the role of a major investor. An LIC director responded, explaining that the LIC had sometimes to sell large blocks of shares at favourable prices as a hedge against the losses it sustained on falling shares. This was published. There was again no reaction from RNG. He respected the editor's discretion.

For quite some years, RNG had been putting *Express* money in shares and by June 1969 held a substantial number of IISCO shares as blue-chip investments with considerable growth potential. On account of subsequent events, IISCO shares could no longer be regarded as blue-chips and so RNG decided to convert the *Express* investments in these shares into 'stock in trade'. Accordingly a partnership by name of Express Traders was formed to take over share investments from *Indian Express* (Madurai) Pvt. Ltd, *Express* Newspapers Pvt. Ltd, and *Andhra Prabha* Pvt. Ltd. However, as IISCO share values continued to fall from November 1970 onwards, the *Express* thought it prudent to sell these shares. In April of the following year, it sold a large number of shares to the LIC at Rs 10 per share. The slide continued and Express Traders continued to sell these shares, which touched a rock bottom price of Rs 4. Whatever shares were left were taken over by the government with IISCO's eventual nationalization in 1976.

Goenka estimated that the overall loss to the *Express* Group on IISCO transactions was of the order of Rs 15 crore, including the cost of holding the shares. The government did not permit these losses to be shown as business losses for tax purposes. Registration of Express Traders under the Income Tax Act was also refused. RNG claims that false allegations of antedating the partnership document and concealment of income were made. The income tax authorities filed a criminal complaint in a Bombay court in 1974, which was still pending in late 1977.

*

RNG was a banker too. In 1954 some time after Ramakrishna Dalmia was indicted over the Bharat Insurance matter and fell foul of the government, Shanti Prasad Jain and Goenka bought his shares in the Punjab National Bank (PNB). Though modern banking had come to India with the British, the Punjab National Bank, which opened its doors in 1895, was the pioneer Indian bank. Shanti Prasad Jain gained a majority holding in the bank and became its chairman but was eased out from that position in 1954 following the Vivian Bose Commission inquiry into the affairs of the Jain Group. Goenka succeeded him. In 1960 the management dismissed a senior PNB executive for misconduct. The latter struck back, spreading a canard that the bank was likely to be restored to the Jains. This led to a run on its Delhi branches. RNG and D.D. Puri were the only directors in town and acted boldly to stave off a crisis. They got Reserve Bank approval to keep PNB branches open even until midnight so that depositors might make withdrawals and be assured that their money was perfectly safe. Within a day confidence was restored and the finance minister underscored the recovery by announcing that the Punjab National Bank was sound and solvent.

D.D. Puri related the story to Prakash Tandon, who was later to become chairman of the PNB. The Reserve Bank governor, being informed of the situation, chartered a Dakota to fly adequate currency notes from Bombay to meet the situation. Even four-year-term deposits were discounted immediately to restore confidence. Overtime was paid and food supplied to all employees to enable them to continue working day and night. Goenka and Puri toured the branches and, standing on stools, addressed throngs of depositors to assure them that their money was safe. They met Nehru, who assured all help, and the finance minister, Morarji Desai, who made a statement that Goenka issued as a press release. Goenka and Puri also arranged for someone to deposit Rs 10,000 in the Daryaganj branch of the bank, following which Goenka got Mahavir Tyagi, a good friend, to ask a question in the Lok Sabha to know whether it was true that the public had started re-depositing money in the Punjab National Bank. Morarji Desai had been suitably briefed and answered in the affirmative![2]

Some time later, T.T. Krishnamachari, the finance minister, was critical of RNG's resort to bank finance for speculating in shares and threatened action against the Punjab National

Bank. To cool things down, RNG yielded chairmanship of the bank to Kamalnayan Bajaj and the matter was smoothed over.

*

While himself in business, RNG time and again assisted others. Lala Sri Ram would often consult him about many matters, often down to detailed information as to the appropriate construction rates for building what was to become Lady Sri Ram College in Delhi. In turn, he would never hesitate to pick the best brains in any field of industry or technology in which he was interested.

RNG had strong faith in Ayurveda and often turned to this indigenous system for his own treatment and that of friends. This was a common interest he shared with Maharishi Mahesh Yogi. While his guest in Delhi in 1980, Mahesh Yogi spoke of setting up an Ayurvedic pharmacy. RNG suggested a scaled up unit. 'But who will manage it?' Mahesh Yogi asked. RNG volunteered to do so, scouted around and purchased the spacious Indraprashtha Gurukul on the Ridge just off the highway between Delhi and Faridabad. The enterprise was started but activity tapered off after Mahesh Yogi's departure.

More significantly, Goenka rallied support for Bharat Ram and H.P. Nanda when Swraj Paul, the British industrialist of Indian origin, made a bid to acquire DCM Ltd and Escorts respectively in early 1983. This was a time when capital was shy in India in what was still very much a licence–permit raj, and wealthy NRI raiders were on the prowl. RNG went to Nanda and asked whether he was prepared to have taken from him a large and successful tractor and automotive enterprise he had built up from scratch as a penniless refugee, only because the company made good profits and therefore had been bought into by the LIC, GIC and other public financial institutions. He said Swraj Paul was well in with Mrs Gandhi and when push came to shove, the public financial institutions would be obedient to the dictates of the government. Nanda agreed. RNG steeled Nanda and Bharat Ram to fight, citing his own example. He advised them to secure the best lawyers and spoke to leading counsel like Fali Nariman and Nani Palkhivala. Writs were filed. Nanda was to say that RNG gave him the courage to stay the course and was always available for consultations and never at a loss for newer stratagems. The *Express* and *Financial Express* gave full support and this gave a lead to the rest of the media.

Barring a few industrial houses such as Tata, Kirloskar and Oberoi, most businessmen were hesitant to cross swords with the government on this issue. The official view was that NRI investment should not be rudely rebuffed. In fact, the Federation of Indian Chambers of Commerce and Industry (FICCI) discussed the matter and advised Nanda to withdraw his writ petition as the government might otherwise take vindictive action against industry in general through taxation and controls. RNG told the FICCI emissary, a leading industrialist himself, that if an NRI takeover was so benign, he should invite Swraj Paul to take over his own flourishing industry! That ended the matter. The great danger seen was that the LIC, GIC and UTI had invested heavily in all blue-chip companies and could evict the original entrepreneurs by siding with NRIs should they come and decide to harvest the plums. RNG saw the issue starkly.

Swaminathan Aiyar, who was then with the *Express*, was asked to look into the matter of the incentives granted to NRIs and the Swaraj Paul raid. RNG gave him no directive but left him to dig into what was an interesting lead. It turned out to be a major story.

RNG had a canny inbred business instinct. He could think big but failed to delegate or build a cadre of professional managers consistent with his soaring ambitions. National Jute is a case in point. In just a few years it had expanded to eight times its original size and had become India's largest jute exporter. But he was an absentee CEO. He was later to admit that, whatever else, he must accept major responsibility for the decline of the National Company. He was not aware that he was being cheated by some of the men around him who then tried to cover up and went down the slippery slope. Even so, he was at least indirectly complicit. As for IISCO, he was carried away by the excitement of the chase. He overstretched himself and finally came a cropper. In both cases some innocent suppliers and brokers paid the price. Maybe they should have been more careful too. But RNG could be hypnotic.

Was Calcutta RNG's Waterloo? Not entirely. He separated a commercial business, the National Jute Company, from the *Indian Express*, his newspaper. The first was ultimately expendable, the other, his lifeline. But then, led by his counsel Rajesh Khaitan, he tumbled to the realization that the two were interlinked. Mrs Gandhi wanted to get National Jute only because she wished to curb the voice of the *Express*. At heart, the issue was freedom of the press. This was to be his defence and core interest ever after.

# 6

# Dark Days to New Freedom

The storm had been gathering. Indira Gandhi had squandered the gains from her Bangladesh triumph in 1971. Cronyism and corruption had bred disillusion that steadily turned to disgust. Opposition and unrest mounted, taking the form of mass movements, first in Gujarat and then in Bihar. The prime minister felt increasingly beleaguered and threatened. A railway strike and the Nagarwala case of embezzlement of Rs 60 lakh from the State Bank had begun to fade from public memory, but then L.N. Mishra, the railway minister, was murdered in January 1975 while the Chief Justice narrowly escaped a bomb attack some months earlier. The Allahabad High Court judgement of 12 June 1975, unseating Mrs Gandhi, dealt her a body blow. She had been disenfranchised for six years and consequently disqualified from holding any elective office for that period. Sanjay Gandhi's goons took to the streets. Jayaprakash Narayan appealed to the police and military not to obey illegal orders. And behind JP stood Ramnath Goenka, the trumpeter sounding the call.

It was patent that the government would react. It did. Not with a thunderclap but as a thief in the night. An internal

Emergency was imposed a little before midnight on 25 June before it was constitutionally promulgated. JP, Morarji Desai and leading Opposition leaders were detained and newspaper offices raided, or their electricity lines cut, to prevent publication and protest. Early next morning, the Cabinet was cursorily informed and meekly endorsed the coup. Censorship was clamped down nationwide. When their Delhi editions appeared on 28 June, the *Indian Express* carried a blank first editorial while the *Financial Express* reproduced in large type Rabindranath Tagore's famous poem 'Where the mind is without fear and the head is held high', concluding with the prayer 'Into that heaven of freedom, my Father, let my country awake'.

RNG was away, hospitalized in Calcutta, stricken with a heart attack. He disconnected the tubes from his ICU bed, stole out and was about to board a taxi when detected and brought back. He was prepared for arrest but was not touched. So he left for further treatment in Madras and then in Bombay, there to ponder his strategy. The story goes that while in Calcutta he had heard the call of Vithal, the God of Battle, from Pandharpur. Feeling better in Bombay, he 'escaped' from Bombay Hospital and drove to Pandharpur, there to have darshan of Vithal. He was later to claim that the strength he derived from this prayer enabled him to survive what followed.

It has been said that during the Emergency, RNG had thought of escaping to Nepal with his son, BD, and daughter-in-law, Saroj. This appears utterly unlikely though it is perfectly possible that he may have not rebutted such a rumour or could even have floated it himself as a feint to throw the authorities off his scent. That would be more typical! It did not take him long to decide that the nation's freedom had been cruelly snatched away and must be re-won. Thirty years after Independence he saw himself once again called to the barricades to wage another freedom struggle. This was war.

He rallied the ranks. Nanaji Deshmukh, Radhakrishna and other Gandhians, George Fernandes, Subramaniam Swamy and still others had gone underground on the night of 25 June or soon thereafter. As in the Quit India movement, RNG was to organize safe havens, movement plans, funds, a communication network and samizdat for the cause. There were obviously difficult days ahead, but nothing like a challenge to stiffen the sinews and summon up the blood.

RNG had had an inkling that something like the Emergency was brewing early in 1975 and had called Kuldip Nayar from the *Statesman*, where he then was, and talked to him about this possibility. Kuldip concurred and said he had heard some rumours too but it would be premature to write a story. However, RNG persuaded him to do so and send the copy to him. A week later, the item had found its way to the front page of *Motherland*, the JS organ! RNG had gradually forged durable links with the JS–RSS through Nanaji Deshmukh and Vijaya Raje Scindia. He had likewise drawn close to the Gandhian and Sarvodaya people through Radhakrishna, Govindrao Deshpande, Narayan Desai and Siddharaj Dhadda, and with socialists like George Fernandes, Madhu Limaye and Madhu Dandavate. It was through this instrumentality that he brought all three elements together under JP's banner.

RNG saw that JP needed a paper to promote his message and movement. Thus was born *Everyman's* and its Hindi counterpart, *Prajaniti* (see also Chapter 4, p.104), financed, staffed, printed and circulated by the *Express* as separate publications, so that the identity and credibility of the *Express* itself should not be compromised. RNG would attend editorial conferences with Radhakrishna, Suman Dubey, Irfan Habib and others. However, he did not agree with all of JP's ideas any more than JP approved of all of RNG's methods and language. But this was similar to the relationship G.D. Birla had with Gandhi. *Everyman's* suspended publication with the declaration of the Emergency. When the Emergency was lifted, Ajit Bhattacharjea, its former editor, suggested its revival. JP concurred. RNG declined. He had no funds. Moreover,

*Everyman's* had served its purpose. It was now time to move on.

With the Emergency in place, BD was anxious to placate the government and asked Kuldip Nayar, who had joined the *Express* in January 1975, if he could not write favourably about Sanjay Gandhi, who was now an extra-constitutional authority and a power behind the throne. Kuldip demurred although BD told him that he had word from one of Sanjay's close aides that he could be made editor in place of Mulgaokar whom it was planned to oust. Other names too had been mooted. Kuldip and S. Ranganathan, a retired ICS official of great standing who was a close Goenka family friend, suggested V.K. Narasimhan.

V.C. Shukla, the then minister for information and broadcasting, and others were playing on BD and Saroj Goenka's fears. Cushrow Irani, the *Statesman* CMD and chief editor, and RNG were soulmates during the Emergency. The two mainline papers stood up to the government and earned its ire. Irani learnt from reliable sources that Sanjay Gandhi's coterie had negotiated a deal through BD and Saroj, with RNG's concurrence. This was that the Congress would buy the *Express* Group of newspapers and the Delhi Express Building for Rs 6.5 crore, leaving Express Estates in Madras and Express Towers in Bombay as well as other smaller properties with the Goenka family. This, he maintains, was told to Indira Gandhi, who flew into a rage saying, 'What! Pay money to these people? I'll make them walk the streets!' RNG's own version to Irani was that he had finally walked out on Shukla and Birla as he would otherwise never have been able to face JP.

Irani's story need not be ruled out. But RNG could equally have been using this as a ploy to prolong discussions while waiting, very much like Mr Pickwick, for something to turn up!

*

Much has been written about the ordeals of the *Express* during the Emergency. The story is best told in RNG's own words.[1]

The government, acting under the personal directions of Indira Gandhi, abused its authority and subverted lawful processes, RNG said, 'to liquidate me and my group of companies economically and to make me an object of public ridicule and shame'. One of the prime minister's first acts on 26 June 1975 was to remove her mild-mannered and democratically inclined information minister, I.K. Gujral, and replace him with Vidya Charan Shukla, who she thought would better serve her Goebbelsian design.

A month later, at a meeting presided over by the prime minister, it was decided that

> The question of inquiring into the Express Group of Newspapers and Ramnath Goenka's industrial empire was to be given immediate attention by the Department of Company Affairs and Ministry of Law and necessary action taken in regard to irregularities and illegal transfers of funds to non-journalistic ventures from the profits of the newspapers.[2]

Indeed, attempts had been made even in 1972 to gain control of the *Express* Group by unilaterally appointing two government directors on its board for a period of two years. The Bombay High Court subsequently annulled the order in 1974 with strictures against the government. However, government directors continued to be on the *Andhra Prabha* board, and they moved the Company Law Board to state that Goenka retained a majority, enabling him to exercise effective management control over his Hyderabad and related group of papers. Quite evidently, the government was seeking management and editorial control over the *Express*.

With the declaration of the Emergency, C. Subramaniam, finance minister, informed RNG that Mrs Gandhi had asked him to inquire whether he would be prepared to sell his papers 'to the Congress Party or its nominees'. Nothing came of this, as has been related earlier in this chapter, but harassment increased. Pressure was applied through the Monopolies and Restrictive Trade Practices Commission. The *Express* filed a writ through V.M. Tarkunde, the great civil rights advocate. This defiance infuriated the government, which vent its spleen through the Press Information Bureau and All India Radio, its captive mouthpieces.

The Congress president, D.K. Barooah, and the Bombay Congress chief, Rajni Patel, then informed Shreyans Prasad Jain that the government planned to detain B.D. Goenka and his wife, Saroj, and possibly also RNG, under the draconian Maintenance of Internal Security Act (MISA), because of the *Express*'s inimical policies. RNG was petrified at the thought of his son and daughter-in-law being incarcerated on his account. Shreyans Prasad sought Rajni Patel's intervention. He in turn consulted the prime minister and concluded that the only solution lay in RNG parting with control over his papers. The warning was blatant and brutal. This was communicated to S. Ranganathan, the retired ICS official, who sought to intervene. BD was summoned by V.C. Shukla and told in no uncertain manner that failure to comply would be visited by punitive tax and other harsh measures. A tax demand of Rs 4 crore was mentioned. The instruments of torture were being readied.

In the circumstances, an anguished RNG wrote to S. Ranganathan within two months of the Emergency, stating that he had taken a decision in principle to part with his newspapers.

> . . . It is not an easy decision for me to take. These newspapers have been my life's work. I have built them up over 43 years and have made the organization the largest in India with a circulation of about a million copies a day. Ordinarily one has to wait for centuries to achieve this circulation in a country like India. Even century-old newspapers here with all their patronage and resources have not been able to achieve anything like this, and therefore it is very difficult for me to make up my mind to accept the proposal made by Shri Rajni Patel. A decision like this is something like my parting with my own son . . .

> Apart from my personal and emotional reactions in coming to this decision, I have been persuaded by the fact that I am now 72 years old and my powers to resist the demands of the Ruling Party, especially at the present time, is almost negligible. I would like to die in peace if possible and would also like to see that the members of my family are not visited with the repercussions of my actions, real or imaginary.

It was at this juncture that BD approached K.K. Birla, the industrialist and son of G.D. Birla, a respected family friend, who claimed he was 'well placed' to assist. Birla, however, now reported that matters had taken 'a serious turn'. R.K. Mishra, the *Express* general manager, met V.C. Shukla and Dinesh Singh, the latter on an old school tie basis. Mishra summed up their conversation in a letter for the record dated 22 October 1975. He said:

> Mr R.N. Goenka was prepared to accept that the [editorial] emphasis had been occasionally misplaced, giving reasonable cause for unhappiness to the Government. But it has not been his practice to interfere with the discretion of the Editor so long as the Editor acted on objective considerations without malice and expressed himself in responsible language within the confines of the paper's traditional policy of independent judgement on issues of public interest . . . Violent departures from these attitudes will destroy the Group's credibility . . .
>
> Mr Goenka . . . would have no objection to an editorial trust which would give guidance to the Editor on broad matters of policy . . . But any device which will interest itself in day-to-day conduct of the paper by the Editor will be found to be unworkable . . .
>
> Mr R.N. Goenka would be quite happy for the cases [against him/the *Express*] to be allowed to proceed in courts of law strictly on merit . . . All he hopes from Government is equal treatment with other newspapers in the matter of publication, allocation of foreign exchange, newsprint and other facilities. He wants no privileges, concessions or favours . . .

RNG was clearly playing for time. The threat of arrests was again held out and at a meeting with Birla, the latter made the point that Kuldip Nayar, who had been detained and released many weeks later on Court orders, could at least be removed. RNG pointed out that Nayar was protected under the Working Journalists' Act. Birla's riposte was that in that case, the editor, S. Mulgaokar, could be sent away! RNG next said he was ready to accept some eminent public persons on his board. But, he added, he could not relinquish complete control as he had borrowed large sums of money on a personal guarantee and his papers were published from eight centres and this called for intimate knowledge of the personnel and problems at each place of publication. He also sought a 'homogenous' board so that he could properly defend himself against the many cases brought against him by the government. Here unfolding was a cat and mouse game par excellence.

At the end of much discussion, RNG agreed to an eleven-member board of directors, five nominated by him and the rest in consultation with him from a panel of names put forward by the government, with K.K. Birla as chairman. There would also be an agreed set of editorial policy guidelines. He accepted this proposal on the understanding that all victimization and harassment would stop and the confrontation between the government and the *Express* Group 'would be transformed into an era of mutual cooperation' in a manner honourable to him and satisfactory to the group companies.

Six officially approved directors were accordingly nominated on the *Express* boards by RNG. These were K.K. Birla (chairman), G.D. Kothari, P.R. Ramakrishnan, A.K. Anthony, Vinay K. Shah and Kamal Nath. The new arrangements were in place by December 1975. Nevertheless, the harassment continued. The income tax department created huge 'paper demands'. Loans were treated as undisclosed income and thereby attracted penalties. The demands outstanding by way of tax, interest and penalties added up to several crores.

The *Express* Group had been accepting loans from the public since 1967 in a category of exempted company deposits. The categorization of these loans was arbitrarily changed by the Reserve Bank to bring them under its regulation, and prosecutions were launched on grounds of alleged contravention of the amended regulations. These loans totalled Rs 10 crore in 1971. Despite the hurdles introduced by the government, they were reduced to Rs 1.7 crore by 1977.

A scheme for voluntary disclosure of income and wealth (VDS) had been introduced by the government in the 1975 budget and RNG was told that all pending tax matters could be settled if he agreed to make a disclosure with a tax commitment of Rs 50 lakh. He acquiesced in the interest of 'buying peace', despite having to incur unjustified tax liabilities. This liability was then arbitrarily enhanced to Rs 75 lakh. The Commissioner of Income Tax, Madras Circle, was prepared to make a settlement on the agreed basis, but pleaded his inability to do so as one matter, pertaining to Express Traders Ltd, fell outside his jurisdiction and would have to be disposed of in Bombay. The Bombay commissioner was sympathetic and said he would abide by whatever overall settlement the Madras commissioner arrived at. The Madras commissioner, however, wanted clearance from the chairman, Central Board of Direct Taxes (CBDT) in Delhi. The latter then told B.D. Goenka that since political figures were involved he needed a nod from the finance minister, Pranab Mukherjee. By now the merry-go-round was in full swing. However, the minister agreed.

Accordingly a VDS disclosure was filed before the Madras commissioner on 31 December 1975. But no instructions reached the chairman of CBDT. In June 1976 RNG was advised that he should refer the one particular matter of Express Traders Ltd to the Settlement Commission. Through this process, issues of concealment of income were raised, ultimately resulting in a criminal complaint being launched against RNG in a Madras magistrate's court in July 1976 after a major confrontation with V.C. Shukla.

*

While the merry-go-round kept whirling, editorial pressures mounted on the *Express* despite the constitution of the new board. When the *Express* approached the government for clearance to start a new edition in Chandigarh, which had been in the works for some time, Shukla asked to know who would be the resident editor there. He also complained of editorial infringements by RNG and charged that Birla was receiving insufficient cooperation. However, all these matters could be smoothened over if Mulgaokar, Ajit Bhattacharjea and Kuldip Nayar were sent away! RNG had suffered another heart attack in March 1976 and was confined to bed until the end of April. Meanwhile a meeting of the boards of the three *Express* companies was convened on 9 April 1976 at which certain changes were made in administrative procedures that lay outside the scope of the agreement reached earlier. These enhanced the management powers of the board. Far more serious was the retirement of Mulgaokar as editor-in-chief and his replacement by V.K. Narasimhan, editor of the *Financial Express*. RNG was deeply pained and outraged when word reached him. Mulgaokar was a person for whom he had enormous respect and the two had become close personal friends.

Efforts were made to induct various others as editor-in-chief of the *Express*, among them Mohammad Shamin, of the *Times of India*, who simply did not qualify, and Suman Dubey, who just was not interested. (Dubey, a fine journalist and a schoolmate of Rajiv Gandhi, did become editor a decade later.) Ultimately, the government agreed to Narasimhan, who seemed a mild-mannered, erudite and inoffensive man, little realizing that they had caught a tiger by the tail. Narasimhan was full of old world charm and courtesy but stood by principles and had a mind of his own. He did take charge, but not in the manner expected! Shukla used Sitanshu Das, a disgruntled senior journalist, to get some information on the Ahmedabad edition of the *Express*. Narasimhan censured this act of indiscipline. Shukla was enraged and now sought Narasimhan's removal. A subsequent noting by Shukla on his ministry's files recorded in the 'White Paper on Misuse of the Mass Media' is interesting. Narasimhan was refused permission to attend a conference being organized by the Society for International Development in Amsterdam in November 1976.

> The then MIB declined permission since he thought that the 'Indian Express matter' was being 'played up' abroad and that the 'personal conduct' of Shri V.K. Narasimhan impelled him to decline permission.

The *Express* case had become a cause célèbre.

Narasimhan encouraged critical comments between the lines and historical, international or literary allusions that made a point without attracting the censor's red pencil. Ajit Bhattacharjea, executive editor, wrote an article on the Supreme Court's habeas corpus judgement. The tone irked Birla, who wanted Bhattacharjea immediately transferred to Gangtok (and Kuldip Nayar to Kohima)! RNG pointed out that editorial transfers were outside the board or chairman's purview and that the Working Journalists' Act did not permit such arbitrary action. Birla remonstrated. Meetings were held. Shukla breathed fire. RNG remained adamant. Threats of detention were renewed and Shukla now insisted on an amendment to the *Express*'s articles of association to make government directors 'irremovable'. Matters had come to a head. It was possibly at one of these meetings that RNG showered Shukla, whose father he had known, with a rich range of choice though somewhat unparliamentary expletives, for which he was famous. This reportedly left the minister cowering. Birla was to receive a similar tongue-lashing.

Reprisals would follow. The Press Information Bureau issued a series of elaborate press notes. The very first was headed 'Large scale tax evasion and fraud by industrial tycoon and newspaper king'. RNG filed for contempt of court proceedings in Madras. His rebuttals sent to AIR and Samachar (the offspring of government's forced amalgamation and virtual takeover of PTI, UNI and the two smaller Hindi news agencies) were not carried. The Congress raised the matter in the rump Parliament and pre-censorship was imposed on the *Express* Group under the Defence and Internal Security of India Rules on 16 August 1976. The result, as mentioned in RNG's affidavit before the Shah Commission:

> Release of pages for printing, after censorship, was deliberately delayed at all eight centres, indicating that the whole manoeuvre was part of an overall design to prevent the said newspaper being brought out in time, or at all, thereby in fact and in reality, crippling and/or stopping the Group companies' activities, causing immense loss and hardship . . .

The *Express* filed a writ in the Bombay High Court. The government found its case unsustainable and quietly rescinded its pre-censorship order on 30 September. Simultaneously, there was a denial of government advertising and pressure was applied on public sector undertakings and private advertising agencies and large advertisers not to release advertisements to the *Express* Group. The *Express* filed another writ in Bombay but the government withdrew these instructions in one of its very last acts in office after its thundering electoral defeat in March 1977.

A little previously, speaking at a press conference in Cochin, Indira Gandhi was reported as saying that there was nothing unethical in government discriminating against some newspapers: 'Why should we support the newspapers of industrialists and big business . . . Customs and traditions have to be discarded. This is like asking us to also give [them] the stick to beat us with.' That was typical of the times. At the start of the Emergency, the prime minister had torn up the AIR Code, saying, 'What is credibility? We are the Government.'

In October 1976, officials of the Municipal Corporation of Delhi (MCD), accompanied by a police posse, forcibly seized and sealed the *Express*'s press on the ground that municipal taxes were in arrears. The MCD's levy of higher taxes was in dispute and the *Express* had a stay order from the Delhi High Court. The seizure of its press was therefore completely arbitrary and in contempt of court, even more so its bid to auction the printing machinery, air conditioning plant and other equipment. A writ application was filed in the Delhi High Court and the plant and machinery were released on its interim orders.

The government juggernaut kept rolling. The Punjab National Bank was instructed not to advance monies for the purchase of newsprint or for working capital. This was the last straw. RNG was ill. Birla called the AGM. He did not expect the ailing Goenka to be present and was surprised to see him there. Under the rules, the appointment of government directors and the chairman required to be ratified by the shareholders within a given period. This had been overlooked. All powers therefore reverted to RNG. He summarily dismissed the board. The old fox had outwitted the lot of them! The farce was ended though pressures continued.

The international press took adverse note of these crude attempts to snuff out freedom of the Press in India. In December 1976, 200 journalists wrote to the prime minister protesting against the persecution of the *Express*.[3] The Gujarat High Court ruling declaring the censorship guidelines ultra vires was itself censored! Extra-constitutional authorities relentlessly and ruthlessly orchestrated every dirty trick in the book in total disregard of legal and ethical norms. The *Indian Express* was a prime target and, within the *Express*, Ramnath Goenka. B.D. Goenka urged compromise and kept a channel of communication alive with Shukla and Sanjay Gandhi. RNG knew of this and possibly even encouraged him to do so. He would always avoid picking a fight, but if it came to a fight he would keep all options open though he fought to win. He believed in the adage 'Never say die; say damn'.

The correspondence exchanged between RNG and K.K. Birla is available as also the minutes of their meetings. Birla has separately recorded his recollections of these events and takes credit for saving RNG from detention under MISA, a course of action, he says, that Indira Gandhi 'steadfastly resisted' against the advice of many around her.[4]

> After becoming Chairman of the *Express* [at RNG's instance], the first job I had to attend to was who should be the Editor of the paper. Mulgaokar . . . was not liked by the Government. I have always held Mulgaokar in high esteem. He is a man of great uprightness and is a fearless journalist . . . I consulted Indiraji . . . As she was busy . . . she directed Sanjay to meet Mulgaokar and report to her. I called Mulgaokar and briefed him in the matter. I gave a lecture to Mulgaokar on the virtues of flexibility and following a middle course in life . . . On my persuasion . . . Mulgaokar met Sanjay but the meeting proved to be infructuous. Mulgaokar was firm in his views. So was Sanjay. When two stubborn people meet, where is the chance of compromise?
>
> After the Janata regime came to power, many people were after my blood. Jayaprakashji regarded Ramnathji as closest to him . . . The story was that Ramnathji had told him not to come to my assistance and that he was going to 'finish' me off . . . Ramnathji is a good friend but a bad enemy. I certainly became nervous . . . What was to be done? I was very close to Bhagwan . . . and telephoned him at Madras to persuade Ramnathji not to harm me. Both Bhagwan and his wife Saroj promised to help me . . . Ramnathji had a lot of respect for father [G.D. Birla]. That might have been one other reason for the cooling off of his temper.

However, fearing that the Janata government might book him under MISA, Birla took anticipatory bail and, as the heading of Chapter Eighteen of his book proclaims, fled India.

One of the terms of the December 1975 understanding

handing over management of the *Express* to a government-controlled board through K.K. Birla was the drafting of a new policy charter for the group. A set of 'broad policies and objectives' was accordingly drawn up by RNG and forwarded to Birla. It paid obeisance to constitutional values, pledged objectivity and adherence to ethical norms, support to the government's new Twenty-Point Programme, support for schemes calculated to build national discipline and national integration, and resistance to 'obscurantism, regimentation and totalitarianism in any form'. It was in pursuance of this that Ajit Bhattacharjea came down on the Supreme Court. Writing in his column, he commented, 'It is not necessary to question the legal rationale of the Supreme Court's majority judgement on the habeas corpus issue to argue that it amounts to a virtual negation of the minimum democratic right of the citizen to protection against possibility of arbitrary detention.' The government was not amused. It was his ringing minority judgement on this matter that won Justice H.R. Khanna undying fame.

Like others, Kamaraj was shocked by the Emergency. He was rather ill and barely able to walk when he called on A.N. Sivaraman, the *Dinamani* editor, in Madras one day. He wanted an opinion on four questions. First, what was the objective situation in Tamil Nadu and would people support an armed uprising against the Emergency? Secondly, would the country as a whole support such an uprising? Thirdly, what would be the attitude of industrialists to such a revolt? And finally, what was the attitude of the people in general as a result of censorship? Sivaraman was surprised and said he would confer with RNG before responding. Goenka's reply was, 'Don't believe Kamaraj and don't reply. He might suddenly change sides.' Obviously RNG and Kamaraj had fallen apart. Sivaraman was to say that a little before the latter's death on 1 October 1975, Mrs Gandhi had sent emissaries to arrange a meeting between Kamaraj and herself. Kamaraj was not unwilling, but his health failed him. The Kamaraj–Goenka relationship had soured at both ends. Some time earlier, Kamaraj had warned Haja Sheriff, a leading Madras Congressman, to keep away from RNG as he was 'a madman and a crook'!

*

Those at the *Express* lived on a razor's edge. None knew what the next day might bring. There were raids, court cases, a long series of pre-censorship orders, stoppages of bank advances and advertisements, financial crises leading to salary delays, newsprint shortages and every kind of uncertainty. The sole, nationalized news agency, Samachar, suspended its service to the *Express*. The Express News Service mustered its personnel to forage for essential news. This was conveyed to nodal centres over the telephone at dictation speed and then sent over the teleprinter network. For the rest, AIR bulletins and foreign broadcasts were milked for copy.

Narasimhan not merely stood by his colleagues but egged them on to be stronger and more forthright in their news reports and comments. He also carried critical Letters to the Editor. Birla was very soon for his ouster but RNG stood behind his editors, with whom he lunched at the *Express* whenever he was in Delhi, especially when Mulgaokar was still there. Trends would be analysed and gossip purveyed to ribald comment and laughter. He was critical of the Emergency and the government. But he would not have his papers black out legitimate news items. He had occasion to pull up the Hyderabad edition for inadequate coverage of Emergency and government news.

RNG was in poor health and the threat of arrest hung over him and his family like a sword of Damocles. This was war by attrition. Payment of salaries was always problematic. Delays were endemic and some members of the staff volunteered to take salary cuts. Yet spirits were high and all felt part of a cause greater than themselves. Exemplifying this was a letter sent by Ajit Bhattacharjea to RNG in June 1976 after learning that he had staved off Birla's plan to send him to Gangtok:

> Only you could manage this without provoking a confrontation. Thank you once again, not only on my personal behalf, but also for enabling the paper to retain some degree of independence and self-respect. Your return to health and the decision to give more time to the paper's affairs has put more strength in us. Without any exaggeration, never has it needed your guidance as much as now . . . Maintaining the *Express* must take precedence over everything else because it represents your greatest contribution to a free nation.

Narasimhan proved a fine helmsman. Yet there was no mistaking RNG's resourceful and courageous leadership, which was acknowledged not only within the group but even more widely outside. He symbolized resistance to the new tyranny. RNG himself reflected on this dark period in an interview with Najmul Hasan for the *Onlooker* magazine after the Emergency was over:

> *Onlooker*: Why didn't you compromise with Mrs Gandhi and her Government and save yourself much of the bother and financial losses?
>
> Goenka: That would have meant compromising with my conscience. I had two options: to follow the dictates of my heart or my purse. I chose to listen to my heart.
>
> *Onlooker*: When all the newspapers gave in, how did you manage to fight?
>
> Goenka: I was prepared to lose money. The other newspaper owners did not want to take the risk. The [*Express*] newspapers have lost about Rs 3 crores during the last two years. My business losses since my problems with Mrs Gandhi began in 1969, would be about Rs 20 crores. Our financial situation had become so bad that if the Government had continued we would barely have survived a few more months.

*Onlooker*: Why didn't they arrest you?

Goenka: You should ask them. I ask myself the same question and do not seem able to find an answer. Probably my earlier acquaintance with Mrs Gandhi had something to do with it. I never met her during the crisis. The last meeting I had with her was either in 1970 or 1971 . . .

*Onlooker*: What are your ambitions?

Goenka: To make the [*Express*] newspaper a formidable weapon in the hands of the people. And then, to die in peace.[5]

In December 1976, Goenka had said that he had exhausted his resources and might not be able to hold out much beyond the New Year. But he had been sustained by Sathya Sai Baba's prediction that events would turn in his favour before that event, certainly before the end of March 1977. And that is precisely what happened. On 17 January 1977, Mrs Gandhi announced that she would hold general elections in March. Her political pundits had assured her that she would win. The life of the existing Lok Sabha had already been extended by a year, and putting off the general election for a second year running would have been exceedingly embarrassing. Some Congress party members made known that they were concerned that things had gone too far. A friend of RNG was privy to dark hints that the coterie around Sanjay Gandhi had even thought of arranging an 'accident' that might 'incapacitate' Goenka. The atmosphere was murky. Meanwhile, international pressure had also been brought to bear on Indira Gandhi through socialist friends such as Willy Brandt, the Austrian Chancellor Bruno Kreisky and British Labour Party contacts. She was beginning to feel caged.

Nani Palkhivala records an incredible experience of clairvoyance or precognition. Travelling on a flight from Delhi to Bombay on 24 June 1975, he happened to be seated next to a simple, khadi-clad person from a Gandhi ashram who told him that he had been told by a clairvoyant in Bangalore that

Mrs Gandhi would lose the Allahabad case only to become 'the most powerful woman in the world'. He further predicted that she would lose this 'extraordinary power' in March 1977 and that Jayaprakash Narayan would be stricken by a fatal illness and pass away within two years. All these came to pass.[6]

*

There has been much speculation on why RNG was never arrested during the Emergency. RNG's own explanation for this rings true. Indira Gandhi knew he had been good to her when her relations with her husband, Feroze, were strained. He had given Feroze a job with the *Express* in Delhi at Nehru's instance and had treated him with great consideration. He had been given a handsome salary for the times and a Humber car, though he only worked limited hours because of his responsibilities as an MP. He had removed him only after the Mundhra exposure, which resulted in his good friend T.T. Krishnamachari's exit from the Cabinet. This had upset Nehru. But the other version that had done the rounds at the time was that Mrs Gandhi herself, as Congress president, had hinted that she would not be unhappy if Feroze were to be eased out of the *Express*.

It was also bruited about that RNG had in his possession some sensitive personal correspondence between Indira and Feroze. He never used this against her in any way and had in fact returned the packet to her. He could not see himself taking unfair advantage of Jawaharlal's daughter. In the same manner, JP had burned the letters his wife, Prabhadevi, had received from an unhappy Kamala Nehru, Indira's mother, with regard to certain family affairs. RNG knew of this too and, reportedly, advised JP to do as he did. Politically, he had congratulated Indira Gandhi on her elevation to the office of prime minister in succession to Lal Bahadur Shastri and she had in response thanked him for his good wishes, adding, 'I shall need your cooperation. I sincerely hope I can count on you.' He had also been instrumental in helping raise party funds for her prior to the Congress split.

Indira Gandhi was aware of all this and was grateful for the respect and consideration shown to her. Furthermore, Mrs Gandhi was zealous of her image and clearly realized that arresting an intrepid, well-known and well-connected publisher like RNG would have adverse repercussions in the international media, which had already given her a bad press. The chief censor, Harry D'Penha, a decent and popular official, in fact told Nikhil Chakravartty, when asked the same question, that 'Madam is not agreeable.'

Employing Feroze in the *Express* was also not a purely altruistic decision. The prime minister's son-in-law obviously carried weight, whether or not he pulled his rank. It was Feroze who signed the lease deed on behalf of the *Express* when it quite legitimately received its building plot on Bahadur Shah Zafar Marg in Delhi. Ironically, it was in Rajiv Gandhi's time as prime minister that the government very nearly seized the Express Building. RNG was to remark caustically that what the father procured the son sought to dispose of in a fine demonstration of guru dakshina!

Moreover, it was RNG's philosophy to do a good turn to anybody, if approached, if it lay in his power to do so at that time. He would do this without thought of immediate recompense. It was good insurance to build up a stock of IOUs even in the most unlikely quarters. Some day, some time, who knows, he might need to encash these unrequited favours.

Thus he considered making Khushwant Singh editor of the *Express* towards the end of 1976 when it seemed that he had almost reached the end of the road. Khushwant was at that time editor of the *Illustrated Weekly* and a known supporter of the Emergency regime. Could he save the paper? Kuldip Nayar was asked to sound Khushwant, who was willing. But then the *Weekly* carried another article by him eulogizing Sanjay Gandhi even as word began to get around that Mrs Gandhi might soon call a general election. Kuldip was discreetly advised to go slow. Khushwant never got the call!

JP had been released on parole on 11 December 1976, just weeks before Indira Gandhi announced general elections. He was seriously ill and the government did not want him to die while in custody. He underwent treatment in Chandigarh and then in Delhi before being removed to Bombay, where he was put under dialysis. RNG was by his bedside at the penthouse, solicitous and encouraging. His doctors said he could be sent home to Patna but would need regular dialysis. The government volunteered partial funding for a dedicated dialysis machine. JP's friends were scandalized and opposed such benevolence, which they feared would be seen as coming to terms with the regime. RNG joined in the drive to collect funds and effect an independent purchase of the machine that was installed at JP's home in Patna.

*

The day Mrs Gandhi announced a general election, RNG knew deliverance was at hand. Only one hurdle remained. Mrs Gandhi had to be defeated. If she were re-elected, that would be the end. But now there was jubilation. The tide had turned. Mrs Gandhi had blinked. Opposition leaders began to be released in March and gathered in Delhi at JP's instance to take stock of the situation. There was a shortage of time and money. Party organizations were in disarray. RNG was indefatigable in helping stitch together a common Opposition front that became the Janata Party. This process had been greatly assisted by the fact that leaders of various political parties had been incarcerated together, enabling them to get to know one another and smooth over programmatic and even some ideological differences. JP's guidance was critical as he represented the national consensus.

There was a backdrop to these events. Once elections were announced, censorship, though not actually withdrawn until a couple of months later, was reduced to something of a formality. The *Express* was quick off the block and, notwithstanding risk of an official backlash, sent out its correspondents and commissioned writers to reconstruct the excesses of the Emergency. What followed was a narrative of ignominy and shame, and of brutal manipulation of the organs of state by a small, depraved coterie to negate freedom, democracy and justice. The group's papers methodically set out to probe and sift what lay behind the veil that had shrouded the country over the past nineteen dark months.

The *Express* at the first opportunity published a speech of Justice Tulzapurkar of the Supreme Court in Nagpur in extenso. This had been censored contemporaneously as it was critical of the Emergency.

There was to be no more silencing the voice of the nation. Altogether, this recitation constituted a searing indictment of the regime and created the political climate in which Mrs Gandhi and her henchmen were called to account. The circulation of the *Express* soared. It crossed 300,000 in Delhi and was sold on the black market, such was the popular demand for what had truly become the people's paper.

JP addressed a huge rally in Delhi on 8 February 1977 calling for Mrs Gandhi's defeat.

RNG remained furiously active behind the scenes throughout the ensuing election campaign. Sceptics thought the Congress majority might at best be blunted. The result was a landslide everywhere but in the South. The Congress was decimated and its top leadership totally cast aside. The *Express* editorial of 21 March 1977 called on all to 'Respect the Verdict':

> After the gruelling ordeal of the past two years and the bitter contest at the polls, the country must enter on a new era of peace and orderly progress. This means that the harsh legacy of the Emergency must be forgotten by both sides. Admittedly

> there have been faults on each side and there is no point in harbouring ill will or rancour. There is no need for witch hunting or for acting in a vindictive spirit. The wounds caused in the past must be healed quickly so that no scars are left behind. It is in a true Gandhian spirit that the parties should act so that a new cooperative approach to the nation's formidable problems may be possible. In a democratic election, there are no victors or vanquished.

This was a call for a new beginning. Narasimhan said he had received for the first time a request from RNG to write in a particular manner and he had readily done so. RNG was also among the first to call on Indira Gandhi after word came that she had lost the election. There was magnanimity in victory.

What now remained was to elect a leader of the Janata Party. Many hats were thrown into the ring, those of Morarji Desai, Jagjivan Ram and Charan Singh among them. Charan Singh found he lacked adequate support and so backed off for the moment. RNG, Nanaji and Madhu Limaye, favoured Jagjivan Ram as he was both a Scheduled Caste leader of great experience with a national image as a good administrator and a flexible person who would be able to keep the motley flock together. But what weighed against him was that he had moved the resolution approving the Emergency in the rump Parliament and had remained in Mrs Gandhi's government almost to the very end, when he broke away with H.N. Bahuguna to form the Congress for Democracy and allied with the Janata Party. Old Congressmen were strongly of the view that the post of prime minister should deservedly go to Morarji, against a countervailing opinion that he would instead make a good President of the Republic.

Finally it was decided to leave the matter to JP and Acharya Kripalani, both of whom preferred Morarji who had suffered, stood steadfastly by Congress ideals and was personally incorruptible though prone to turn a blind eye to the doings of his son, Kanti. They were strengthened in this resolve when

Charan Singh also cast his lot with Morarji. The Jana Sanghis had meanwhile been misled into believing that JP wanted Jagjivan Ram and therefore declared in favour of him. Nanaji Deshmukh saved the situation by doing the Jana Sangh rounds early next morning to correct the faux pas. The elected MPs gathered at Rajghat to take a pledge of unity. Morarji was selected. Jagjivan Ram felt hurt and threatened non-cooperation but finally came round some days later. RNG was disappointed. He would rather Jagjivan Ram had been sworn in as prime minister, but he went along with JP's decision. A little thereafter word came that the new prime minister planned to appoint V. Shankar, a retired civil servant known to have been close to certain business interests, as his Principal Secretary. RNG was wild. 'You know what that means,' he said. 'The Birlas are back.'

However, everything said, the country had emerged out of the tunnel. The Emergency was formally lifted on 27 March 1977. A new chapter was beginning.

# 7

# Triumph and Tragedy

March 24, 1977. The day the new Janata government was sworn in under Morarji Desai should have been a proud and celebratory occasion for all at the *Express*. In fact it was not. Instead, there was consternation and bewilderment. RNG fulfilled a personal pledge. He removed V.K. Narasimhan, who had led the *Express* editorial team with finesse and courage, to restore Mulgaokar as editor-in-chief. The move was understandable as Goenka had been virtually blackmailed into removing Mulgaokar during the Emergency. What rankled was the manner of his reinstatement and Narasimhan's removal. It was sudden and ungracious, without any previous consultation with Narasimhan, who was alerted to the change in the imprint line on a special supplement by agitated colleagues. An initial query suggested that this was inadvertent. But when Narasimhan entered the office the next morning, he discovered Mulgaokar ensconced in his chair. He immediately turned about and left the *Express*, never to return.

Sumer Kaul, an assistant editor, Kuldip Nayar, Ajit Bhattacharjea and others drafted a note that they presented to RNG. The latter explained that he had sworn to restore

Mulgaokar as soon as he possibly could and was honour bound to do so. This was preordained and should not have occasioned any surprise. The deputationists agreed but said that Narasimhan should have been consulted and suitably provided for in a manner that caused no hurt and recognized the tremendous service he had rendered. RNG admitted he had perhaps acted in haste but pleaded that he had meant no offence. Kuldip was sent to assuage Narasimhan's feelings. But the latter did not relent, said he wanted nothing from RNG and never even collected his provident fund dues from the *Express*.

Later RNG said he would be prepared to reinstate Narasimhan as editor of the *Financial Express*, which C.P. Raghavan, assistant editor, had been looking after, with his status and perks untouched. This was not communicated to Narasimhan who shortly thereafter left for Bangalore and in due course became editor of the *Deccan Herald*. He never spoke about this episode to the press. Nor did he blame RNG, knowing how pained he had been at Mulgaokar's ouster. He only wished RNG had not gone about the matter quite so shabbily. Nevertheless, he always admitted that but for RNG's rock-like stance, no editor would have been able to withstand the relentless onslaught of the government. A note was subsequently published paying tribute to Narasimhan. But the damage had been done. Both RNG and Mulgaokar stood diminished by this sorry episode and the *Express* lost some of the sheen it had acquired.

A Letter from Narasimhan, 'Bidding Farewell', was published in the *Express* some weeks later. It concluded with the statement that

> the Indian press can serve the great public of India adequately only if the professional pride and integrity of journalists are strengthened.

Speaking of the black period of the Emergency, the new information minister, L.K. Advani, remarked that when the

Ramnath Goenka as a young man. He started life as a modest trader in Calcutta, in 1919–20.

With his wife, Moongibai, who died in 1966

PRICE ONE ANNA

# THE INDIAN EXPRESS

VOL. I.] MADRAS—MONDAY, SEPTEMBER 5, 1932 [ NO. 1.

This toilet cream keeps the hair in good condition.

EVANS'
LIMES & GLYCERINE

MAXIMUM BENEFIT FOR SMALL PAYMENTS

Rs. 40,000 to 40 CLAIMS
at
Rs. 1,000 Each (Maximum Benefit)

A CERTIFICATE IN
THE RELIANCE MUTUAL BENEFIT SCHEME
PROOF AGAINST POVERTY AND MISERY

BOTH MALES AND FEMALES ARE ELIGIBLE
FOR
MEMBERSHIP

Admission Fee Rs. 5-8-0 only.

The Reliance Assurance Co., Ltd.,
New Tharagupet. BANGALORE CITY.

GLORIOUS HEALTH

DRINK
NESTLÉ'S
MALTED MILK

Banish Weakness and
Lack of Strength -
with SANATOGEN

Buy a bottle of Sanatogen to-day!

SANATOGEN

Sanatogen is NOT touched by hand

WEST END WATCH CO
BOMBAY CALCUTTA

THE
UNITED INDIA LIFE ASSURANCE
COMPANY, LTD.

TRUSTEE: OFFICIAL TRUSTEE OF MADRAS

M. K. SRINIVASAN, B. A., B. L.,
Managing Director.

The World's most Popular Soap

More Sunlight Soap is used than any other soap in the world. In almost every country it is the most popular soap for all washing and cleaning. The reason is that Sunlight is absolutely pure and pure soap washes cleaner and is safer for clothes.

Use Sunlight Soap in your home and see how safely and economically it does its work.

SUNLIGHT SOAP

The first issue of the *Indian Express*, 1932

# INDIAN EXPRESS

Largest combined net sales among all daily newspapers in India

## Text of declaration

## Opposition leaders among 676 arrested

# Emergency proclaimed

NEW DELHI, June 26

PRESIDENT Fakhruddin Ali Ahmed declared a state of emergency this morning on account of a threat to the security of the country due to internal disturbances.

## Bihar bandh flops

## Situation 'by and large peaceful'

NEW DELHI, June 26

THE general situation in the country on the first day of the proclamation of the new national emergency was "by and large peaceful", the Principal Information Officer of the Union Government told newsmen here today.

## No alternative – State Cabinet

# PM: Nothing to panic about

## States told to make full use of DIR

## Huge rally at Rae Bareli

## Cong. suspends Shekhar, 5 others

## Nandini stays as PCC chief

## Domestic power cut is withdrawn

By A Staff Reporter

THE Maharashtra Cabinet on Thursday decided to lift the power cuts on major categories of consumers, including domestic consumers, with immediate effect.

## BPCC: Govt. can't keep quiet

## CMs hail firm action

## Scrutiny of press matter

## About right to move courts

## Karnataka power

## Ban on Assembly

## Power failure

Weston offers you the largest finest range of TV sets in India

Weston TV

INDIA'S MOST EXCLUSIVE TV SET

The Emergency is declared: the quiet headline belied the stormy months ahead for the *Express*

A family group. Ramnath Goenka is standing third from left, with his son, Bhagwandas, extreme right. Seated in the front row, second and third from left are his wife, Moongibai, and daughter-in-law, Saroj.

Ramnath Goenka with Jayaprakash Narayan

# Nationwide raids on Express offices

## Staff members roughed up | Things can get worse: Officials

## Govt waited for session to end

Express News Service

NEW DELHI, Sept 1

Government agencies raided offices of the Indian Express all over the country on Tuesday, the morning after the monsoon session of Parliament ended.

Hundreds of men from the income-tax, customs and the Directorate of Revenue Intelligence spent the day rummaging about in Express offices, in simultaneous raids ordered by the Central Government.

Journalists came rushing to 11 centres of the Indian Express where the raids were carried out. For most of them it was a ringside view of the Government's strong arm in action.

(According to a UNI report, besides the Express offices, the residences of the group's chairman, Mr R. N. Goenka, the executive director, Mr Major Kumar Soothalia, the Finance controller, Mr R. Kumar, the imports manager, Mr M. Gurudoss and electronic data processing department manager, Mr T. P. S. Manian, were also searched.)

The editor of the Indian Express, Mr Arun Shourie, told pressmen that the action was an "infringement on the freedom of the press". He said that this was the first time since the emergency that the offices of Indian Express had been raided by Government's investigating agencies.

Mr Shourie said the raids on the classified section was probably carried out because "I was in touch with some of my informants on the Bofors issue through classified advertisements in the past four weeks".

Express photographers were attacked by the raiding officers at several places. In Bombay the camera of the photographer was

ates and uneducated buggers". In Bombay, an officer threatened "things can get worse if you don't co-operate". In Vizianagaram, press workers were kept out for 90 minutes.

**BOMBAY:** The raids by the DRI on the Indian Express here took a bizarre turn when some officials tried to tamper with and censor news copy flow in the teleprinter section.

Two officials stationed themselves in the teleprinter section to monitor incoming and outgoing messages. They did not even allow the day's news budget from Bombay to be creeded to other centres of Indian Express, which is a routine activity.

While one official placed himself at the entrance to the teleprinter section, the other started reading the messages coming in from other centres.

When this was objected to by the resident editor, Mr Hari Jaisingh, the officials acted tough: "The treatment could get worse if you do not co-operate".

When the editor's efforts to get the prying officers out of the teleprinter section failed, he contacted his lawyers, including Mr Mahesh Jethmalani, to move the court for seeking eviction of the DRI officials.

Just then the entire city press corps and photographers reached Express Towers at Nariman Point. Mr Jethmalani also arrived after Mr Jaisingh's call.

A heated exchange between Mr Jaisingh and the officials led by DRI assistant director, Mr G. B. N. Iyengar, on the one hand and between Mr Jethmalani and the officials on the other, followed.

While the argument was on, photographers of various newspapers took out their cameras to click, but were

tant director, Mr G. B. N. Iyengar, escorted Mr Vivek Khaitan, executive director of Indian Express, Bombay, to the DRI offices for further interrogation.

In the meanwhile, senior executives of the Indian Express and their lawyers led by Mr Mahesh Jethmalani apprehensive of arrests, sought anticipatory bail for Mr Khaitan.

However, the search party found nothing incriminating or contraband in the third floor of the building, which houses the accounts, circulation, advertisement and administration departments.

Later the Bombay High Court granted anticipatory bail to Mr Vivek Khaitan effective up to 2 P.M. Wednesday.

The order directed the DRI to release Mr Khaitan on bail in the

More reports on Page 4 and 9

event of his arrest and not to interrogate him in the night.

Mr P. B. Vakil, counsel for Mr Khaitan, moved Justice Din Shaw Mehta at his residence for the anticipatory bail.

**HYDERABAD:** Over 30 personnel representing income-tax, excise and customs and Revenue Intelligence departments swooped down on the Indian Express and Andhra Prabha offices here.

They overruled the protests of the time-keeper who wanted them to obtain the permission of the manager before undertaking any search. The officials warned the time-keeper against making telephone calls. Two men stood guard on the lady telephone operator preventing all internal and external calls while the raid lasted.

EXPRESS UNDER SIEGE: Scores of policemen laid siege to the Express building (top) on Tuesday to assist Revenue Intelligence officers in their raid and (bottom) BJP activists protesting against the raid — Express photograph.

The Ajitabh connection

During the *Express* investigation of the Bofors arms deal, the offices of the newspaper were raided in eleven cities.

Ramnath Goenka, with Khushwant Singh and C.R. Irani of the *Statesman*, leading a march along the Central Vista near India Gate in protest against proposed curbs on the press through the Defamation Bill, 1988

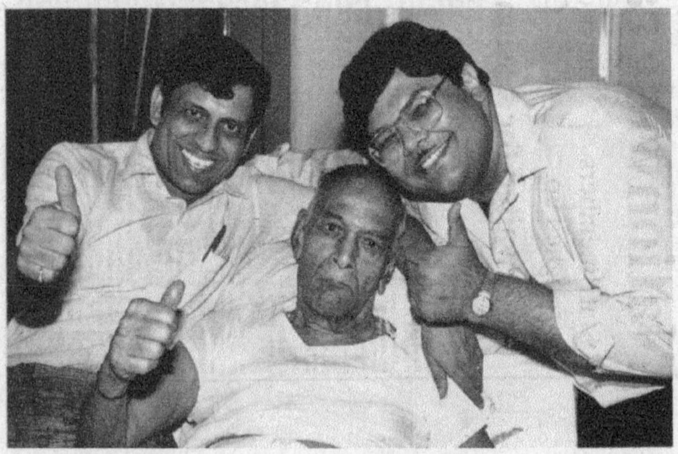

Ramnath Goenka towards the end of his life, flanked by trusted adviser S. Gurumurthy (left) and grandson Vivek Goenka

Two faces of Ramnath Goenka

Enjoying the company of hostesses at a teahouse in Japan

and spending a quiet hour in his study

The street named after RNG in Mumbai, with the Express Towers, Nariman Point—the nerve centre of his empire—in the background

Press was asked to bend, it had, with honourable exceptions, crawled. Goenka's *Express* was an outstanding exception. RNG did not now claim his pound of flesh from a government he was instrumental in bringing to office. The finance minister told Parliament in June that there was 'no proposal under consideration of the Government to withdraw the court cases against Ramnath Goenka and the *Express* Group of newspapers'. Yet RNG obviously did expect some consideration, though no favours. This was not forthcoming.

*

In June 1977, workers of the *Express* Group went on strike, resulting in the declaration of a lockout preceding closure of the paper in Delhi. Congress members, seeking to get their own back on the *Express*, raised the matter in Parliament and Delhi journalist unions went on a token one-day protest strike, shutting down most papers in the capital. The matter was finally settled in a couple of weeks.

In an explanatory note to readers on 7 July, RNG set out the facts and sought to dispel what he saw as a disinformation campaign by his detractors:

> The dispute arose over two notifications of the Government of India of April 1, 1977 relating to payment of interim relief to journalist and non-journalist staff of all newspapers in the country. The *Indian Express* had pleaded incapacity to pay the interim relief in full and had secured an unconditional stay . . . until further [Court] orders.
>
> . . . Barring a dozen newspapers in the country, all the others have failed to honour the notifications because of incapacity to pay, and disputes have either been settled by partial payment, or agreements, in no case above 50 per cent, or are pending in court.
>
> On June 21, the management made a fresh offer, undertaking to pay 100 per cent interim relief from October 1, 1977 if in the intervening period, the circulation of the

> *Indian Express*, which had surpassed that of the *Hindustan Times* during February and March 1977 and had since declined, was at least brought to within 5000 copies of the *Hindustan Times* again. This offer was rejected by the employees and it was decided to close down the establishment in Delhi, subject to all the legal obligations.
>
> The reason for the peculiar state of affairs at Delhi is in part political. The political forces which were displeased with the *Indian Express* because of its independent stand and policy during the Emergency, wanted to seize this opportunity to hit the *Indian Express*. Questions were being continually put in Parliament. The Minister for Information and Broadcasting and the Minister for Labour made statements which were far from helpful and, on the contrary, aggravated the situation. There are a large number of newspapers in the country who have not implemented even partially the two notifications but the *Indian Express* was singled out for this discriminatory treatment.
>
> . . . [An] offer made on June 26, which is the basis of the agreement now reached to end the strike, was that the *Indian Express* was prepared to pay 100 per cent interim relief from January 1978, 50 per cent being payable from April 1 to the end of the year. The offer was made in the hope that the financial position of the *Indian Express*, which had suffered grievously during the 20 months of the Emergency on account of persecution by the then Government, could be stabilized to some extent in the breathing spell of nine months.

Goenka went on to explain that the *Indian Express* had sustained huge losses during the Emergency, those of the Delhi office alone being just under Rs 80 lakh. The debts of the group now exceeded Rs 10 crore and all properties of the group were encumbered, with large sums also being obtained as unsecured debt. A Chandigarh edition was being started without fresh capital investment by cannibalization of existing plants from other centres. The equipment was installed in 1975 but publication could not then begin because the authorities refused to authenticate the required declaration. The objective of starting the Chandigarh edition was to make the Delhi edition viable in the hope that their combined circulations would be the largest in northern India and would therefore command higher advertising rates. Continuing, he said:

> The kind of difficulties faced by the *Express* Group can be understood by the systematic denial to it of facilities available to other newspapers. The case of the *Hindu* is pertinent. The *Hindu* has been able to go ahead with facsimile transmission at several centres. This reduces costs because only skeleton staffs are required to man extra centres of publication. In the face of this competition, the *Express* also sought permission to import machinery for facsimile transmission. This was granted but subsequently cancelled by the previous government. As a result, the *Express* had to pay about Rs 2 lakhs a month for its staff at each centre whereas the *Hindu*'s expenditure on staff at many centres is negligible. Another instance of discrimination practised against the *Express* Group is that since 1969, no import licence of plant and machinery was extended to it in spite of several applications. There was also the systematic denial to the *Express* Group of Government advertisements it should have commanded by reason of its circulation . . .
>
> I only hope that the Government in its attitude to the Press is not adopting the same method as the previous Government, though in a more subtle and sophisticated form.

The discussion in Parliament turned vicious. Parvathi Krishnan (CPM) said Goenka had started new editions in Hyderabad and Cochin during the Emergency and now one in Chandigarh and applied for permission to start two other editions in Patna and Lucknow. She wanted an inquiry into the finances of the *Express* and appealed to JP to 'quit Express Towers' in Bombay, where he was currently residing. K.P. Unnikrishnan went further. He again reverted to the sins of 'Seth Golmal Ramnath Goenka' and lambasted him for his allegedly nefarious deals, blackmail and criminal activities, although now 'a great defender of [the] Janata faith'. He charged the government with 'absolute collusion' with Goenka who had 'infamously' removed Narasimhan, 'a great and competent journalist'. He cited the Bhabatosh Datta Fact Finding Committee on Newspaper Economics as saying that the *Express* Group was in a constant state of metamorphosis. 'It was a private limited company, then it became a public limited company, and again it was transferred into other different companies. At one time there were 410 companies in carrying on this tamasha called the Express empire.'

The Bhabatosh Datta Committee (1975) had with misplaced zeal urged the government 'to resume efforts to control the prices of newspapers on the same lines as prices of other essential commodities' as well as their advertisement rates. It detected tendencies towards monopoly and restrictive trade practices in the *Express* Group as evidenced in the close link between the *Indian Express* Bombay Ltd and the *Jansatta* of Ahmedabad and Rajkot, especially through investments made by Express Traders. Further evidence of restrictive practice was the compulsion on advertisers to place their advertisement in two or more editions of the group at a higher rate on grounds of larger circulation. It advocated de-linking and diffusion of ownership, partly through allocating equity rights to employees, and a check on use of newspaper profits for non-newspaper purposes. It reiterated the first Press Commission's recommendation that every paper should, if possible, be constituted as a separate unit. It also suspected that newspaper owners, who also own news agencies, were keeping the charges low with a view to getting an advantage for their papers.

The committee had a close look at trading in shares by the *Express*. Its study showed that Express Traders had made an accumulated loss of Rs 6.3 crore between 1967 and 1973. It computed Rs 4.77 crore of additional liabilities over and above these losses carried by the *Indian Express* during this period on account of its holdings of IISCO and other shares and the operations of Express Traders. All this collated data was now grist to the mill.

It had also been alleged in Parliament by Bhupesh Gupta (CPI) that RNG had undisclosed bank accounts abroad. He denied this vigorously. Two years later, a probe was ordered against the *Express* under the Monopolies and Restrictive Practices Act for formulating a standard agreement with its distribution agents in various centres in the South as a means of impeding competition in the matter of retail newspaper sales. It would seem that RNG was never to get out of the woods.

The circulation of the Delhi *Express* had started declining after the peak it had touched at the fag end of the Emergency. The 1977 strike had not helped. RNG was worried. Ajit Bhattacharjea argued that *Express* salaries were low and therefore the paper did not attract the best talent. Moreover, anyone showing promise was soon lured away by lucrative offers from rivals. In the circumstances, he urged playing up selected stories and writers coupled with a bright, eye-catching appearance. This is what had made it popular earlier. 'It was the Manchester *Guardian* policy as compared to that of the *Times* or *Daily Telegraph*,' Bhattacharjea pointed out, adding that 'with our limited resources, to attempt to be bright as well as comprehensive is to be neither'. RNG was to remember this in an elaborate directive he issued later.

Funds were needed by the Janata Party too. When the party was in the process of formation in 1977, it was strapped for funds. RNG had spoken to Saroj and Bhagwandas and had then gone to Morarji Desai to pledge the family jewels for the cause. Morarji rebuked him, saying, 'Are you mad? Have I reached that stage where I will take an Indian woman's jewellery to fight elections?'

Goenka had other concerns. Bickering within the Janata Party and false moves by the government were both reasons for anxiety. Indira Gandhi had gone on the offensive after her botched-up arrest and now contemplated returning to the Lok Sabha through a by-election. RNG was soon busy in a stop-

Indira campaign. Word had got around that she might contest a by-election in Tanjore. RNG believed that the only person who could defeat her was Karunanidhi and so got to work on the DMK leader and made elaborate plans for filing his nomination should Mrs Gandhi trick everybody by doing so at the very last moment. Her movements were tracked and it seemed at one stage that she might get to Tanjore by helicopter via Hyderabad. At the last moment word came that she had changed her mind. She was later to stand from Chickmagalur in Karnataka. The Janata Party parliamentary board was reluctant to oppose Mrs Gandhi as the party elders were not sure if they could think of a winning candidate. George Fernandes decried such defeatism and said he would find a candidate.

Fortunately Ramakrishna Hegde was then heading a Janata government in Karnataka and had introduced a genuinely decentralized panchayati raj, which had aroused great hope and interest as a harbinger of wider and more meaningful popular participation in governance and 'value-based politics'. RNG had got to know and like Hegde and assured him of every support through the Bangalore edition of the *Express* and the *Kannada Prabha*. Now Virendra Patil was persuaded by Fernandes to stand from Chickmagalur. He pleaded lack of resources but RNG promised to take care of this aspect and threw himself into the electoral battle. Alongside George Fernandes, RNG played a central role in the campaign, organizing funds, printed material and volunteers and monitoring every detail. Yet the odds were great. Nanaji then said the BJP and RSS wanted to take over the campaign in considerable segments of the constituency where their cadres were active. Fernandes was disinclined to accept the offer but RNG prevailed on him in the larger interest of defeating Mrs Gandhi. In the event, Patil lost. RNG's nemesis was back in Parliament, a wounded tigress biding her time for the kill.

JP was distressed. He was in poor health and had thought his life's work was over. But the Janata government appeared to be unravelling. The principal leaders were at loggerheads and scarcely cared to hide their mutual disdain for one another. Charan Singh described his colleagues as a 'bunch of impotent people' unable to punish Indira Gandhi. Morarji called for his resignation, and Charan Singh quit the Cabinet in June 1978. JP issued a public statement calling for a return to rectitude and discipline on the part of the squabbling Janata leadership. He was able to coax Charan Singh back into the Cabinet in January 1979 as deputy prime minister. But by then the rot had gone too deep.

Failing health compelled JP's return to Jaslok Hospital, Bombay (after insinuations about mis-treatment in Chandigarh, which he personally disowned), to be watched over there, as always, by RNG. As he hovered between life and death, RNG pleaded with Chandra Shekhar, the Janata president, that when the end came, JP must get a state funeral. Morarji, Charan Singh and Jagjivan Ram were disinclined, standing on protocol. Seeing this as an act of meanness and ingratitude, RNG wept like a child and beseeched Chandra Shekhar to intervene. The Janata president accordingly got Nanaji Deshmukh to call up Kedar Nath Sahni, Delhi's chief executive councillor, to declare that JP would get a state funeral in the national capital, while Chandra Shekhar called up all Janata chief ministers to instruct them to declare state mourning on JP's death in their respective states. RNG was overwhelmed.

On 22 March 1979 JP suffered cardiac arrest but was revived with prompt shock treatment by Dr Ashwin Mehta. This started a rumour that JP had passed away. An intelligence report was flashed to Delhi and Morarji interrupted the proceedings of the Lok Sabha to announce the 'sad news', only to return post-haste to state that that had been a false alarm. The end came in October.

*

Nineteen seventy-nine was a bad year for RNG. Even before JP's passing, Morarji Desai's government fell on 15 July 1979. The Janata Party had fractured on account of the overweening ambitions of its main actors. Charan Singh took office as prime minister with Indira Gandhi's support, an opportunistic alliance that could never have endured. The rug was pulled from under his feet in August 1979 and he was reduced to a caretaker until a general election was held in January 1980.

Morarji was a stern disciplinarian and quite incorruptible. He was a withdrawn man, dogged by unhappy family circumstances. His son, Kanti, who stayed with him and acted as some kind of personal secretary had, however, acquired a reputation for misusing his privileged position. Morarji would have none of it and to prevent tongues wagging suggested an informal inquiry. This was entrusted to RNG. Ten weeks later, RNG reported that he had been unable to find any evidence of Kanti Desai's culpability.

RNG admired courage and was drawn to George Fernandes and Subramaniam Swamy during the Emergency, when both of them evaded arrest and went underground. Fernandes, however, was subsequently arrested and booked for his role in the Baroda Dynamite Case. This had brought them closer and now they shared the same burning desire for the Janata experiment to succeed. But the party was falling apart. H.N. Bahuguna quit, then Biju Patnaik. Devraj Urs's supporters decided that they would absent themselves during the vote of non-confidence in Morarji's government that was moved on 11 July 1979 by Y.B. Chavan. Defectors swelled. Fernandes was the only minister to stand by the prime minister. But the next day he advised Morarji to resign and make way for another so that at least the party might be saved.

A year earlier, in 1978, Nanaji had also advised Morarji to lay down office in favour of a younger man. Who then, Morarji had asked. Atalji? Nanaji replied that the Janata Party would not accept that, and suggested Chandra Shekhar, the party president. The following day Nanaji declared at a press conference that no one above sixty years of age should be prime minister. The old guard was outraged. Nanaji took sanyas and retired from active politics. He was later to say that he had throughout acted in consultation with RNG.

RNG too was distraught as he saw the government tottering on the brink. He too felt the Janata Party must be saved and was moved to write to Morarji. A handwritten draft of a note written on 10 July 1979 survives:

> I am ashamed of myself that I have not been able to do much for you or the country. I had promised to see you after your victory. Unfortunately that does not appear to be possible. All the forces are arraigned against you and I see no escape from it. They are determined to go to any extent to hurt you and your friends if you do not voluntarily retire. This is a spectacle that I would not like to live to witness.
>
> Sensing some of it I had decided to retire. I am still of the same opinion. The whole atmosphere is sickening. It is my firm opinion that you should also retire. It will help matters. Highly placed persons are all out to dishonour you and I would be the last man to see it. I am writing this with my eyes wet.

Whether the letter was actually dispatched is not certain. But the lines penned portray the pain and sorrow of a man who saw his world in ruins.

Goenka's cup of sorrow was not yet full. Within days, on 19 July 1979 the genial Bhagwandas, the first natural male offspring in his family over three generations, died of a sudden heart attack in Bombay at the relatively early age of fifty-six. RNG was heartbroken. He had never been outwardly close to his son, who had in fact feared more than loved him. However, a lineal descendant was a precious gift. And now that too was gone, cruelly snatched away, adding to the emptiness of his lonely life.

The news was broken to RNG in Delhi. Joined and comforted by close companions, he immediately flew to Bombay where arrangements had been made to take the body to Madras where BD's wife and children waited. There he lay in the Express Estates for a last darshan by friends and mourners, before being consigned to the flames. The old man wept.

The Janata betrayal, JP's going and his son's death caused a surge of emotion that burst forth in a series of three signed articles on 'The Current Situation' that RNG wrote in the *Express* in November 1979. The first analysed the central issue. JP had 'led a captive nation to its second liberation' but the sapling he had planted had been cut down. A leader, 'second only in moral stature to Mahatma Gandhi', had been betrayed by self-styled leaders who had 'pursued self-aggrandisement at the expense of our national interest'. He alleged that the '"emergency" treatment of JP inflicted on him a permanent disability that ultimately led to his death last month'. He denounced Indira Gandhi (an 'unabashed liar') and her son Sanjay, and asserted that the central issue of March 1977 remained, that of 'democracy versus dictatorship', aided by defections. He described the five-month-long caretaker government sworn in by the President under Charan Singh as 'a constitutional aberration', usurping 'the rightful claims of the Janata Party with 205 members solidly behind Mr Jagjivan Ram'.

The second article dwelt on 'Janata's Handicaps and Performance'. He handed out a good report card to the Janata government and castigated Charan Singh for bringing in a preventive detention law 'designed to scare traders and thereby swell the electoral coffers of the parties now in government'. He warned that Charan Singh's 'half-century old economic theories' would stifle industrial growth, create widespread shortages and raise prices. Biju Patnaik, George Fernandes, Raj Narain and Madhu Limaye were named for chaotic, populist and mischievous statements that hobbled the Morarji government. Not least was the communalist and RSS dual-membership 'bogey' that had enabled Mrs Gandhi to rise from the ashes. Jagjivan Ram was a sober, level-headed leader who recognized that 'a socially responsible private sector has a vital role to play'. He was not an ideologue and 'is today perhaps the only authentic democratic national leader acceptable to all sections of people'.

The third article was titled 'The Real Communalists' and tore apart the appellations 'communal' and 'secular' that were constantly bandied about. The secularists claimed to be the sole protectors of the minorities who had been pocketed as so many vote banks, the article pointed out, adding that the Congress had a vested interest in the backwardness of Muslims and traded on their ignorance and isolation. RNG went on to observe that the lot of the Harijans was improving by the day 'without being drawn away from the national mainstream' so that today Jagjivan Ram stood out as the most acceptable national leader. He stoutly defended the Jana Sangh and RSS against the communal charge and claimed credit for persuading JP to look on them with a kindly eye, even to the extent of saying, 'If the Jana Sangh is fascist, I am a fascist.' It had become part of the vocabulary of the Left to abuse the Jana Sangh and RSS and make them whipping boys for all social issues. The cacophony of charges about RSS involvement in communal riots remained unproven and RSS-baiting was 'a game played by authoritarians and defectors to perpetuate communal tensions and disharmony'. RNG's article concluded:

> The Janata Party with all its inherent limitations as a political party is still the best instrument for reversing this process of self-destruction and taking the country towards people-oriented decentralized politics that is rooted in the values for which our two freedom struggles—the one under Gandhiji and the other under JP—were waged.

An *Express* editorial simultaneously inveighed against the smear campaign against the Janata Party and its current leader. Mrs Gandhi had alleged, on the basis of a new book, that the CIA had an agent in her Cabinet in 1971. Raj Narain had named

Jagjivan Ram as that person. The American journalist, Seymour Hersh, was later to charge that Morarji Desai was a CIA agent. Both allegations were dismissed with the contempt they deserved. Politics had fallen to a new low.

*

The general election of January 1980 returned the Congress-I to power. Mrs Gandhi was back in the saddle. An item high on her agenda was the role of the media. Following the Emergency excesses, the Janata government had in 1978 appointed a Second Press Commission under Justice P.K. Goswami with liberal terms of reference calculated to strengthen the freedom and independence of the Press. The commission was due to submit its report in March 1980, after two extensions, but resigned as soon as the new government took office, to be replaced by another team under Justice K.K. Mathew. The terms of reference of the new body and its general orientation were subtly different. Work virtually commenced afresh and the publication of its report in April 1982 was to arouse considerable controversy and a divide among its membership.

An invitation to RNG to tender evidence before the Mathew Commission was politely turned down by him. He wondered if the commission could override the jurisdiction of the statutory Press Council, which was seized of many of the matters included in the commission's terms of reference. Notwithstanding that, the *Express* figured quite prominently in the commission's report and was cited to justify some of the recommendations. These were powerfully repelled by four dissenting members—Girilal Jain, Rajendra Mathur, Professor H.K. Paranjpye and Justice Sisir Kumar Mukherjea. The majority had recommended de-linking and diffusion of ownership of papers with circulations in excess of 100,000 on grounds of monopoly.

The *Express* commented editorially:

> The Report asks 'whether commercial journalism can ever be free journalism', a preposterous postulate which leads to an assault on both circulation and advertising as something dangerous . . . The extraordinary conclusion that emerges is that only impecunious papers without a real reach are truly free.

The Minority Report pointed out that Ramnath Goenka was no longer associated with the jute and steel industries and had not been found to be a 'national monopoly house' by the Indian Institute of Public Administration. Indeed, the irony is that during the Emergency Mrs Gandhi's government had insisted that K.K. Birla, a big industrialist and owner of the *Hindustan Times* Group, take over the management of the *Express* Group! It pointed out that the Majority Report had conjured up a 'horrifying picture of monopoly' on such slender evidence as that Goenka's son, Bhagwandas, had been married to Saroj, daughter of Shreyans Prasad Jain (brother of Shanti Prasad Jain and owner of the Bennett Coleman Group). It concluded:

> In our opinion, the Report has prescribed multiple penalties and deterrents. Steeply escalating import duties on newsprint . . . an arbitrary news-to-advertisement ratio . . . a price-page schedule . . . One wonders why a whole armoury of weapons, each of them deadly enough, is being recommended against the best of our newspapers. If all of them are triggered off together, our Press Commission may well come to be known as the Press Annihilation Commission.

The Majority Report was silent on the internal Emergency and the trauma of censorship, showing the extent of its bias. On the other hand, the Minority Report gave examples of recent exposés by the Press, many of them unearthed by the *Express*, to highlight the watchdog role of the media.

If Mrs Gandhi was out to punish her tormentors in the Press, it did not take much time for the *Express* to feel the heat. Jagmohan was appointed Lieutenant-Governor of Delhi on

17 February 1980. That very day, a Sunday, he called for the files pertaining to the *Indian Express* building on Bahadur Shah Zafar Marg. These were delivered to him, whereupon he convened a press conference on 1 March at which he stated that the Express Building extension was in contravention of several municipal by-laws and in disregard of the Delhi Master Plan. A notice followed to the *Express* to show cause as to why the building should not be demolished, together with a charge of unauthorized deviation from the approved building plan. On 7 March the Land and Development Office passed an order of re-entry and slapped another notice for unauthorized construction of an additional block on a vacant parking lot in front of the building.

Apart from anything else, Jagmohan had a grievance against the *Express*. The paper had carried a story alleging that as vice-chairman of the Delhi Development Authority he had witnessed the Turkman Gate demolition with Sanjay Gandhi from the Ranjit Hotel building, just before the Emergency and later made some communally loaded remarks. Jagmohan filed for defamation. It transpired that his informants had misled the *Express* correspondent. Jagmohan was able to prove that Sanjay Gandhi was not in Delhi on that particular day and that he was not in the Ranjit Hotel at the time. The *Express* apologized.

This time around, the *Express* obtained a stay order and finally won the building case before the Supreme Court. But in order to gain time, RNG played a delicious extrajudicial gambit that stopped the government in its tracks. The story is truly hilarious and points to the audacity and genius of the man. RNG had two objectives in mind: to play for time so that the building might be completed in a few weeks, and then to prevent the government attaching or demolishing the structure.

Following the death of Bhagwandas, RNG had gone abroad and visited Maharishi Mahesh Yogi's World Government of Creative Intelligence headquarters, located at the Maharishi European Research Institute in Switzerland. He was 'profoundly impressed' by his methodology of transcendental meditation (TM) 'and the great work he has initiated to revalidate by the aid and test of modern science the truths expounded in the Vedas'. The Maharishi had acquired a massive following around the world, including celebrities such as the Beatles and Hollywood stars. Moreover, his spiritual exertions had earned him a vast fortune. In a letter to Mrs Gandhi, RNG testified to the efficacy of TM from personal experience. 'It is,' he said, 'the one thing that has enabled me to overcome the extreme stress that followed the death of my son.' He went on to write her a whole tutorial on TM!

Now, fearing that the threat to the Express Building posed a clear and present danger, RNG invited the Maharishi to be his guest in India and there enlarge his world network and develop his plans to establish a Vedic university. If all rentals in the Express Building had been frozen then why not allow the new building to be used for some greater purpose rent-free? Nothing loath, the Maharishi arrived post-haste with 3470 disciples on one count. The Express Extension Block was converted into a TM centre by day and a residence for the Maharishi and his immediate entourage by night. Makeshift electricity and water supplies were arranged, curtains hung, furniture and mattresses provided and a special vegetarian kitchen set up. *Express* managers and TM acolytes vied with one another in serving the cause.

There would be meditation and lectures in the forenoon and 'flying' (levitation) lessons in the afternoon. No journalist or photographer was allowed access to the Maharishi. At nightfall, busloads of exhausted but exhilarated devotees would return to their hostelries around the city. The Express Building was spiritually charged. None could touch it. Nonplussed officials gazed in wonder at the spectacle, not knowing how to react.

RNG slapped his thighs in high mirth and said he would like to see who would dare evict the Maharishi and his ecstatic followers from the Express Building. It was pro tem sacred ground. By the time the TM congregation dispersed, the Express Extension Block was not merely complete but had been occupied and consecrated. The case could drag on. It did. The government had been completely outwitted. According to the grapevine, the *Express* was richer by some photocopiers and printing equipment and bouyed by the prospect of possible funding to finance the purchase of much-needed stores and equipment for the expansion plans, for which the Extension Block had been constructed.

It seemed that the Maharishi might be tapped for further investments in the *Express*. RNG now wrote to Saroj Goenka in Madras on 21 June 1981 on a variety of property issues:

> According to me the Delhi building can be given to [the] Trust immediately. When I discussed with Sitaram and Gurumurthy, they did not raise any objection. We are thinking of donating the Delhi building to charity. If we do not donate it to charity, we will have to pay 65 per cent of the income to taxes and only 35 per cent will be left with us. With that, we cannot do very much. So far as the Plaza on the Madras property is concerned, I am all in favour of it. We can make it a commercial project. I can arrange the money through Maharishi. If we make it a commercial proposition, it will be more or less impossible to create a B.D. (Goenka) Centre, unless we are prepared to call the commercial centre as B.D. Centre.

It was in answer to Indira Gandhi's speech cautioning the country against 'gurus who have their ashrams abroad and come here from time to time' that RNG had written to say that if she had the Maharishi in mind, it was his duty to enlighten her about his following and activities in India. The Maharishi had the powerful and famous in India as his disciples. Men like Justice Krishna Iyer, K.B. Lall, and Justice P.N. Bhagwati were, with RNG, on the board of the Maharishi Yogi Trust for Vedic Learning.

RNG was ambivalent about Mrs Gandhi. On her return to office in 1980, he had told Kuldip Nayar that he wanted to make up with her and would consequently need to make compromises that might disturb some people. He was also anxious to mend fences with Sanjay Gandhi. He was later to urge that the family tiff between Indira Gandhi and her daughter-in-law Maneka was of no real public interest and should therefore not be played up. At the same time, he was embattled in the Express Building case and on other fronts and was determined to confront the prime minister. He would blow hot and cold.

It was at this juncture that tragedy struck Indira Gandhi. Her younger son, Sanjay, was killed in a flying accident in Delhi on 23 June 1980 while piloting a powerful new light executive aircraft.

RNG was quick to condole the bereaved mother and said he could understand her grief as he too had lost a son recently. More than that, he wrote a long and eloquent article in the *Express* entitled 'An Explosive Situation' in which he paid fulsome tribute to Sanjay and called for national unity at a time of peril.

> When Sanjay Gandhi hurtled from the sky and concluded his brief personal Odyssey in the Delhi dust, the country and his own party suffered the loss of a youthful and dynamic leader of the future. His death has come at a time when it can be least afforded, at the precise moment when India needs inspiration, fresh purpose and a new impetus.
>
> Mr Gandhi made the mistakes of a young man: he was spirited, outspoken and impatient of delays, and he wanted everyone else to work at the same pace as he did. He therefore, naturally, acquired enemies as well as friends. Yet his was a firm, resolute and decisive personality. He was not afraid of responsibility or of criticism. He flew high and he flew fast, and eventually he flew to his death.
>
> Our sympathy for the young man himself, his brave mother and devoted young wife, must be transmuted into

> positive action, as he himself would have wished. Grief solves no problems, and India already has too much to mourn for.

He then focussed on the despair he saw all around him. There had been four elections in three years; a rupee float; rising prices with the oil shock and drought; agricultural and industrial stagnation; labour unrest; the rise of the black market and an underworld mafia; the frustration of unemployed youth turning to violence; dissension in the Congress; and fragmentation of the Opposition.

> The situation today, politically and economically, is explosive. It is as potentially deadly as a threat of war . . . Today, we face once more a time of adversity, a sterner trial than we have ever seen before. The country needs a leader, and fortunately the only person who can possibly lead India, Mrs Gandhi, is once more at the helm of affairs.
>
> A leader cannot achieve the salvation of a country alone . . . There should be no pre-conditions, either by Mrs Gandhi or the Opposition, should the two forces unite to attempt a solution to the apparently insoluble. For Mrs Gandhi, too, will understand that only a politically united nation can face the tasks of today.

He was calling for reconciliation and a national government at a time of trial. There was little response. However, he did suggest to Mrs Gandhi that they keep in touch. She accordingly designated Mohammad Yunus, retired diplomat and family friend, as a contact. Thus RNG became a regular visitor at Yunus's home when they would quietly spend long hours in conversation on all manner of subjects. Interviewed after RNG's death, Yunus revealed that RNG had on one occasion shown him a dossier on Mrs Gandhi's government with linked official files that he had obtained from his own moles within the administration. The papers documented misdemeanours by ministers and bureaucrats, some of them rather damaging. He wanted Yunus to inform Indira Gandhi that he had this information. To prove the point, he gave some file numbers to

Yunus to pass on to the prime minister who, in turn, was astonished by the revelation. Yunus felt that RNG did this not to threaten Mrs Gandhi but to help her clean out the Augean stables as he wished to serve the country. It was Yunus's impression that, despite everything, Indira Gandhi and RNG had mutual admiration and respect for one another and the latter was genuinely grieved when she was tragically assassinated.

*

Towards the end of 1980, RNG felt Mulgaokar was tiring, and set out to search for a new *Express* editor. Ajit Bhattacharjea was looking after the editorial side, including leader writing, while Kuldip Nayar ran the news service. There were resident editors in the major centres. Mulgaokar wrote his column and was otherwise available only if required. He had essentially assumed an advisory role and RNG felt he might be formally designated an Adviser. Arun Shourie, who felt restless in the World Bank during the Emergency and returned home as an intense polemicist, burning with zeal to take up cudgels for causes he held dear, was introduced to him through JP and Radhakrishna. He joined the paper in 1979 as executive editor and was left to do his own thing, though used by RNG as a troubleshooter.

S. Nihal Singh was ready to leave the *Statesman* and had been offered the editorship of the now defunct *Illustrated Weekly* in Bombay when RNG corralled him to succeed Mulgaokar in January 1981. Ajit Bhattacharjea and Kuldip Nayar put in their papers as they saw no reason to be superseded. RNG wished them success elsewhere. He asked Kuldip what he planned doing. When Kuldip replied that he might start a syndicated column, RNG immediately made a bid for it. He appreciated his news-getting qualities. Yet when Arun Shourie reported to RNG that influential people were talking about Nayar's and Bhattacharjea's departure from the paper, he cynically retorted, 'When a family loses a young son, he is forgotten after the eleventh day!'

RNG told Nihal Singh that Shourie was a 'race horse' and would have to be reined in; Mulgaokar also warned him that he would have a problem on his hands. Nihal Singh discovered this soon enough as he was a hands-on editor and did not approve of a loose cannon as his deputy. However, he found an élan in the paper, and in RNG a publisher larger than life, with Shourie often closeted with him and assisting him in various ways. S. Gurumurthy, a brilliant young chartered accountant and exceedingly astute amateur lawyer, had taken over as RNG's financial adviser in Madras during the Emergency period, but was now also slowly on the way to becoming a very close and trusted counsellor in all matters. Prabhash Joshi, who had joined the *Express* via *Everyman's*, was another member of the staff who enjoyed the confidence of RNG.

Late in 1981 a storm broke over the conversion of some backward class Hindus to Islam in Meenakshipuram in Tamil Nadu. RNG was incensed and sent Nihal Singh a note for a critical editorial on the event. Nihal Singh discarded this and wrote a more balanced piece. RNG did not demur.

In the post-Emergency reorganization of the *Express*, many bright sparks were recruited and then promoted to field positions that gave them considerable latitude to follow their nose for news. Shekhar Gupta was moved from Chandigarh to the North-East, where he earned a name for himself. Likewise, Arun Sinha in Patna, N.K. Singh in Bhopal, Coomi Kapoor in Delhi, Ashwini Sarin as a roving correspondent, Leela Menon in Kerala, and Vipin Pubby and Rajan Bala as sports writers in succession to old masters like Ron Hendricks. Raghu Rai was chief photographer. Saeed Naqvi was sent to Madras to coordinate the southern editions. It was a bright and eager team.

RNG was keen to shift the emphasis from editorial writing and analysis to hard news. Investigative reporting was to see its day. It was not that newspapers had never carried exposés. However, in the early post-Independence era, the giants of the freedom movement were still in office. Their pronouncements and what the governments said or did made news. Parliament was a major news forum and keen parliamentarians would dig up scandals which made headlines. The judiciary too commanded great respect. The legislative, executive and judicial branches stood on a pedestal and the Fourth Estate was basically content to report their doings in the belief that they might be in error but were not venal. After 1967 things had changed. This was now a more fractious, self-serving, corrupt society. Standards had fallen and hallowed institutions were seen to be hollowing out. The Emergency climaxed these trends. The Fourth Estate now felt it incumbent to expose the lapses of the other three great estates and redeem cherished values. RNG certainly thought so. He saw the *Express* as ombudsman, whistle-blower, social auditor and muckraker, duty bound to expose the misdoings of those in power or authority and hold them accountable. Freedom of the press cast a duty on the media to ensure the people's right to know. And so started a series of exposés and campaign journalism. Moreover, these would be good for circulation.

Ashwini Sarin had been taken on *Everyman's* staff, and when that folded, the staff was absorbed in a tabloid called *Indian Express International* being printed in Canada and distributed overseas under a man named Sondhi. The venture did not survive more than a few months. Sarin was transferred to the *Express*. In 1979 he staged a mildly riotous act 'under the influence of liquor', hopefully to be arrested and sent to jail. The authorities obliged. He spent four days in Delhi's Tihar Jail and came out to write a series of inside stories about the crudities and brutality of prison life. He had earlier written of rural women being paraded nude. These reports were shocking.

In 1980 the *Express* broke the horror story of the Bhagalpur blindings of undertrials by the police while imprisoned. Was it that police and public alike had no faith in the criminal justice system as, once out of jail, these anti-social elements would resume their life of crime, and hence should be incapacitated? Arun Sinha in Patna got a tip-off and went to Bhagalpur, investigated the facts and wrote a story that was front-paged. Parliament was rocked. Arun Sinha, later joined by Arun Shourie, followed up with more reports. Some Bhagalpur residents took out a protest march in support of the police! Sinha dug deeper. He found many victims were innocent rural youth and discovered a nexus between feudal rural elites, some of whom had migrated to the towns, and the police. Caste-class conflict in rural Bihar had bred tensions in which criminal elements had also come to flourish.

Sinha was given a cash award of Rs 2500 and promoted by the *Express* but began to feel that the paper was more interested in sensational events than with the underlying socio-political factors. He had to struggle to get these stories into print and a subsequent report he filed on the Dhanbad coal mafia don Suraj Deo Singh went on an inside page while a story he filed on reasons for the economic backwardness of Bihar was held up for weeks. However he derived encouragement and pride from words of commendation by RNG.

Ashwini Sarin dropped another bombshell with his story of Kamla, entitled 'Buying Girls from a Circuit House' and datelined 26 April 1981. The opening paragraph read:

> Yesterday I bought a short-statured, skinny woman belonging to a village near Shivpuri in M.P. for Rs 2300. I find it hard to believe that I have returned to the Capital this morning after buying this middle-aged woman for half the price one pays for a buffalo in Punjab.

This was the price of stark poverty and its contribution to the flesh trade. The effect was electrifying. Everybody in the Central and state administration sprang to action. The *Express* had taken the precaution of sending a sealed letter to five public figures with details of what was intended and with a note to state that the seal should not be broken until so advised. The day the story broke the Madhya Pradesh police sent a police posse to arrest Sarin. Justice Bhagwati passed a restraining order on the police and the Supreme Court took up the case under a public interest litigation suit. The Delhi administration placed Kamla in a remand home from which she subsequently disappeared.

Vijay Tendulkar wrote 'Kamla', a Marathi play based on the event. This was translated into several languages and played in theatres all over the country. A producer called Mundhara made a film from the play. The *Express* sought a stay on its release, alleging plagiarism without due attribution but with material changes that depicted the reporter and the newspaper proprietor in a bad light. The matter went to court but was dismissed on the ground that there can be no copyright for real events, and that dramatists and film producers enjoy a measure of artistic licence. However, Sarin too got a cash award and a commendation from RNG, who named him his James Bond.

Arun Shourie followed up with an exposé of A.R. Antulay's Indira Gandhi Pratibha Pratishthan (Maharashtra) to encourage talent in the field of literature and the fine arts. The pratishthan was to have a fund of Rs 5 crore, with the state government contributing Rs 2 crore and the remaining amount being collected as donations from the public. A heated debate followed in Parliament and it was alleged that the funds raised were being improperly used for party purposes. A stay was obtained against the trust. Antulay resigned as Congress chief minister of Maharashtra on 12 January 1982, following a Bombay High Court ruling that he had allotted cement (a controlled item) to certain parties in consideration of donations made to his trust.

Vidya Subramaniam was later to do a story on a 'rail job racket' that resulted in an investigation into railway recruitment.

The *Express* did, however, come to grief over a story published in April 1980 in the Bombay edition, on a gang rape that ended in suicide. The story was plagiarized from a report published three months earlier in *Sakal*. The *Express* ran a half-baked apology but its defence collapsed when the entire story was shown to have been a fabrication.

Arun Shourie wrote two stories in 1981 from Bangalore, where his family had gone for medical reasons, both of which created a furore. The first related to publication of a snippet of conversation over lunch with the former Congress chief minister of Kartnataka, Gundu Rao, containing unflattering comments about various Congress ministers and others. Nihal Singh, the editor, demurred about the prominence and positioning Shourie desired for the piece. Incensed, Shourie offered the article to *Sunday*, a weekly newsmagazine published by the Ananda Bazar group from Calcutta, which carried it, to Gundu Rao's great embarrassment. The second story included a highly offensive remark about Mrs Gandhi uttered by C.M. Ibrahim, a former Karnataka minister, which he thought he had clearly made off the record. Nihal Singh refused to publish the piece. Despite this rejection, the article was passed on to an unsuspecting Dina Vakil, editor of the *Sunday Standard* (as the Sunday edition of the *Express* was then called), in Bombay, who ran it. Nihal Singh was taken aback and took up the matter with RNG, but got little satisfaction.

Nihal Singh had made a number of staff and editorial suggestions but RNG paid little heed or was otherwise preoccupied at the time. He seemed to be getting nowhere with institution building. He also felt uneasy with a 'second editor' in the paper who was constantly at the elbow of the boss. RNG seemed to encourage creative tension among senior staff so that they would come to him to arbitrate their differences. Nihal Singh wanted none of that. He resigned and left the paper on 31 May 1982.

The next editor was B.G. Verghese, who was with the

Gandhi Peace Foundation after being dismissed from editorship of the *Hindustan Times* by K.K. Birla on account of pressures from the regime in the run-up to the Emergency. The matter had gone to the Press Council, which was itself abolished during the Emergency for the embarrassment the case had caused. Verghese had known Arun Shourie for some years but was introduced to him by RNG with the stock remark that here was a 'race horse' that would need to be kept on a tight rein.

A problem arose within days. Shourie had written a story based on records of proceedings of the Public Undertakings Committee (PUC) of Parliament on the import of 500,000 tonnes of high speed diesel at fixed prices from a Hong-Kong-based Kuo Oil Co. in 1980, at a time of volatility in oil prices in the wake of the global 'oil shock'. A loss of Rs 9 crore had been incurred. Verghese inquired if the PUC had presented its report or was still in the process of completing its work. In the latter case there would be a breach of privilege and violation of a valuable parliamentary convention whereby such committee reports were presented as unanimous documents after members had spoken their minds confidentially in committee, irrespective of party labels. Shourie was impatient with what he thought was mere sophistry. He declined to have this checked by the news bureau chief, H.K. Dua, or anybody else, and preferred to 'withdraw' the story.

In days, a missive landed on Verghese's table with a copy marked to RNG, who was away in Bombay and en route to Ahmedabad. In it Shourie expressed his unhappiness at the withholding of the story. He went on to suggest that RNG was tired and broken after his exertions during the Emergency and was trying to make up with Mrs Gandhi. Indeed he needed to be saved from his own actions and it would be appropriate were Verghese and he jointly to take charge. He suggested that Verghese had been influenced to stop publication of the Kuo Oil story by RNG, which was simply not the case.

Verghese did not know what to make of this extraordinary

epistle. He did impress on Shourie that what he had done was unfortunate, even as RNG called up from Ahmedabad, speaking with a mix of fury and anguish. He felt deeply hurt especially as he had treated Shourie 'as a son'. He was no longer prepared to put up with such tantrums and indiscipline and wanted Shourie to be served with a letter of dismissal. Verghese tried to pacify RNG. He agreed that Shourie had acted impulsively, but pleaded that he be given another chance.

RNG was unrelenting over the ensuing days. Shourie was unrepentant. In fact, he went further. He sent copies of his unpublished series to some fifty Members of Parliament on *Express* stationary and leaked his version of the episode to the media. The fat was in the fire. The *Express* too ran the story, once it was established that the PUC had presented its report. Parliament and the Press alike had a field day, the Kuo Oil deal and the *Express* both making news.

An uneasy lull ensued. In July 1982 the Bihar Press Bill was introduced to amend the Indian Penal Code and Criminal Procedure Code, with the object of curbing scurrilous writing, yellow journalism, sensationalism, blackmail, unwarranted invasion of privacy and writings calculated to divide communities and cause social unrest. The chief minister, Jagannath Mishra, argued that the situation warranted 'some kind of self-restraint and self-censorship'. He added that no step which seeks to 'put hurdles in our way of promoting socialism shall ever be encouraged. . .' The national media was up in arms. The *Express* wrote editorially that the chief minister's remarks illustrated

> The tendency among politicians . . . to confuse 'government' with 'nation', 'personal interests' with 'national aspirations' and to shield error and misdemeanour behind 'security'.

It opposed sweeping powers under which stories like the Bhagalpur blindings, Naxalite encounters and the depredations of the Dhanbad coal mafia would be actionable. Indeed, it was

Jagannath Mishra who had argued that the Bhagalpur blindings had wide 'social sanction'.

The wounds of the Kuo Oil episode were yet to heal when *Surya*, a journal started by Maneka Gandhi and now bought out by Dr J.K. Jain, the surgeon, BJP member and friend of RNG, published in October 1982 the Goenka–Shourie correspondence on this matter accompanied by an unflattering commentary. Goenka was very angry with Jain and refused to speak to him for months. Taking her cue from that, Shobha Kilachand (now Shobhaa Dé), editor of *Celebrity Magazine*, Bombay, bearded RNG in his penthouse in October. He was reluctant to talk, then said he was speaking conversationally and not granting an interview, but was finally forthright in his comments. *Celebrity* published 'Goenka vs Shourie: The War without Victors'. RNG protested breach of trust. Shobha Kilachand said she had been impelled by the fact that 'the current developments are an important milestone in Indian journalism'. She had put on record 'only that which will not harm his or Mr Shourie's interests'.

Goenka said he had been embarrassed. What had he said?

> I can vouch for his [Shourie's] absolute integrity and honesty. He is one person who can never be bought . . . But, Arun is not a news-getter . . . When he says that during the last three years the *Express* has flourished, I'd like to remind him that we have been on the scene for 50 years and will continue to be there in spite of him. As far as his 'scoops' and exposures are concerned—the Antulay story was 100 per cent my story. All the facts and files were given to me by my sources. The credit for the other two big breaks should be given to N.K. Singh [he probably meant Ashwini Sarin] and Arun Sinha. Arun Shourie is a very competent man, but he totally lacks balance. A newspaper cannot be a one-man show. Even his writing is far too emotional. He takes twenty sentences to say something that can be said as effectively in two . . . We have always pursued truth and justice—we didn't have to wait for Arun for that.

Further:

> I am a Marwari—I believe in compromise and discretion . . . I have always considered the country's national interests before anything else. If I appear as if I am backing Mrs Gandhi today—I have my own reasons. The country is in a chaotic state already. We have no opposition worth speaking of. If she steps down, what will follow is anarchy. I am here to see that I don't contribute to that.

Shourie replied:

> I think my letter to George [Verghese] cleansed the atmosphere. It has cleared many doubts on a subliminal level. Yes, I know Ramnathji was deeply hurt. But I also know that he now understands the motives behind the letter.

Shourie surmised that the letter was leaked to the prime minister's house, from where it was given to two magazines.

RNG sacked Arun Shourie a few weeks later. He addressed a statement 'To Our Readers' on 21 November 1982:

> . . . There was and is no change in editorial policy. The only factor that counted was the need for compatibility between senior Editors and organizational norms and discipline. Mr Arun Shourie had been a tower of strength to me personally. But that does not answer everything . . .
>
> This paper is nobody's personal property, but belongs to society at large . . . It will continue to perform its mission . . .

A love-hate relationship had ended—temporarily.

Through all his four years at the *Express* until 1986, Verghese felt RNG was a troubled man. It was a difficult time for him in terms of family, health, property, the future of the group, finances, court cases, acute newsprint problems and concerns for the future of the country. The two got on well but he was later to say of his editor, 'Verghese is a saint. But saints should be sitting in the Vatican!'

Verghese thought the paper should devote more space and attention to problems of economic and social development and change, which RNG thought dull and expendable. RNG was also worried about the critical stand the paper took on India's intervention in Sri Lanka, especially after pro-LTTE mobs attacked the Madurai office and there was public resentment in Madras, where Rajmohan Gandhi had taken over as resident editor. RNG was also in some disagreement with the line on Kashmir, Pakistan and Bangladesh and said that critics felt the paper was being soft on India's neighbours. But he would always say he was merely expressing or reporting certain views and that ultimately it was for the editor to decide.

In response to a letter from RNG on the subject, Verghese replied:

> I was rather surprised by the contents. We have possibly carried the liveliest debate of any Indian newspaper on the Shah Bano–Shariat issue and related matters . . . Additionally, we have permitted and encouraged contrasting views, as we always do, but this has helped clarify issues.
>
> Likewise on 'Pakistan's involvement in Indian affairs'. . . About Pakistan and our neighbours generally, I readily admit that I strongly favour an active and sustained policy of normalisation of relations. It speaks ill of the foreign policy of any nation if it is at loggerheads with all its neighbours and is distrustful of and distrusted by them, diplomatic niceties apart. It adds to our security problems and distracts attention from urgent tasks at home. Mrs Gandhi spoke of a 'foreign hand' every day. This became an alibi for failure to deal with these problems . . .

RNG was pleased with Operation Blue Star in 1984 and hailed Mrs Gandhi's stern action against Bhindranwale and his Khalistani zealots who had barricaded themselves within the Golden Temple in Amritsar. Vir Sanghvi recalls RNG's remark at a dinner he hosted that very evening in Bombay that 'this was the Devi's greatest triumph, even more than Bangladesh'. But he was rattled by reports of mutiny at the Sikh regimental centre in Ranchi, with some recruits marching on the capital.

He telephoned Verghese in Delhi to get his assessment and

then said, 'I have talked to Girilal Jain [then editor of the *Times of India*]. He has said that if the *Express* blacks out this bit of news, the *Times* will do likewise.' Verghese was aghast and said that facts were facts and that the paper's credibility would be gravely damaged if it blacked out the news. Rumours would take hold and worsen the situation. He said the item would not be sensationalized and would be treated with due sensitivity.

Meanwhile, the *Express* had been facing an unprecedented newsprint crisis. The number of pages was reduced, and the Delhi edition would literally await the arrival of a truck of newsprint reels by some clever exchange or bargain to print the next day's paper. RNG was at his wit's end. The government was playing games, teasing him. The day Indira Gandhi was assassinated in October 1984, RNG telephoned from Bombay to say that he was absolutely fed up and the Delhi and Chandigarh editions should not appear the next day! Verghese was astounded and protested that a huge story of the gravest import had just broken and the paper simply could not shut down. If necessary, only a two- or four-page paper might be printed but come out it must. RNG quickly realized that he had spoken out of extreme frustration. In the event, the *Express* carried a special supplement that was on the streets by early afternoon and had a full-fledged edition next day.

Punjab had virtually been cordoned off during Blue Star and subsequent operations. Movements were restricted. Some areas had virtually been declared out of bounds as battles raged around a number of gurudwaras that had been converted into strong points by Khalistani elements. As soon as the embargoes were lifted, the *Express* sent out teams of reporters and photographers to assess the damage and reconstruct the story of the preceding days. In Delhi, the paper announced an *Indian Express* Relief Fund and raised Rs 17 lakh and took a direct part in relief, rehabilitation and rebuilding of mohallas that had been torched by arsonists during the shameful anti-Sikh pogrom that followed Mrs Gandhi's assassination. The effort was carried out under the auspices of a distinguished citizens' committee headed by L.P. Singh and including (then) Air Chief Marshal Arjan Singh, Nirmal Mukarji, K.F. Rustomji and P.R. Rajgopal.

On Mrs Gandhi's death, the *Express* had carried an editorial and followed this up with a series of letters from readers, and articles assessing the life and work of the fallen leader. Many were critical. In order to restore balance, Verghese requested A.N. Dar, resident editor in Delhi, to write a piece, as he had known her well. He dwelt on the many positive contributions she had made. RNG was enraged. He stormed in anger and said his life's purpose had been undermined by this eulogy. Verghese said he assumed full responsibility and had cleared the article, which was unobjectionable and reflected a valid point of view that the *Express* was bound to carry. If anything, he was prepared to resign. RNG cooled off and later apologized. But his reaction reflected his many quirks and contradictions, for deep down he respected Indira Gandhi. She was, like him, a fighter, indomitable.

Rajiv Gandhi became prime minister the very day his mother was assassinated. Constitutionally, there could not be an executive vacuum. There had to be a government in office to aid and advise the President. RNG was pleased. A new chapter had opened.

When Verghese had accepted his assignment as editor, he had told RNG that he would retire at the end of three years when he would be due to superannuate. RNG had laughed off the suggestion. He now repeated his desire to retire in mid 1985. RNG remonstrated, said editors did not need to superannuate, and ultimately sought a year's time during which to find a suitable replacement. Verghese agreed and finally left in June 1986. He did not quite approve of the manner in which the *Express* was preparing to mount a campaign against Reliance Industries Ltd. RNG came along one morning with an unsigned news analysis item that was to launch the campaign and asked if it could be published under a byline like that of J.D. Sethi, a former Planning Commission member. Verghese replied that if Sethi had not in fact written the piece it could not be fathered on him. It could, however, be published as 'From a Correspondent'. This was done after some strong language had been edited out. Subsequently, some letters critical of the item were also published.

It was left to Verghese's successor, Suman Dubey, to take on from there.

# 8

# Managing a Growing Empire

By the late 1980s, the *Express* was a huge, sprawling multi-edition, multi-lingual chain, the like of which had been unknown in India any time before. Managing it was difficult enough. Doing so efficiently was even more challenging, a task not rendered any easier for lack of a sound organizational structure and a cadre of professional managers.

The *Express* empire just grew. In some ways it was initially more or less an accident. Ramnath Goenka was in business but was quickly drawn to politics. The passionate nationalist in him soon decided that the freedom struggle needed greater voice and he felt it incumbent to do something about it. Opportunity came in Madras when Sadanand found himself in distress and RNG took over the *Express* and *Dinamani*, Thereafter, one thing led to another as new editions were started.

Speculation and trading provided a living income, with something to spare for investment. But the real back-up was to come from real estate, for which RNG had a keen eye. Coming late to the major metropolitan centres, RNG knew that his would not be the first paper in Madras, Bombay or Delhi. The answer, to his mind, therefore lay in starting editions in smaller towns from where he might penetrate the countryside, thereby achieving larger aggregate sales in any region. This would make him competitive in the advertisement market. He also wanted to go beyond English-speaking elites and reach the less sophisticated vernacular reader. Hence his insistence on the use of simple rather than classical Tamil and non-Sanskritized Hindi. Similarly, *Loksatta* was to become the market leader in Maharashtra because of its wide network of mofussil correspondents.

RNG branched out to Calcutta in 1944, launching the *Nationalist* in collaboration with Shyama Prasad Mookerjee, and then going on to launch the *Eastern Express* and a Bengali sister paper, *Bharat*, on his own as he felt the *Nationalist* was oriented towards the Hindu Mahasabha, whereas he was of a Congress bent. But even at that time he had thoughts of spreading further afield, with editions in Delhi, Lahore and Karachi.[1]

Editions were to sprout in Bombay, Delhi, Vijayawada, Bangalore, Ahmedabad, Cochin, Chandigarh, Hyderabad, Vizianagaram, Pune, Coimbatore, Calicut and Trivandrum in steady succession, with Gujarati papers in Baroda and Rajkot. The group would soon be publishing in six Indian languages and would break into financial journalism in 1961 with the *Financial Express*.

RNG had set his heart on a Malayalam paper from Cochin. In 1977 he had even called for a project report and started working on the plant and machinery requirements. But this was not to be. He was still looking for the right editor when he fell ill. Friends had sought to dissuade him from such a venture on the ground that there was no scope for another Malayalam paper in Kerala. He was not convinced. His argument was that the Kerala papers had a religious or ideological orientation and that it was for the *Express* to launch a secular newspaper.

As mentioned earlier, RNG was conscious of the need to make readers feel that his papers voiced their concerns and aspirations. He therefore encouraged his editors to espouse local and regional views despite this sometimes leading to divergent editorial views among papers in the group. Thus *Dinamani*, *Andhra Prabha* and the *Indian Express* took different positions on the formation of Andhra with reference to the future of Madras city and the sharing of river waters, while the *Express* and *Loksatta* adopted different editorial lines on Samyukta Maharashtra.

Goenka's newspapers were not primarily intended to be profit centres, but to serve the cause. Nevertheless, it was necessary at least to break even. Profits would come from advertisements and advertising from circulation. Distribution was therefore the key. It was essential to reach the reader before rival papers got there. In order to do so, RNG started van editions to service areas unserved by rail or to reach these places before the morning trains arrived. He would accordingly study bus and railway timetables, work out printing schedules to match and chart the routes his vans should follow, with agents and subagents positioned to take delivery and complete local distribution ahead of the competition.

He was very much a hands-on person and would not accept anybody's say-so. When a van driver told him that it took four hours to get from Madurai to Kodaikanal, RNG drove to the hill station himself and completed the run much quicker. The driver defended himself saying that RNG had done a single trip whereas he had to make a daily run. Moreover, he had a wife and children to support and should not be asked to risk his neck! At other times, RNG would check the number of level crossings on a given route and the timing and duration of gate closures. After allowing for such involuntary delays, he would lay down a schedule.

His knowledge of these matters was unique. In January 1960 he wrote to J.S. Mani, a manager in Madurai:

> Now that we have decided to send a van to catch the boat mail and other trains in Trichi in the evenings instead of at Madurai, I suggest the following arrangement.

> The van that leaves the evening for Trichi should come back and stop at a place about 20 miles from Trichi from where a road goes to Pudukottai. The van for Trichi, which leaves in the morning at 11.30 should take the Malur road and unload the parcels meant for Pudukottai, Karaikudi and other places in the van that will be waiting in that place on its way back from Trichi. The van should go to Pudukottai and Karaikudi and deliver the parcels and come back to Madurai. I think that the van that will leave Madurai in the morning at 1.30 would reach this place at about 3.15 at the latest. If the parcels are loaded at 3.15 into the van, which will travel through Karaikudi and Pudukottai back to Madurai, we will be able to deliver all the parcels on that route before 5 a.m. Places like Sivaganga, if necessary, may be covered by bus from Madurai. You can also send all the parcels for the Trichi-Erode line in the van to be delivered at the Trichi Junction Station, where the van will reach in any case long before 4 a.m in time to catch the 4.15 a.m train by which the Madras papers also go to these places.

A month later, T.K. Thyagarajan in Chittoor got this note:

> We should not send a van from Chittoor all the way to Chingleput. If necessary we must arrange it in such a way that a van waits at Conjeevaram at some point or other to take parcels from the Madras van and transport it to Chingleput. The Conjeevaram Agent used to himself take his copies from the level crossing. There is no reason why he should not do it now.

The planning was meticulous.

Close tabs were kept on other departments as well. He told managers at Vijayawada and Madras that he was not satisfied with the account-keeping and stock registers. He demanded a monthly account of income and expenditure under itemized heads and was very emphatic about the accounts 'being properly maintained, scrutinized and checked'. He also sought a confidential report on the performance of every individual member of the staff for his personal information.

RNG knew that quality production and printing was necessary for circulation and to attract advertisements. Hence he was for modernization of plants and the use of the latest technology. These were departments in which Bhagwandas, his son, was more interested and adept. This was something in which RNG was prepared to invest. Apart from other benefits, he felt that technology was labour and cost saving. He would therefore put his money more readily on machines than on men. The one was an investment, the other an expenditure and a headache. Labour tended to get unionized and bred 'communists'. He would fight them.

He wrote to T.S. Krishnan in Bombay in 1958 and recalled having dispatched an Inter-type heading machine from Delhi a year back on the suggestion of a John Dickenson representative who had certified these to be 'the best machines . . . in the world of their type'. He wondered why the machine was not installed and running and wished the matter to be looked into immediately. He added that he had been asked

> to buy a Ludlow for Bombay. I shall do so. But this does not mean that the most valuable property of the Company should be thrown into the dustbin.

On one of RNG's visits to Europe in the late 1960s, Sitanshu Das, the *Express* representative and correspondent in London, met him and suggested the purchase of a facsimile plant from the *Daily Mail*, which was closing down its edition in Manchester.

Goenka visited the equipment manufacturers who laid on a demonstration for him. RNG was suitably impressed and even discussed opening a letter of credit. Thereafter, nothing moved. When Das queried him later, RNG replied that he had thought it over and felt facsimile would not work. It implied centralized production and the loss of a sense of local ownership and content. Facsimile was still a novelty at the time. RNG was later persuaded that his fears had been exaggerated. Local and regional content could be maintained alongside decentralized printing and distribution. When he did take the decision nearer the Emergency, the government was obstructive.

B.D. Goenka had engaged a technical man, K.K. Sen, earlier working in Switzerland. After the Emergency the two of them developed a proposal to switch from hot metal to offset. An import licence granted during the Janata regime was utilized to procure the requisite machinery at a cost of about Rs 3 crore. Unfortunately, BD passed away and the plans were kept in abeyance. K.K. Sen found nothing moving and resigned.

RNG was interested in finding out about printing technology in Japan, and dispatched P.N. Rajgopalan there to study various systems and report back. He himself favoured flexography regarding which he had got some information from Germany. He found this cheaper but wanted to make cost comparisons with other systems, satellites included—for which he had made a tentative $200,000 bid after trials on the *Tribune* and *Metro* satellites in Bombay. BD's technical expertise would have been most useful at this time.

Labour was a constant worry for RNG. He was a poor paymaster and always suspicious of unionization by lurking 'communists' and lesser breeds of Leftists. He would say the more he paid, the more that was demanded. His first principle was to keep numbers down and keep everybody on a short leash.

Illustrative of the wary eye he kept on recruitment was a letter he wrote to D.P. Sonthalia, his manager in Delhi in 1958:

> I really do not know why you require two more packers. Out of the 45,000 copies, more than half is sold in Delhi, for which no packers are required. For the balance 20,000 copies or less that you sell in the mofussil, if you cannot do with 9 packers I am amazed. We pack as many as 1,80,000 copies a day [in Madras] and we have 21 packers in all. Bombay packs about 60,000 copies a day, apart from weeklies, and they have only 13 packers . . . It is easy to add to numbers; but it is impossible to get rid of them.

. . . We cannot forget that addition of men requires more money . . . We just cannot go on increasing expenses.

He also questioned the number of teleprinter operators employed.

The teleprinter machine works for about 14 hours and you have 3 operators. You have only one channel to feed. Even if one man is absent, two operators can take 7 hour shifts each. And when the man is not absent you have an extra man . . .

From Pothan Joseph's time onwards, editors had complained that the *Express* could not retain its brightest people as they were paid a pittance and soon lured away by rival papers. The *Express* therefore became a training ground for others and was left with the mediocre or raw hands. Some did of course stay out of loyalty and because of the undoubted élan of a paper that broke out of the conventional mould. It offered excitement, opportunity and a different experience.

However, RNG would treat senior staff relatively more generously, throwing in various perks to make up an acceptable package, and thereby seek to win their loyalty. Moraes and Mulgaokar were kept in comfort after retirement until the end of their days. But the middle-level staff, who constitute the backbone of any paper, were invariably a discontented lot. Admittedly, his constant skirmishes with the government strained the group's finances, but this was a secondary factor.

RNG would insist on recruiting beginners as trainees and then taking them as probationers after a test. After another test they might be confirmed. Yet another test was required for promotion. While this was intended to prevent ad hoc recruitment and promotion, it also meant constant uncertainty in the minds of staff and a feeling that they were being made to run an obstacle race.

The enforcement of wage board scales did a great deal to improve the salaries of journalists who were also categorized as 'workers' under the Industrial Disputes Act. At the same time it imparted rigidity to the structure through excessive job classification that inhibited legitimate rewards and punishments. His final solution for getting rid of those who fell from favour was to order their transfer to Bombay, where they would find it difficult to get suitable accommodation at reasonable rents or would have to live so far out that they would spend hours commuting and finally throw in the sponge. That was his 'Gulag'.

RNG was not inclined to employ women staff, though the *Express* was perhaps the first paper to take on a woman under Pothan Joseph in Bombay. Women, he felt, were undependable. They would get married and quit. If they stayed, they would have babies and take maternity leave. They could not be put on night shift and thereby disturbed the rotation of staff; nor could they be given rough beats. Beyond all of this, they would require separate toilets! Yet he was later to appreciate that the women on the *Express* staff made a fine contribution to the paper.

Goenka hired or retained expatriate staff at various times as they had experience and technical expertise and could write good English, on which he put a premium. Though he presumably had to pay them competitive salaries he was canny enough to know that they would themselves want to depart home after a while and were unlikely to create any labour problems for him. Among these, William Farrel and Pike were engineers and Wilmot, the press superintendent. The process department was started under Edward Fielding. Harry Miller, the British son-in-law of one of his close Madras friends, Parthasarathy was the chief photo executive. The competitions editor, A.J.V. Munro, managed Squarewords, a popular daily teaser in Delhi.

Hamilton, from whom RNG purchased the *Morning Standard* in Bombay, continued as manager for some time. The paper metamorphosed into the *Indian Express*, Bombay, and was edited and managed for a while by Ewing and Claude Scott.

Quite some years later, while on a visit to London, Dom Moraes at his request arranged for him to meet some bright British journalists over lunch. As narrated earlier, some were recruited but few lasted any length of time. One that survived in the *Financial Express* for some time was Kevin Rafferty. Rushworth, who came in to revamp the *Express* in Bombay, along with R.V. Pandit and N.J. Nanporia, was an early casualty.

With the steady expansion of the *Express* as a multi-edition newspaper, structural change was inevitable. The first step was regionalization, with editions being grouped under regional editors. This was facilitated by the development of the *Express* teleprinter network. When Frank Moraes took over in 1958, he was designated editor-in-chief. The editorial headquarters of the paper shifted to the capital. Delhi was the prime news centre as the seat of the Central Government, Parliament and the Supreme Court and the focal point for the conduct of the country's international relations and management of its security concerns.

*

In 1963 RNG decided to place the Delhi and Bombay editions and the southern region under senior editors. Prem Bhatia was located in Delhi and D.R. Mankekar in Bombay and a search was initiated for a suitable person for the South. All three regional editors were to work under the direction and control of the editor-in-chief. These arrangements more or less continued until after the Emergency by when RNG had suffered his first heart attack. Thereafter he began gradually entrusting greater responsibility to his son, Bhagwandas.

However, in the first instance RNG thought he should take stock of developments and plan a second phase of restructuring to meet emerging challenges and changing circumstances. This he did in a sixteen-page letter to Mulgaokar on 26 November

1978 from Kottakkal in Kerala, his favourite health resort, where he had gone for rest, recuperation and some rejuvenative Ayurvedic therapy. He started with an analysis of the paper's strengths and weaknesses.

The *Express* boasted the largest combined circulation among dailies and could therefore 'attract good authors who want their message to reach the largest number'. It had a very large newsgathering network and could draw on the strength of its editions in Gujarati, Marathi, Tamil, Telugu and Kannada. It was in a better financial position than during the past decade and was 'no longer on the wrong side of the government', which freed it from 'daily irritants'. Despite this, the paper was rapidly losing its place, as in Delhi where it now ranked third, thus impairing its ability to attract advertisements. Against this background he spelt out his thoughts for the future. The *Indian Express* had become the second or third paper everywhere with strong competition from established papers in each region. To become the first paper anywhere, the paper would have to acquire a distinct character of its own. To this end

> we will have to break the tradition that almost all newspapers have faithfully followed since British days of being obsessed with politics and governmental news. Obviously, political news and decisions taken by the Central and State governments are important but our political reporting consists of accounts of palace intrigues, shifting group loyalties and activities of personalities involved in the power game. This reporting is devoid of social or economic content. We report events or decisions verbatim but seldom educate the reader about the background . . . and the impact of these events on the life of the people. In sum, we deal with politics and other happenings as a privileged game of a few chosen individuals in which the Indian people are mere spectators.
>
> This has resulted in neglect of many important areas of human activity in which large numbers of people are involved. What we should do is to give social and economic content to all news and analysis . . . we can bring all news nearer the

> people . . . and make it more meaningful. At the same time, we will have to give equal, if not more, space to news and investigative stories [of] social, economic and cultural [interest] from the district level to the national capital . . . [This] would help the *Indian Express* to develop into a different [kind of] paper with a distinct personality. It would also pay dividends in circulation because the relationship between the paper and the people would become deeper and more important . . .

RNG accepted the fact that many reporters and correspondents would not be equal to the task. But he expected some would make the grade, given clear directions and mentoring.

This apart, what was required was restructuring, monitoring, a more relevant content and training of personnel. The contours of the new structure that he went on to outline reflect his views on the changing social scene.

> We became a multi-edition paper because we were the youngest national newspaper. When we started in Madras, the *Hindu* was 55 years old. In Bombay, the *Times of India* had deep roots and a well-settled clientele. The *Hindustan Times* of Delhi enjoyed the same reputation of pride and place. To achieve financial viability and stay in competition with these papers we opened editions to nullify the other advantages that they had. This strategy has paid us rich dividends in the South and gave us an advantage over our rival [the *Hindu*]. Our rival had to follow suit.
>
> But the situation is now changing. In addition to the national dailies, we are facing tough competition from regional English and language dailies. English is no longer the medium of instruction at all levels. It is still the language of administration at the highest level, but Indian languages are fast replacing it everywhere else. Decision-making is still in the hands of the English speaking elite but I feel its alienation from the people is nearly compete.
>
> Nationalism has taken a back seat and State or local ties have emerged as the more powerful driving force. You and I may dislike and regret this, but we cannot ignore it. Regional identities will have to be recognized and the feelings of

> people of different regions will have to be respected to draw them into the national mainstream.
>
> With the encouragement given to the various languages by the Central and State governments and the spread of education, the language papers have obtained a readership, which they never had a decade ago. Technological advances in printing and communication have made these language papers as professionally competent and financially viable as any English national daily. In their States, they are as powerful and influential as national dailies are in Delhi. The new language elite in this country has given respectability to these papers. In their areas of circulation they are capable of making national English dailies a luxury.
>
> In this situation, our regional editions cannot survive unless they are made to come up as newspapers in their own right. The fact of their being part of a national chain can be turned to advantage in one way alone—they must be at least as good in their regional and local coverage as the regional papers and, taking advantage of our national and international network, must outscore them in their national and international coverage.

Keeping these considerations in mind, RNG suggested certain structural changes. He proposed resident editors for all editions who would be capable of writing and commenting on regional and local issues, thereby developing their publications as 'autonomous units of a national chain' under the guidance of the editor-in-chief. These resident editors should gather in Delhi periodically to confer with him and review progress. Except for the editorial page and the OpEd page, resident editors should have a free hand to develop all other pages within the broad framework of the *Express*'s policy. Six or more editorials a week should be sent up from the regions. This would provide a balance between comments on matters of national and regional interest.

RNG proposed regional news bureaus at Delhi, Bombay, Madras, Calcutta and, perhaps, Chandigarh. These would be responsible for regional coverage, selecting and summarizing regional copy to be filed to other regions. Regional news bureau chiefs should work under the direction of the Express News Service (ENS) editor and their copy should be processed and disseminated through regional ENS desks. The Delhi bureau of the ENS should concentrate not merely on all-India news but on stories of regional interest emanating from Delhi. All copy must be filed at the earliest so that the items could go in the dak editions. Photo coverage should be similarly treated.

Progress would have to be monitored if it was to be sustained. There should be accountability for errors and delays and performance of all staff carefully maintained so that

> should demands for increasing bonus or wages, restricting the recruitment of people from outside the organization, etc., gather force, and should they be referred to an arbitrator, we would have enough material to substantiate our feeling that we cannot distribute largesse across the board as many members of our staff are just not doing or are incapable of doing their job properly.

He wanted the work of reporters and correspondents watched and compared with agency copy and coverage in rival papers to see whether they were malingering or providing some value-addition. Marked papers, their own and of rival publications, should be posted up for general information, and stories missed should be followed up and carried in the earliest ensuing edition of the paper. Delays in dispatch and transmission were not to be countenanced. Teleprinter circuits must not be cluttered with advertisements and news messages must be given first priority. But the weekly lottery results, a public craze at the time, were an exception.

In order to ensure a shift in reportage from happenings in ministries and the doings of ministers to the life and concerns of the people, staff could be redeployed. Instead of attending routine press briefings

> we should employ reporters who will be prepared to travel extensively anywhere in the country to report in depth about

> special aspects of people's lives, whether these be the rapidly changing caste situation in Bihar, the mood of the Sikhs in Punjab, the changing Church in the South or agrarian tensions in Andhra.

Moreover, Delhi must carry these stories for more balanced and comprehensive coverage. Likewise, investigative stories should be 'cumulative', with due follow-up, so as to add meaning and punch. Thus a series could be published on conditions in hospitals, schools, prisons, slums, the courts and so forth in various places and regions and then brought together in an analytical piece that would provide national perspective. Experts could be engaged to write on problems of special concern such as police reform and urban development. Likewise good experimental work being done by small social and cultural bodies and non-governmental organizations (NGOs) should be highlighted. Specialized international journals of high standing should be tapped and permission sought to reproduce outstanding articles. Foreign correspondents previously stationed in India and now back home could also be requested to write on foreign relations with an Indian angle. The *Express* man in London, B.K. Tiwari, might be suitably replaced by an Englishman and stringers employed in Japan, the Middle East and elsewhere.

> Lead articles on the editorial page should be used more for news analysis and for providing variety to the paper and less for political punditry. Today, four of our six days are blocked by regular in-house columnists and three of these four days are used mainly for general political comment. The Chief Editor alone should have a regular weekly column.

RNG emphasized the importance of training in building up professional cadres. This must be an immediate priority. He said he would like to start a regular training establishment for newcomers and to provide refresher courses. Such a training centre was subsequently established in Bangalore under T.J.S. George but only to be given over to the *Hindu* in Madras to become what is today the much-acclaimed Asian College of

Journalism, housed in the very building on Mount Road into which the *Express* had moved after the 1940 fire.

He also wanted managers at every centre to be held to given circulation and advertisement targets.

To assist in implementation of these reforms he suggested that the deputy chief editor be relocated in the South.

Here was an exhaustive and thoughtful blueprint for action. Things were set in motion. Over the years, resident editors were gradually appointed at all centres. Bright, young reporters were promoted on transfer and promising newcomers recruited. They were encouraged to travel and do investigative stories. Among the rising stars, in the early 1980s were Shekhar Gupta, Arun Sinha, Ashwini Sarin, N.K. Singh, Coomi Kapoor, Leela Menon, Vipin Pubby as a sports writer, Sapru as a science writer, Kanwar Sandhu as a defence analyst, and many others. Arun Shourie was appointed executive editor in 1979. A series of good stories kept coming in. However, consistency was lacking. Resources and newsprint remained nagging problems. RNG was impulsive, had strong likes and dislikes, would listen to tales and play off one person against another.

Nihal Singh, editor-in-chief from early 1981 to mid 1982, was troubled by the lack of coherence between the various *Express* editions and sought to streamline the organization and get better staff on the desk. RNG would agree but little action followed. Finding himself unable to make much headway and concerned about having a somewhat freewheeling deputy in Arun Shourie who had RNG's ear, Nihal Singh decided to call it a day (see also Chapter 7, p.187).

B.G. Verghese followed in June 1982. He too found RNG intent on further expansion while pleading lack of resources to improve salaries and attend to basic issues plaguing various centres. RNG remained concerned about circulation in Delhi and falling advertisements and Verghese kept urging that it was more important to improve quality and standards and thereby gain circulation rather than stretch resources further by starting more sub-standard editions. The whole approach seemed mistaken. Likewise, he found RNG's spending hours with railway and bus timetables and seeking to revise printing schedules to reach some remote areas quaint and unproductive. The whole management structure was 'primitive', lacking autonomy and delegation. Again, RNG was impatient of attention being diverted to social and developmental reporting. Though he had advocated this, his preference seemed otherwise. Ill health and other worries also impeded constructive implementation of his blueprint.

*

Until R.K. Mishra, a former Burmah Shell executive, joined as general manager in Delhi in the 1970s, the *Express* Group probably never had a truly professional manager. RNG had from the start concentrated all powers in his hands and inducted family members, trusted retainers and loyalists to assist him. As the empire expanded this clearly would not do. His own time was divided between the *Express*, politics and his other businesses. These diversions were distracting. He had started grooming his son to take over in due course but the Emergency intervened.

Then followed the tragedy of B.D. Goenka's sudden and untimely death in 1979. RNG was devastated. His hopes and dreams seemed to crumble, though in his son's lifetime he had outwardly, at least, been a somewhat distant parent.

Filled with grief, guilt and withdrawal symptoms, he impulsively parted with a controlling interest in the *Express* Group in favour of his daughter-in-law, Saroj. He was later to retrieve control. Saroj Goenka had been inducted into the *Express* board in 1963 in place of her father, Shreyans Prasad Jain, a close friend and respected counsellor to RNG, but essentially remained a housewife. She was now designated managing director and began to devote herself to the task.

The first task, however, was to rationalize the structure of the many *Express* companies post-Emergency in view of changes in Company Law. At a meeting of the board he chaired in late 1979, RNG noted that the sad demise of B.D. Goenka, 'a human dynamo in the context of his work as Chief Administrator of the *Express* Group of companies, [had] created a near-crisis in the management . . . and a vacuum in the top managerial position wherein the federal set up in the . . . Group was coordinated'. Hence, in the absence of this 'towering personality', an alternative organizational structure was necessary.

The board noted that *Express* Newspapers Pvt. Ltd and Ace Investments Pvt. Ltd, a subsidiary of *Indian Express* (Madurai) Pvt. Ltd, did not publish newspapers but were financiers and dealers in property, shares and securities, hired plant and machinery and so on. It accordingly resolved to amalgamate and merge into a single corporate entity all publication companies in the group in order to avoid duplication of secretarial, administrative and other responsibilities and hive off the non-newspaper companies to constitute a separate entity.

As was his wont, RNG recruited senior bureaucrats as executives as he valued their experience and contacts within the government and their ability to operate the licence–permit system and perhaps even to overawe their erstwhile juniors in the service if and when necessary. He employed Iravatham Mahadevan as a manager and editor in the 1970s in Madras and later took on K.S. Ramakrishnan as a group management consultant, based in Madras, and then S. Srinivasan as general manager in Bombay. All three were IAS officers of the Tamil Nadu cadre. He however parted company with Ramakrishnan later when the chief minister, M.G. Ramachandran, nominated the latter to the Rajya Sabha. He did not wish to have a political party affiliate in the organization as others of a different political hue might doubt the paper's independent credentials.

However talented these officials, they were administrators, not managers. Saroj Goenka applied herself to learning the ropes and in her own words 'worked like a coolie' to grasp the intricacies of the business, learning from the staff. Her ideas and ambitions were recorded in two interviews she granted.[2] She wanted to see the *Express* become the country's leading paper in her lifetime and wished to expand into magazine journalism. But the first task remained to consolidate the *Express*'s position in the South. She had plans for an evening paper in Madras, a Hindi daily in Bombay and several regional film and other magazines. Her father-in-law was looking after editorial matters while she maintained oversight over the entire group management.

However, as managing director, Saroj Goenka was content largely to confine her interest to the southern editions. RNG moved to Bombay and, as chairman, continued to take a close interest in every aspect of the working of the group. Tensions soon developed and were apparent in the correspondence exchanged between the two on a variety of issues.

Labour troubles were brewing. RNG decided to face a strike in Delhi in October 1987, refusing to concede a 1.5 per cent increase in bonus, a gesture recommended by some senior editors and managers. This would have cost Rs 30,000 against the lakhs lost through the work stoppage. Some of his responses were feudal.

In 1980 he wanted to declare a lockout and close down the Madras edition as he had done once before in 1959. Saroj Goenka and Mahadevan were opposed to so drastic a step. He responded to Saroj Goenka's urgings for a compromise on labour matters in a letter written in February 1980:

> Your letter of the 26th has obviously been written in anger . . . Labour problems have now become a part of life and the earlier we solve it the better for all concerned. As a general principle we should avoid a strike at all costs. In spite of our best efforts, if a strike takes place we should try to compromise

> as soon as possible. If a compromise on fair terms is not possible, then of course we will have to face the consequences. [In the matter of] confirmation of staff and transfers, under no circumstances [am I prepared] to give up my legal rights. So far as bonus is concerned, I did not tell Arun [Shourie] to agree to 17%, but I told him to bargain and if necessary to go up to 17%. However, after your telephone, I sent a message to Arun to withdraw from that position.

He cautioned against placing implicit faith in whatever might be said by persons around her. He spoke from experience but it was for her to take her own decisions. 'After all, you are the boss.'

He again addressed Saroj Goenka through Mahadevan with regard to the continuing stalemate in the South, stating, 'we must close down our Madras establishment . . . to save me from bankruptcy'. Madras was losing money and with the sharp rise in newsprint prices, losses would mount to Rs 2 crore per annum. That decision was stalled but ten months later, RNG again wrote to say that they had been 'compromising with the workers on all points to buy peace at heavy cost'. Despite accepting the Palekar award, 'appeasement' had only worsened the situation. For a number of months the papers were being inordinately delayed and claims for unsold copies were fast rising. Closure was the only answer as in 1959. The threat worked and the strike was called off.

In Bombay, more drastic measures were employed when the maverick labour leader Datta Samant sought to take over the *Express* union in 1981, and resorted to a go-slow and intimidatory tactics. As recounted earlier, loyal workers were prevented ingress by scattering itching powder across the entrance. Here again, the general manager, N.M. Dugar, counselled tact and reasoned argument. But in the face of Datta Samant's recalcitrance, rival workers were imported through the RSS-affiliated Bharatiya Mazdoor Sangh (BMS) to overawe the opposition and enable loyal workers to resume work.

To strengthen the Madras office, two names had been suggested from which to select a senior executive, those of S. Srinivasan and S. Guhan, both IAS officers. RNG fancied the latter but Saroj Goenka said she found him 'rigid, fashionable and modern'. He was likely to insist on 'luxurious' standards with regard to office modernization 'which we can ill afford'. RNG said he had made elaborate inquiries before coming to the view he had communicated. However,

> if you have no faith in my decision, I cannot help it . . . You can do whatever you like as long as we have a manager in Madras. You refer to Guhan as a modern man who will try and modernise everything. In my opinion, it is high time we do it. We are suffering today because we have not modernised ourselves. Ours is a Marwari shop, which we cannot afford to continue under changing circumstances.

Srinivasan was appointed.

RNG was uneasy about losing management control of the South though Saroj Goenka insisted he was consulted in all matters. He wrote to inquire about progress in the installation of certain equipment and told her:

> If you and Madras think that I have nothing to do with the South, I will be quite happy even to retire from the organisation. But as long as I am alive, I would like to be kept informed. I do not want to interfere in day-to-day affairs, but overall knowledge of the whole organisation is due to me and I must have it if I am there as Chairman.

Some time later he was again to write to her regarding a certain appointment. He urged her 'not to turn down my suggestions without considering them in depth. After all, I admit that you are the final authority.'

Each felt the other was being unduly influenced by a coterie around them.

RNG had after some study desired that the publication of *Andhra Prabha* be shifted from Bangalore to Madras. As Saroj

Goenka was not convinced, he wrote once more in an effort to win her consent.

> If we transfer AP to Madras, we will definitely have the advantage of increased circulation both for *Indian Express* and *Andhra Prabha* in the districts of Chittoor, Kadappa and Nellore and also in the City [of Madras] where there is no Telugu paper. The only place where we may not improve our position will be Anantapur, but Anantapur can be fed by Hyderabad. But in any case, no other newspaper can reach Anantapur before us.
>
> If you people do not agree with me, please do not hereafter refer to me any matter concerning the South. I am not interested in arguing things when the matter is as clear as daylight to me. If you want I can withdraw from the North also and you can look after the affairs of the company. As it is I am over-worked because only problems come to me. I am going to die one of these days, so why not take over from me before I die rather than wait for the day. However, the decision is yours . . .

Impatience would pass. Yet the relationship was never relaxed. He would needle his daughter-in-law on petty issues. On one occasion he was distressed about some dhotees Saroj Goenka had purchased for him:

> In regard to Rs 4104.75 for the dhotees purchased for me, I am sorry the cost is too much. During Diwali there is a commission [discount] of 20% on the khadi items purchased from Khadigram . . . Had we purchased the dhotees from Khadigram we would have saved Rs 1000. We lost Rs 1000 because of our purchase from Mohan Vasthra Bhandar.

Every paisa does count, but the note was churlish. The mania for economy was manifest again when he invited guests for a dosa meal at the penthouse in Bombay and complained that the caterers, Woodlands, had cheated him on the price!

However, even Homer nods. RNG was prepared to admit mistakes when he realized he was in error. He had misjudged the space required to accommodate the equipment required to introduce photocomposing in Hyderabad. He wrote to Saroj Goenka that 'the fault belongs to me. We all make mistakes. You will appreciate that it is not possible to visualise all the difficulties we may come across!'

Things seemed ready to move forward with regard to a technology upgrade at the time of BD's death in 1979 and it was decided to go in for photocomposing as well, starting with Madras and Delhi. However, the matter was still hanging fire in 1983 as additional import clearances were awaited.

In September of that year he shared his anxieties with Saroj Goenka:

> I am as much puzzled as you are in the matter of photo-typesetting. The problem is far bigger than what I ever thought it to be . . . The printing machines must also be able to use photo-typesetting. For instance, if we have photo-typesetting then we must have offset machines or we must use Napp. If you go in for Napp, it is quite costly. If we go in for flexography, we have to buy fresh equipment for making the plates. All these things are very costly. I am in the dark and am praying to God that He gives me some light.
>
> Our competitors are making lots of money and are improving in all directions. They are adding new publications to their existing units. *Hindu* is planning to produce a Photo weekly. *Deccan Herald* is thinking of producing an English weekly. *Free Press* has started a paper in Indore and is thinking of starting one in Jaipur. *Times of India* will start their Lucknow edition next month and they are thinking of starting an edition from Bangalore. We appear to be the only unfortunate ones. This makes me spend sleepless nights. I do not know what to do. I am consulting my friends.

Speculation about the future of the *Express* had commenced soon after BD's demise. The grandsons were inducted into the management to assess their capabilities. But senior editors and close friends had also begun to canvass the idea of a trust. RNG's own view was that the *Express* was more than a family concern and had become something of a national institution.

He would worry about how it would uphold that tradition in future. A draft trust deed was virtually drawn up around 1990 with Achyut Patwardhan, Nanaji Deshmukh, Venu Srinivasan, Nusli Wadia and Gurumurthy as possible trustees. Neither Wadia nor Nanaji believed that a trust was the answer. Nanaji's experience was that trustees often worked to promote their own interest. His advice: 'Don't appoint ten commanders.' RNG was inclined to agree.

Yet, RNG was never categorical and would continue to discuss the matter when broached later. Verghese recalls mentioning the matter and being asked to propose names. He put forward an illustrative list of the good and the great. RNG's response was to ask whether this body of men and women had greater stature than those making up the *Statesman*'s ill-fated management and editorial board of trustees who were unceremoniously bundled out in the late 1960s. The *Tribune* Trust was cited as a workable model, but that was seen as part of an old tradition that could not be easily replicated. RNG also feared that a motivated government might masquerade as the camel that occupied the tent.

The *Express* itself had drawn editorial attention to the potential mischief inherent in the Maharashtra Public Trusts (Management, Acquisition and Common Good Fund) Act, 1982.

> One is . . . left breathless by the provisions governing the temporary and permanent takeover of public trusts irrespective of whether they are religious or charitable. Not only are the prescribed grounds . . . vague and sweeping, [but] temporary takeovers, which are to last three years, appear to be so in name only. The trusts can irrevocably go out of the hands of the original trustees, because at the expiry of the three-year period, the government-approved administrator will hand over charge to new trustees to be appointed 'under any scheme framed by the Charity Commissioner and, if no such scheme is framed, to the trustees appointed by the State Government'.

However, the public trustee hurdle could have been overcome. Even before the relevant legislation was amended in 2000 to withdraw overriding powers from the public trustee, it would have been possible to form a private trust, rather than a public charitable trust, in which voting rights would not vest in the government. RNG ultimately took the view that without monetary involvement, trustees would be like bureaucrats on the boards of public sector undertakings. Yet he went along with discussions on creating a trust as a ploy by which to fend off other pressures until he was absolutely clear about what he should do with BD no more.

An alternative or interim suggestion was that RNG appoint public interest directors in order to create a more broad-based *Express* board, providing a balance to family representation. This was to happen later when Nusli Wadia and Venu Srinivasan were inducted.

Till the end of his days, the *Express* essentially revolved around one man, Ramnath Goenka. Even such time as he could devote to the affairs of the group was attenuated by parallel preoccupations with politics and business. Dabbling in National Jute and Indian Iron and Steel compelled him to attend to their affairs, even if only intermittently. This did those enterprises no good while diverting time and energy from the *Express*. Both suffered as he had no professional managers anywhere. Inspiration and genius can achieve great results. But without truly structured and sustained managerial and editorial underpinnings, the *Express* empire remained vulnerable and a hostage to fortune.

# 9

# Litigant Par Excellence

Ramnath Goenka was a practical man who believed in the maxim 'disobey and explain' rather than 'obey and complain'. Complaints might go unheard forever and could be as futile as talking to the wind. On the other hand, explanations, if required, could be pondered over and then vigorously defended in a cultivated spirit of injured innocence. This was a recipe for litigation from which lesser souls might shrink. But RNG was made of sterner stuff and, while not necessarily looking for trouble, was not the one to shy away from a good fight. It was invigorating and sharpened the wits. Above all, it was fun.

Of course the man had his share of worries. Some take tonics or go to spas to revive their drooping spirits or failing health. RNG went to court. It rejuvenated him. There was in the process something of the thrill of the chase, even if he himself was the quarry. He had the gambler's instinct and the will to stake all. He also had immense faith in the Courts and always believed that at the end of the day he would get justice. And if perchance that failed, he had insured with the gods, for he knew his cause was transcendental and its pursuit the stern call of duty.

Indeed, litigation was central to RNG's life and being, and it kept him going even while buying time. He would provoke legal action. On the other hand, the government and his opponents would seek to fix him by making all sorts of charges, placing him under constant investigation or pressure, using this to deny the *Express* bank credit, pin him down and break him. He fought more cases and spent more time in court and litigation than perhaps any other man in India. He was surrounded by legal advisers and read the law and judgements with close attention, so as to be one step ahead of his opponents.

Thus, donned in shining armour, Ramnath Goenka would set forth for battle. He would cut corners and be called to account. His sturdy independence displeased many who sought to settle scores with him. Political persecution led to vindictive prosecutions through the 1970s and 1980s. By one count RNG was in his lifetime involved in some 600 cases big and small, surely a record of sorts. He had the best of lawyers, whom he cultivated in Madras, Bombay, Delhi and Calcutta. Men like Srinivasa Iyengar, Thiruvenkatachari, Fali Nariman, Ram Jethmalani, V.M. Tarkunde, Nani Palkhivala, Chimanbhai Patel, Soli Sorabjee, H.M. Seervai, Bholanath Sen and Arun Jaitley were among those to whom he turned for legal advice and who, in turn, were glad to assist him in fighting political vendetta and upholding the freedom of the press.

Swaminathan Gurumurthy joined him during the Emergency essentially as his financial adviser. But such was his legal acumen that RNG depended on him heavily for preparation and scrutiny of briefs and affidavits. RNG himself had an acute grasp of the law and would cut through the dense jungle of legal niceties to get to the core of any matter. He would pore over laws and law books, peruse judgements, make notes and burn the midnight oil to draft briefs for his lawyers to consider and polish. Many were impressed by his intuitive knowledge of what would appeal to the Bench.

The cases filed against RNG related to a variety of issues ranging from wage fixation, newsprint allocation and proposals for a price-page schedule, to matters relating to customs, income tax, company law, foreign exchange violations and so forth. In all these he would convert the issue to one of infringement of Article 19(1)(a) pertaining to freedom of the press. His position was that anything that restricted newsprint would curtail circulation or the number of pages that could be printed and thereby limit the reader's right to know. A limitation on advertising, customs duties or sales tax would by the same token entail raising costs, thus affecting the economics of publication, quality of news or the ability to gather news, and thereby be tantamount to a tax on information. He would therefore move all issues from the realm of commerce and finance to a ringing defence of freedom of the press against malign attack or trespass by those in authority. The Courts were sympathetic to this line of reasoning and in case after case held freedom of expression, and the freedom and independence of the press deriving from it, to be paramount. Indeed, the Supreme Court was virtually to hold freedom of expression to be the first among all freedoms and, subsequently, list it with other fundamental rights among the basic features of the Constitution, which it declared unamendable.

As one of the doughtiest champions of freedom of the press in India, RNG was in the forefront of those who contributed to its expansion. This he did through persistent litigation on behalf of the *Indian Express*. The outcomes went towards building up the case law surrounding freedom of speech and expression.

Perhaps the first major case he fought was against the Audit Bureau of Circulation (ABC), which had challenged the *Express* circulation figures in Madras. He contested the ABC audit and took the matter right up to the Supreme Court, which vindicated his position.

In 1958 the *Express* along with other papers challenged the

Wage Board Act before the Supreme Court. The Wage Board was set up consequent to the recommendations of the first Press Commission in response to the plea that journalists were treated as sweated labour. The *Express* pleaded that in 1957 it employed 331 working journalists, including 123 proof-readers. Under the Wage Board award, its existing wage bill would rise from Rs 9.78 lakh to Rs 15.21 lakh, with an additional Rs 1 lakh in payments to stringers. Retrospective application of the award to May 1956 would greatly add to the overall burden.

The concepts of 'basic', 'living' and 'fair' wages were pitted against the principle of capacity to pay. It was stated that higher wages would restrict employment. This would be tantamount to restricting freedom of the press and also result in curtailment of circulation. Laying an excessive and prohibitive burden on newspapers would impede the growth of the press and force existing papers to seek governmental aid, which would rob them of their independence. The grouping of newspaper chains would also create difficulties for weaker units. Everything considered, the Act would infringe Article 19(1)(a). The Court upheld the plaint.

The *Express* was involved in litigation in 1961 when a strike in Madras was followed by a lockout and closure of the unit. The *Express*, *Dinamani*, *Andhra Prabha* and *Screen* were published in the city until April 1959 when RNG announced his decision to close down, giving a month's wages in lieu of notice. He proposed to relocate in Chittoor, just across the border in Andhra Pradesh. An industrial dispute in Madras a couple of months earlier had been resolved through adjudication. Continuing labour troubles, however, made RNG think of retrenching sixty-nine workers and moving the *Express* to Vijayawada by selling the *Indian Express* to its sister company, *Andhra Prabha*. The workers objected to what was seen as a subterfuge and the state home minister intervened to prevent this from happening. Simmering unrest finally led to a strike. This was the last straw for RNG, who declared a closure. He purchased a paddy field in Chittoor, got it levelled, built some sheds and started publishing from there within two years. The *Express* did not return to Madras until 1965. Chittaranjan, who was later to join Nihkil Chakravartty in starting *Mainstream* in Delhi, was one of the principal union leaders behind the strike. The workers tried to form a newspaper cooperative and did start a Tamil paper, which however failed.

In 1962, a major court battle was joined on the page-price schedule on which the *Express* and some other papers came together with *Sakal*, a leading Marathi paper published from Poona, in petitioning the Supreme Court. Article 19(1)(a) was invoked on the ground that a higher cover price would affect circulation while a reduction in pages would curtail news content and leave less space for advertising, thus hurting both the reader's right to know and the economics of newspapers. It was argued that the protection of small papers could not justify putting impediments in the way of larger ones.

A decade later, the *Express* was back in court with the *Hindustan Times*, *Times of India* and others to challenge newsprint control. The government's stand was that the country did not produce all the newsprint it required, necessitating increasingly large imports from around the world to meet both rising circulations and the demands of new publications. Limitations of foreign exchange for sustenance of the economy as a whole did not permit open licensing and free import. Bulk purchases of newsprint were therefore made through the State Trading Corporation and allotted to individual papers on the basis of quotas linked to previous circulation, with some allowance for growth.

The *Express* and other papers challenged the government's newsprint import policy for 1971-72. They took the line that newsprint control was not a 'reasonable restriction' permissible under Article 19(2) of the Constitution as it abridged the fundamental right of freedom of the press by curtailing pages, circulation and advertisement space. Objection was also taken to the newsprint policy for 1972-73 as it brought white printing paper, an indigenously produced alternative being used by newspapers, within its ambit. The newsprint policy was bad because it barred 'common ownership papers' from starting any new paper even within the paper's authorized newsprint quota, limited the maximum number of pages to ten and prohibited inter-changeability between different papers under common ownership. Further, smaller papers were permitted a 20 per cent increase in pages up to a maximum page limit of ten pages while larger papers were prospectively barred from increasing the number of pages, the page area or periodicity by reducing their pages as previously allowed. Thus no flexibility or adjustment was permitted and these papers were put in a straitjacket. Such discrimination against larger papers constituted an unreasonable restriction.

The Supreme Court ruled that liberty of the press was an essential part of freedom of speech and expression. It held that the 1972 policy was arbitrary, treated unequals as equals and tended to discriminate against more efficient and innovative papers. Loss of circulation and advertising would affect economic viability and therefore violate Article 19(1)(a). In sum, the verdict was that newsprint control could not and must not become an instrument of newspaper control.

In 1986 the *Express*, along with the *Hindu*, *Statesman* and *Times of India*, challenged the imposition of customs duty on newsprint. The burden was said to be excessive and likely to stifle newspapers. A 15 per cent ad valorem duty had been imposed on newsprint with effect from 1981-82. Newspapers were in turn classified in three categories by order of circulation, namely, small (with sales up to 15,000 copies), medium (with sales between 15,001 and 50,000) and large (with circulations in excess of 50,000). The 1982 budget then levied a duty of nil, 5 per cent and 15 per cent respectively on newsprint allocated to newspapers in each of these three categories.

This burden, over and above that imposed by the Palekar

Wage Board award, was found to be excessive. The Supreme Court called upon the government to reconsider the duty.

In all these cases, the *Express* was involved in common cause litigation affecting newspapers or certain categories of newspapers at large. These were class actions resulting in landmark decisions of the Court that went a long way towards both clarifying and amplifying the ambit of Article 19(1)(a) and freedom of the press. However, the *Express* was separately engaged in fending off a variety of governmental pressures and charges through literally hundreds of cases instituted against it. The rift with the Central Government began with the Congress split in 1969 and manifested itself more openly from 1971 when RNG came to Parliament as an Independent supported by the Jana Sangh and then went on to back Jayaprakash Narayan.

This was the beginning of what RNG saw as a series of fishing expeditions by various limbs of government to uncover whatever dirt they could on him and his companies. By now he had acquired ownership of the National Jute Company and was buying heavily into Indian Iron and Steel. The net was spread wide. The attack was orchestrated with one issue after another surfacing in Parliament, the media and the courts.

A Company Law Board inspector visited the Madurai office of the Express in 1971 and, having gone through the books, said he could not attest to the genuineness of a particular transaction involving the purchase of 2500 tonnes of white printing paper from a Radha and Company in Calcutta. The CBI raided the premises soon after and a criminal case was registered by the Special Police Establishment against RNG, B.D. Goenka, Saroj Goenka and three employees on grounds of forgery and cheating. The allegation was that the accused had obtained credit facilities from the Punjab National Bank by pledging non-existent stocks of paper on the basis of fabricated accounts and invoices. The alleged offence was said to have been committed in 1968 and the issue was whether or not the stocks hypothecated to the bank actually existed.

The defence argued that the stocks were verified by the bank which itself had made no complaint and had been repaid its loan in full with interest. RNG would say that the CBI was used as a tool by the government to compel the Punjab National Bank to discontinue credit to his companies.

The matter was publicized with gusto by *Patriot* and AIR. Meanwhile K.P. Unnikrishnan and other Congress and Leftist MPs alleged in Parliament that Goenka and his family had also misused funds belonging to the Tirupati Temple Trust for nefarious purposes. All these charges were refuted.

On the misuse of the temple funds, the Speaker of the Lok Sabha had in 1969 said that the charge that Tirupati funds were used to corner Indian Iron and Steel shares had been looked into:

> The Deputy Minister, Shri J.B. Muthyal Rao, was instructed by me to go to Tirupati, look into the registers, talk to the officers of the Devasthanam and the Andhra Pradesh Government and report to me . . . He had been to Tirupati along with an officer of the Ministry of Law and they had a series of detailed discussions with the Minister of Religious Endowments, Government of Andhra Pradesh, and officials of the Tirupati Devasthanam. They had also gone through the registers of investment and books of account maintained by the Devasthanam under the statutory provisions applicable . . . The registers were seen to be duly audited by the Assistant Commissioner of Local Fund Accounts. As a result of these discussions and examination . . . it was seen that there has been no misuse of funds . . . Therefore . . . there is no truth in the statement that the funds of the Tirupati Temple were misused, as alleged.

In the other matter, the CBI investigations revealed that Radha and Company, the Calcutta firm from which the white printing paper was allegedly purchased, did not exist. The person who had signed the invoices on behalf of Radha and Company turned out to be a clerk in the *Express*'s Madras office, who ultimately turned approver in the case. RNG and Saroj Goenka were acquitted. Bhagwandas and two *Express* employees were convicted, the former just before he passed away in 1979. Appeals in the case of the others were still pending even after the demise of RNG.

This case first came up before the special Metropolitan Magistrate, Madras in December 1974. Ram Jethmalani appeared for the *Express* and was assisted by Gowrikantan, the *Express* auditor in Madras, and his young articled clerk, Swaminathan Gurumurthy. This was the beginning of Gurumurthy's association with RNG and the *Express*.

In 1972 the government, acting under the Companies Act, appointed two directors on the board of *Indian Express* (Bombay) Ltd for two years without a show cause notice. This bid to gain control over the paper was challenged in the Bombay High Court. The government wilfully delayed its responses until the term of the official directors had expired. The court passed strictures on the government and ordered that costs be paid to the *Express*.

*Andhra Prabha* Ltd and *Indian Express* (Madurai) Ltd had similar experiences, with government directors being appointed to their boards. RNG filed writs alleging mala fide efforts by the Congress to infiltrate the management of his papers, but by then the Emergency had been imposed and all stops were pulled out in persecuting and prosecuting Goenka.

From then on raids became a familiar routine. RNG had his moles in various branches of government at the Centre and in the states and would often have some forewarning. Trusted staff members in Madras recall being summoned from home at night and being told to pack up sensitive papers and documents, load them in waiting vehicles and then personally drive furiously to unknown destinations, without stopping for anyone or worrying about who might be following them! An apocryphal story is also told of one of his aides being increasingly troubled by multiplying cases against the *Express*. RNG told him not to worry as both he and the judge visited the same dancing girl! Here was a man who could laugh off his woes.

At various times, the government endeavoured to bring the *Indian Express* Group within the scope of the Monopolies and Restrictive Trade Practices Act. It stretched definitions to bring the *Express* Group within the ambit of the Act in the first place and then levelled vague and unsubstantiated allegations to suggest that it had violated the same Act. The *Express* went to court and matters dragged on. The object, as before, was harassment. Finally the government dropped all pretence and virtually issued an ultimatum that the paper should either be sold to the Congress or placed under a board of directors dominated by government appointees. Failure to comply was accompanied by threats of arrest of RNG and his family, and prosecutions on other counts. RNG played for time, appeared to compromise by accepting the board imposed on him under K.K. Birla, but finally threw off these shackles and defied the government to do its worst. Mrs Gandhi backed off, fearing the backlash of adverse public opinion mounting within the country and abroad.

*

The most critical instrument of the Emergency regime was, however, censorship (the editorial impact of which has been dealt with in Chapter 6). This was used in the most brazen and cynical manner. It commenced, totally illegally, with the cutting of the electricity supply to newspapers along Bahadur Shah Zafar Marg, Delhi's equivalent of Fleet Street, on the night of 25-26 June 1975. Thereafter censorship guidelines were imposed, accompanied by threats of grave consequences should these be infringed. More drastic action was to follow. Pre-censorship was imposed on the Cochin edition on 13 November 1975. This was extended to the Madras and Bombay editions on 24 February 1976 and further extended to all editions of the

Group on 16 August. Pleas that this was unwarranted and illegal fell on deaf ears. Pages would deliberately not be cleared by indicated deadlines or would be returned at the last moment with large chunks of material arbitrarily censored for no reason at all. Since blank spaces were disallowed, this would entail composing fresh matter. The whole object was to so delay printing as to virtually deny publication. Alternatively, late printing ran the risk of economic attrition on account of a huge accumulation of unsold copies.

RNG decided to get each edition to maintain a register, meticulously detailing the time at which matter was sent and cleared and the nature and extent of material censored. The schedules of other papers were also logged and their contents monitored to prove gross discrimination. A writ petition was filed in the Bombay High Court in August 1976 against the Union Government and its chief censor, Harry D'Penha. It was shown that the front page of the *Express* in Delhi was sent to the censor for scrutiny at 11.40 p.m. on 16 August but was only cleared at 6.35 the next morning. On 17 August the petitioner sent all pages for the city edition for clearance between 7.30 p.m. and 11.30 p.m. but the censor cleared the last page only at 6.20 a.m., by when all the rival papers were on the streets. Corresponding timings were given for the dak editions. Similar compilations were made for the Bombay and Ahmedabad editions and the five southern editions published from Madras, Madurai, Bangalore, Cochin and Hyderabad.

It was further argued that the pre-censorship order violated Article 301 of the Constitution by imposing crippling restrictions on the trade, business and calling of the petitioner and preventing him from printing, distributing and circulating his papers and journals. None of the matter censored had or was shown to have any bearing on the defence of India, civil defence, public safety or maintenance of public order for which the order had been promulgated. An affidavit filed by the *Express* observed that the harassment that had been detailed was part of 'a deliberate policy with a view to prevent publication of the paper under the guise of pre-censorship'. It cited examples of the tactics employed:

> News items, which our editors have put on a particular page, are required to be transferred to another page without rhyme or reason. This is not the function of the censor.
>
> Unobjectionable news items published in other newspapers are deleted from editions of the *Indian Express* and *Sunday Standard*.
>
> It has been the practice of the *Indian Express* to have at the end of the editorial column a feature called 'Think it over'. The following quotation from Mahatma Gandhi . . . was deleted by the Censor: 'After I am gone, no single person will be able completely to represent me. But a little bit of me will live in many of you.'

Among items perversely deleted were 'Mettur Levels Decreasing' and 'Drought Will Decrease Coconut Yield'.

Likewise, interesting items from the *Express* of '25 Years Ago', carried as a regular feature, were often deleted. Even copy cleared by the censor for dissemination by Samachar, the nationalized news agency under government control, was required to be separately cleared once again when carried in the *Express*. In Vijayawada, items cleared by the censors as galley proofs were required to be cleared a second time when made up in pages.

In a spirit of accommodation, the *Express* proposed as an alternative that the government should either ensure that publication was not delayed and copy refused for publication be so attested and duly returned or post censors in all *Express* offices so that matter could be cleared on the spot. The government panicked at the prospect of its absurdities inviting the ridicule and wrath of the court and sought desperately to conclude a bargain whereby it would accept the compromise, provided the paper withdrew its petition.

On 30 August the *Express* petitioned the court stating that it was unable to carry on and would be left with no option but to close down its papers and throw 5000 persons out of work, thereby denying more than a million readers of newspapers of their choice. The government thereafter assured the court that it would ensure that pre-censorship would be conducted in a manner so as not to delay publication of the *Express* editions. The *Express* reported to the court a week later that the assurance had been honoured.

On 30 September 1976, the pre-censorship orders on the *Express* were finally withdrawn.

Earlier, on 23 March 1976, a ban on government advertisements in the *Indian Express* was revoked after a writ petition was filed in the Bombay High Court.

On 1 October 1976, on the eve of the annual public holiday on Gandhi Jayanti, the Delhi administration cut off electricity supplies to the *Express*. The paper immediately went to court. The petition was heard and withdrawn on 4 October when the Delhi Electric Supply Corporation pleaded it had repaired a 'technical defect' and restored the electricity connection.

Then on 6 October the Delhi High Court upheld the *Express*'s contention that its press in Delhi had been padlocked for alleged non-payment of property tax. The court held this action improper and ordered that the seals and locks be removed.

These decisions were reported in *The Times*, London, the *New York Times*, *Newsweek* and other leading international journals. Everywhere, the government did its worst but failed to cow down the *Express*.

In 1977 yet another criminal case was filed against Goenka in relation to Express Traders Ltd, Bombay. The charge was that prior to 1967, *Express* (Madras) Pvt. Ltd had dabbled in shares, mainly of the Indian Iron and Steel Company, whereas *Indian Express* (Madurai), *Indian Express* (Bombay) and *Andhra Prabha* Pvt. Ltd were in the newspaper business. Then some time in 1967, the *Express* (Madras) Pvt. Ltd converted the IISCO shares held by it into investments. Thereafter, in collaboration with *Express* (Bombay) Pvt. Ltd, it cornered a large block of IISCO shares before their prices fell sharply, causing the two companies heavy losses of about Rs 85 lakh in the accounting year 1970-71. Since these share holdings were investments, these losses could not be set off against losses on other income under the Income Tax Act.

In the circumstances, Ramnath Goenka and other *Express* officials, in collaboration with certain Income Tax personnel, allegedly entered into a conspiracy and fabricated documents purporting to show that a company called Express Traders Ltd, Bombay, had been formed on 1 October 1970 initially through a partnership comprising *Express* Madras Pvt. Ltd and *Express* Bombay Pvt. Ltd but subsequently enlarged in April 1971 to include *Express* Madurai Pvt. Ltd and *Andhra Prabha* Pvt. Ltd. Thereafter the tax returns of Express Traders were filed setting off pro rata among the four newspaper companies almost Rs 85 lakh of the capital losses said to have been suffered by it. In short the speculative losses of the newspaper companies were transferred to Express Traders at the cost of the exchequer in terms of evaded tax.

It was further alleged that some income tax officials joined hands with *Express* officials in falsifying the records. Two others, V.L. Teli, a vendor who pre-dated the stamped paper he sold the *Express*, and T.P. Shirke, an income tax receipt clerk, turned approver.

Some of the concerned officers handling the *Express*'s income tax returns disallowed the share of losses in Express Traders alleged to have been made by the various *Express* companies. They maintained that Express Traders was not in existence during the relevant period.

On the other hand, RNG asserted that after thwarting his efforts to seek election to the IISCO board in 1970 in order to prevent further mismanagement of that ailing company, the government did nothing to improve matters. Consequently, IISCO could no longer be considered a blue-chip investment. The *Express* companies accordingly decided that IISCO shares should not be held as 'investments' but converted into 'stock in trade'. The group companies however decided that the circumstances were conducive for the resumption of trading in shares and therefore went on to form a partnership firm by name of Express Traders consisting of the group companies, namely, *Indian Express* (Bombay) Pvt. Ltd, the holding company, and its three subsidiaries, *Indian Express* (Madurai) Pvt. Ltd, *Indian Express* Newspapers Pvt. Ltd, and *Andhra Prabha* Pvt. Ltd.

However, the price of IISCO shares continued to fall from November 1970. The *Express* Group therefore felt it prudent to sell its IISCO holdings and a large block of shares was in fact sold to the LIC in April 1971 at Rs 10 per share. The share prices continued to decline and touched rock bottom at Rs 4 per share, entailing huge losses to the *Express* Group of companies. IISCO was eventually nationalized in 1976.

RNG charged the Central Government with failing to act as a true guardian of the interest of shareholders and indeed supported what it recognized to be an inefficient IISCO management only to harass Goenka out of sheer spite. The losses to the *Express* Group on this account, the Shah Commission was later told, amounted to Rs 15 crore, including the cost of holding the shares.

Deposing before the Shah Commission, RNG maintained:

> Not content with inflicting this enormous loss on me, the Central Government saw to it that the losses on this account which in law and in fact were business losses, were not allowed in income tax assessments. Registration of the firm of Express Traders under the Income Tax Act was unlawfully refused; the genuine business losses suffered by it was not entertained and computed on grounds wholly unsustainable in law or in fact. False allegations of ante-dating the partnership

> document were raised and a charge of concealment of income was made. [Finally] a complaint was lodged [on these grounds] by the Income Tax authorities in a court in Bombay in September 1974.

The case was still pending years later.

*

Another major case was decided in 1986 with regard to the bid by the government to take over the Express Building in Delhi on grounds of violation of the municipal zonal plan and building by-laws. In the early 1950s RNG had mooted the idea of developing a 'Fleet Street' for newspaper offices in Delhi. The idea gained ground and the *Express* was allotted Plot Nos. 1 and 2 on Bahadur Shah Zafar Marg in Delhi for the construction of an office and press. Since this site was later sought for the construction of Pyarelal Bhavan, in memory of one of Gandhi's closest aides, RNG readily agreed to exchange it for Plot Nos. 9 and 10, reportedly at the request of Jawaharlal Nehru. After taking possession of the new plot it was discovered that an underground sewage line ran diagonally across it, rendering a triangular portion unsafe for construction. The *Express* therefore built on the remaining portion, using the 'unsafe' area for parking, on the basis of what it claims was a clear understanding that it would later be permitted to build on that portion too if the drain was diverted or other means found to enable construction.

Shortly after the Emergency, RNG wrote to the housing minister in the Janata administration, Sikander Bakht, seeking permission to construct an annexe on the hitherto unbuilt area for publication of a Hindi paper. Bakht cleared the proposal on the basis of a floor area ratio (FAR) of 300, which would be suitable for a three-storey building as recommended by his officials. RNG demurred and said the minister himself had spoken of an FAR of 360 but that the *Express* had in mind an

FAR of 500 that would enable it to construct a five-storey structure. Both the Municipal Council of Delhi (MCD) and the Land and Development Office (L&DO) objected to any increase in the FAR above 300 and a counter-offer was made to Goenka that he could be given land elsewhere if he so desired. RNG was adamant and finally an FAR of 360 was sanctioned along with a no objection certificate to go ahead with construction. The wrangling did not end until 1979 when construction commenced on the basis of 80 per cent coverage and only a single basement instead of the double basement the *Express* had sought.

The Janata government fell and with the return of the Congress to office, the new Lieutenant-Governor of Delhi, Jagmohan, reopened the matter and set up a fact finding committee that reported that the annexe had a covered area of 18,000 square feet in excess of the sanctioned plan which was itself 55,748 square feet more than the legally permissible area! The government first sought to seal and then demolish the annexe and meanwhile barred the *Express* from collecting rentals from its tenants in the Express Building. The *Express* took the government's 'terror tactics' to court, pleading violation of Article 19(1)(a) and freedom of the press. Hearings commenced in the Supreme Court in April 1982 and continued for seventeen months. Judgement was delivered in October 1985 with an interlude of comic relief when at RNG's canny invitation Maharishi Mahesh Yogi and his followers filled the annexe for several months with ecstatic sessions of transcendental meditation (see Chapter 7, pp.172–74).

Justice A.P. Sen, with Justice E.S. Venkatramaiah concurring, described the government's action as arbitrary. It betrayed non-application of mind and constituted a threat to freedom of the press. It held the *Express* office on Bahadur Shah Zafar Marg not to be 'public property'. The *Express* had been granted permission to construct a new Express Building with an enhanced FAR of 360 by the DDA, which the *Express* contended, also specifically permitted a double-basement. The building was not violative of the Delhi Master Plan in terms of the D-II zonal development plan under the MCD building bylaws. Therefore, the notice to the *Express* by the Zonal Engineer (Buildings) was in excess of his authority as the annexe was not unlawful. The court passed strictures on the Lieutenant-Governor, saying he had taken an undue interest in the case, and rejected his plea for promissory estoppel. The *Express*'s case was upheld. In the matter of conversion charges, however, the court rejected the assessed levy of Rs 3.3 crore and said these charges should be suitably determined.

Jagmohan's plea was that far from bringing out a Hindi paper, the *Express* was renting out its premises and unless he took speedy action, RNG would complete the building and present the government with a fait accompli. This in fact is what happened and the Hindi *Jansatta* only commenced publication in November 1983. He also said that the notice to resume the building was struck down because this could only be done by filing a civil suit. Such a suit was filed later and the case was still pending after many years. After RNG's death, the property on Bahadur Shah Zafar Marg passed on to Saroj Goenka. With the compounding of damages, the government demand now runs to some colossal figure. But to seek damages today may be whistling in the dark.

Shortly after the Supreme Court had ruled in favour of the *Express* in the building case, the minister for law, H.R. Bhardwaj, criticized the former housing minister Sikander Bakht in the Lok Sabha for his part in the Express Building matter. RNG replied in a statement on 30 November 1985, calling the minister 'delinquent'. He scorned the implication that the *Express* had bribed Bakht and said that if such a charge were made outside the privileged sanctum of Parliament, he would have called it 'concocted falsehood, vicious and defamatory' and taken Bhardwaj to court. He pointed to inaccuracies in the minister's statement, such as calling

A.P. Sen's order a 'minority judgement', and concluded, 'In just two days, Mr Bhardwaj has done the greatest damage to Mr Rajiv Gandhi who has tried hard to create a clean image after a decade of the politics of confrontation and intrigue.'

A motion of privilege was moved in the Lok Sabha against Ramnath Goenka's 'overreaction'. However, the Speaker ruled that, in keeping with tradition, the House would best uphold its dignity by taking no further notice of the matter.

*

At a very different level, the *Express* got involved in a corporate war with Reliance Petrochemicals Ltd (RPL). The issue pertained to RPL's issue of 12.5 per cent convertible debentures for a very large petrochemical complex at Patalganga in August 1988 for the manufacture of mono-ethylene glycol (MEG), high density poly-ethylene (HDPE) and poly vinyl chloride (PVC). The *Express* had published some articles impugning the action of the Controller of Capital Issues in granting the necessary sanction for this mega issue. Reliance got an injunction against further publication of articles on this topic by the *Express*. However, once the issue was over-subscribed, the paper sought and was granted relief from the 'gagging order'. RPL pleaded that the further articles constituted contempt as the debenture issue was still pending in certain high courts and was therefore sub judice.

The RPL debenture issue was for Rs 593 crore, inclusive of a permissible 15 per cent retention of the amount over-subscribed. Since there were other plaints in some high courts, RPL had asked that all the suits be transferred to the Supreme Court. In an interim order on 19 August 1988 the Supreme Court allowed the mega issue to go forward without let or hindrance. A few days earlier, on 15 August the *Express* carried an article entitled 'Infractions of Law Has Unique Features: RPL Debs'. While RPL urged unimpeded administration of justice, the *Express* took its stand on freedom of speech and expression. The point in contention was whether the *Express* should be permitted to write before the mega issue closed on 31 August, although the issue had already been over-subscribed, as investors could still withdraw their applications.

A bench of two judges held that continuance of the injunction on the *Express* was unnecessary. H.M. Seervai, however, was later to comment that aspects of the judgement possibly rested on certain faulty premises.

Earlier, in June 1988, the *Indian Express* and the Gujarati language *Jansatta* in Ahmedabad were seized by the Gujarat government, which objected to a certain report. RNG issued a strong statement condemning the action as 'the latest illustration of the growing hostility of the Solanki Government towards the press'. The *Jansatta*, he said, had a public mission to perform and would not be deterred. What the paper printed on 10 June was factual and not prohibited by law. 'I am reiterating this. If it is an offence, I dare the government to prosecute me.' The offending report, according the *Express* editor in Ahmedabad, Hari Jaisingh, was the naming of eight persons burnt alive in a certain incident. The government held that this could have incited feelings of enmity and hatred among different communities.

Prior to this, the *Express* had been involved in a rather unusual case in the Bombay High Court where it sought a restraining order in December 1984 on a certain Jagmohan Mundhara to prevent him from screening a film, *Kamla*, that the *Express* claimed was plagiarized from the news story it had carried by Ashwini Sarin on the purchase of an impoverished woman in Shivpuri, Madhya Pradesh, in 1981 (see also Chapter 7, pp.180-81). The film producer stated that his film was scripted from a stage play of that name by Vijay Tendulkar that had been showing to packed theatres around the country for quite some time. The tables had been turned. On this occasion it was the *Express* that sought a gagging order against a film producer who, in a sense, pleaded freedom of expression.

Ashwini Sarin's celebrated story 'Buying Girls from a Circuit House' had appeared in the *Express* in April 1981 and had caused a national outcry. Vijay Tendulkar had dramatized it and the play had thereafter been translated into many languages. It sought to portray the ugly consequences of stark poverty. The *Express* claimed copyright but took the further plea that the film showed the journalist and the newspaper proprietor, whom it claimed would be popularly identified with Ashwini Sarin and Ramnath Goenka, in a bad light. The plaint was that the film was defamatory, derogatory of the press and at variance with the facts. The *Express* sought an injunction against screening of the film and a sum of Rs 5 lakh in damages.

The court admitted that the film followed the *Express* story line, but said that it emphasized a more universal theme of human bondage, especially of Indian women. The court ruled:

> There cannot be copyright in an event which has actually taken place. There is a distinction between the materials upon which one claiming copyright has worked and the product of the application of his skill, labour, capital, judgement and talent to these materials. Ideas, information, natural phenomenon and events are common property and are not the subject of copyright. Further, the form, manner and arrangement of a drama or movie are different from a newspaper article. Therefore no infringement of a copyright is involved.

While the court dismissed the copyright plaint it upheld defamation and granted the *Express* the right to sue. It also directed Mundhara to delete certain portions of the film.

Many years earlier, RNG had wanted to start an edition from Bangalore and had purchased four acres of land in the Rajmahals area from the Maharaja of Mysore for that purpose. In 1960 the Karnataka government gave notice that it proposed to acquire this land for some public purpose. Thereafter RNG approached the chief minister, Nijalingappa, for a suitable site and was allotted the *Express*'s present plot on Queen's Road near the Vidhana Souda in compensation. Construction of an office commenced in 1963 and was completed over the next two years when the *Express* planned to shift its Chittoor edition to Bangalore.

Getting wind of this, the *Deccan Herald* put up somebody to file a declaration for publication of a Kannada Indian Express, which the district magistrate, Bangalore, rightly declined to entertain. A few days later the *Express* filed its declaration on 29 April 1965 and began preparations to commence publication in Bangalore. The *Deccan Herald* thereupon filed a case seeking a stay on the *Express* as it was shifting its edition from Chittoor and would harm the interest of a local paper like the *Herald* which was said to be protected under some obscure law. V.K. Krishna Menon donned his lawyer's robes to argue the case for the *Deccan Herald* while Thiruvenkatachari appeared for the *Express*. The *Herald* plaint was thrown out.

*

All this was as nothing compared to what followed later. The government had begun to fume as the *Express* mounted its campaign against Reliance and on other matters. On 1 September 1986 some 600 sleuths descended on eleven centres of the *Express* in countrywide raids. But the roar of pain that followed the publication in 1987 of President Zail Singh's letter to Prime Minister Rajiv Gandhi could leave no one in doubt that a wounded tiger was at large. Rajiv Gandhi was furious. The letter charged him with breaking all conventions and constitutional norms by refusing to meet the President and keep him informed on crucial matters of state, even while permitting his henchmen to denigrate the Head of State with impunity (This episode has been covered in detail in Chapter 10). The Express Guest House in Delhi was raided on 13 March

1987, and Gurumurthy arrested in Madras and his partner Jankiraman in Bombay.

It was alleged that the paper had been tipped-off in advance as Directorate of Revenue Intelligence (DRI) agents recovered 'secret documents' on the basis of which these raids had been conducted. This was refuted by Vivek Khaitan (now Goenka), executive director in Bombay. A statement issued by him said that, having failed to discover anything in what was a 'fishing expedition', the DRI had resorted to a disinformation campaign. The so-called secret documents were no more than the 'dossier' that was distributed to several newspapers, MPs and government offices at least six months earlier 'by an ostensibly anonymous, but in fact easily identified, source . . . In fact, in the days following the raids, we had been amused to notice that some of the statements in DRI press handouts . . . had been bodily lifted from this "dossier"', which had allegedly been circulated by Reliance.

A few days later, the charge that the *Express* was operating secret funds abroad was emphatically answered by RNG. He explained that this charge flowed from a payment of $200,000 made by Dr Briner, an eminent Swiss jurist in Geneva, 'to keep alive the machinery supply contract that would have lapsed because of the delay in Government sanction of an import licence and permission for foreign loans'. Renegotiating the deal, had it lapsed, would have meant paying higher prices. He described the charge as a self-serving argument against the *Express*'s insistence on acting against persons who stash away funds abroad. For its part, the *Express* was prepared to risk 'the most hostile investigation' the government might mount. 'State aggression of this kind' was only to be expected when corrupt officials had no answer to serious charges against themselves. He said the campaign orchestrated by the government and 'lavishly publicised' by its information and broadcast organs went beyond the legitimate limits of the law enforcement function and were intended to discredit the *Express*.

> The *Indian Express* does not look for soft options . . . In decades of vigorous life [it] has seen many rulers, Indian and alien, who have come and gone, a few of them known for their domineering ways. Persecution at the hands of rulers who have need to conceal their actions is not new to the free press and certainly not to the *Indian Express*. The paper has suffered more under the indigenous dispensation, to usher in which it came into being. The official attempt to liquidate the *Express* during the Emergency and even earlier, is part of the nation's history and would require a volume by itself. But with every such setback the *Indian Express* became mightier and better qualified to perform its mission. The present attempt of the Government will lead to the same result, strengthening and sharpening the paper, as every such effort has in the past. Its fight against corruption in high places and against the buccaneers in business will continue even if the full might of the State comes in the way. For to guard the people's right to know is our commitment.

Next, strikes were engineered against the *Express* in Delhi. RNG reacted strongly in a statement that appeared on 16 October 1987, rebuffing those trying to silence it in its performance of public duty.

> In the fifty odd years the *Express* has been on the scene, it has had to face the onslaught of those whom it has taken on as part of its public duty. During the last six months, it has been tirelessly seeking to bring into the open shameful secrets and fraudulent activities of a number of powerful men. This has led the authorities to initiate arrests, raids and other forms of harassment. These have been almost universally condemned as wanton assaults on a free press.
>
> Having failed to silence the paper by these means, the powerful combination of interests the *Express* has taken on has decided to continue its war on the *Express* by other means and to engineer a strike that will prevent the paper from appearing. It is their ultimate weapon. I have no doubt that this too will fail as all else has, for the *Express* has the public on its side and the public interest at heart.

The pressure on the *Express* continued relentlessly. On 16 November 1987, RNG came out with another statement in the *Express*. It was titled 'To My Last Breath'.

> In the last 48 days, eleven prosecutions have been launched against the *Express* Group. Twenty-six show cause notices have been issued. Several of us, including me, have been interrogated again and again.
>
> The customs authorities have detained equipment in Bombay. An official of the Directorate of Revenue Intelligence has said . . . that equipment and newsprint being imported by the Group is liable to be seized and auctioned . . . A strike was engineered . . . and now comes the news that the Government has in effect expropriated the building of the *Express* [and] all equipment in it . . .
>
> . . . The *Express* will return to [the Supreme Court] for justice, for protection against this lawless, this vindictive Government . . . I will not yield to such highhandedness; to my last breath I shall fight for the principles, for the freedom that we fought for under the banner of Mahatma Gandhi. This much I pledge to every reader of the *Express* Group and to everyone who loves freedom in our country.

It was a stirring cri de coeur.

Among the new crop of cases filed in October–November 1987, the first related to the purchase of Hong Hua web offset presses from Taiwan in May 1984, allegedly resulting in evasion of customs duty to the extent of Rs 20 lakh. The charge was that fourteen offset units were imported under open general licence by declaring a printing capacity of 35,000 copies per hour whereas available evidence suggested that the capacity was no more than 20,000 copies an hour. The *Express* said that the output of these Taiwanese machines had proved disappointing, partly because they were used in conjunction with some older equipment, resulting in reduced performance. As far as duty payments were concerned, the *Express* had not purchased the complete set and the customs department had in fact refunded some of the amount initially paid. RNG pointed out that several other newspapers in India had purchased the identical equipment and paid the same rate of duty as had the *Express*. Yet the Directorate of Revenue Intelligence had thought fit only to prosecute the *Express* and none other.

A second case pertained to a suit filed against the *Express* in October–November 1987 in regard to the import of a Dr Hell's colour scanner from West Germany through Goenka's former private secretary, Renu Sharma. Here too the allegation was that excess payments had been made, over and above the foreign exchange sanctioned for the letter of credit, and that there had been a significant evasion of customs duty. Renu Sharma was no technical expert but was said to have been assisted by her brother, who was knowledgeable in this particular line. The transaction may have been above board but the episode resulted in Renu Sharma's severance from the *Express*.

There was yet another customs case and as the prosecutions mounted, Gurumurthy wrote a two-part article in November 1987, captioned 'What It Means to Stand Up', giving a connected account of the travails of the *Express*. Nearly 200 proceedings had been launched against the group over the past fifteen months. The burden of this was enormous:

> Thousands of pages of legal drafting; hanging around for days in the corridors of different courts in different cities; inspecting and taking copies of thousands of records that have been seized and kept in different places; endless correspondence with totally unresponsive and frightened officials, bankers, taxmen and customs officers. These are the endless activities to which this paper is reduced, to the neglect of its other central activities.

Among the departments involved were the DRI, Company Law Board, Enforcement Directorate, Income Tax and Chief Controller of Imports and Exports. In contrast, Reliance had been untouched despite unrefuted evidence of malfeasance, Gurumurthy complained. Then followed another effort at 'strangulation'. As Gurumurthy wrote:

> The *Express* had planned to come out from six more centres by using facsimile transmission to reach more readers. It had sunk Rs 20 crores in facsimile and related equipment. A hostile state could hardly afford this accession of strength by the *Indian Express*. So the customs refused to clear the equipment. It also demanded three times the duty another newspaper has paid for identical equipment. The *Express* moved the Bombay Court and got directions to the customs authorities to clear the machinery [after a four months' delay].

However, the government scuttled the operation of the equipment in the South despite having granted written sanction and accepted advance rentals from the *Express* for the Madras, Bangalore and other circuits. Twelve hours before the commissioning of facsimile transmission, the leased communication circuits were snapped 'on orders from above'. Next the Company Law Board ordered an investigation into the *Express* under Sec. 237 of the Companies Act, after an earlier inspection under another Section. The State Bank was 'advised' not to release working capital it had sanctioned and backed out of its commitments on term loans. Advertisements were blocked from government sources. The income tax department called for so many details from one centre that almost four tonnes of paper had to be transported in a van. Fax connections were severed.

Ramnath Goenka was prevented from going with a PTI delegation to China in 1987, and had to decline an invitation to attend an International Press Institute executive meeting in Istanbul as permission was delayed and a Rs 5 lakh bank guarantee demanded. His passport was impounded, something that greatly pained him. Contrast this, Gurumurthy asked, 'with the indulgence shown to Win Chadha, who stealthily smuggled himself and his son out of India when the Bofors affair exploded'. Gurumurthy concluded:

> This then is what it means—more appropriately what it costs—to stand up to those who do not want to hear tunes

> other than their own. But it also means that there are strong and courageous men willing to incur the cost of facing the worst from raw state power.
>
> But in this confrontation, they are not alone. There is, after all . . . a judiciary with a roused conscience to strike down illegal state acts. And you are there, the readers of this paper, who provide it the strength to fight and keep on fighting.

*

While all these cases were matters of Goenka or the *Express* versus the state, RNG was also involved in a lingering case of personal litigation. In his early years, he had partnered Murli Prasad, a dubash in Madras who later moved to Hyderabad. The allegation is that sometime in 1936, RNG took a loan of about Rs 6.5 lakh from him but failed to repay the amount. Murli Prasad passed away in 1947 and the family became insolvent. In 1982 his son, Narendra Prasad, filed a suit for recovery stating that this money had been utilized by RNG to build up his newspaper assets to which he now laid claim. RNG's version was that he owned nothing and that what he had received from Prasad was in fact repayment of a loan earlier taken from him. The case still lingers, unsettled.

S.B. Kolpe, an *Express* trade union leader who had fought many a hard battle with RNG and had nothing kind to say about this 'manipulator', referred to this case in some of his polemical tracts, 'Goenka: An Investigative Report' and 'Goenka Unmasked'. Years later, Nicholas Coleridge, a British author, interviewed RNG when he was ill. Goenka was unable to speak for long and so Coleridge turned to Mulgaokar, who happened to be present.

> I mentioned the case to Mulgaokar when I visited Ram Nath Goenka in his Penthouse and Mulgaokar smiled, raised his eyes to the ceiling, and said, 'Ah, Kolpe,' as though I had

> referred to an exasperating and somewhat dotty aunt upstairs in the attic. 'Ah, Kolpe. A man of great principles. And like so many people of great principle, given to wishful thinking sometimes.'[1]

Court cases apart, the *Express* was taken to the Press Council by Harkishen Singh Surjeet and Madhu Limaye, both political notables, in 1990. They complained about a tendentious front-page signed article by Arun Shourie that was misleading and put them in a false position. This was contested by the *Express*. But at the conclusion of prolonged adjudication, the council found that the respondent had not verified the facts, on which the article was based, from either of the complainants who had been named and both of whom had categorically denied the contents. It observed that

> Journalists and editors are human beings and liable to error. They cannot arrogate to themselves the infallibility of god who can perceive everything and everywhere all that may be happening or transpiring between persons behind a veil of secrecy.

The council accordingly 'disapproved' of the appending by the *Express* of a post-script to a denial by each of the complainants, stating that the '*Indian Express* stands by its report'.

When RNG was served with a demolition order on the Express Building in Delhi in 1980, he sought and obtained a stay from the Supreme Court. It so happened that just about that time, the *Express* had carried a series of articles by Arun Shourie on the so-called Transfer of Judges case, on which judgement had been delivered by Justice Bhagwati. The Justice felt that the article was offensive and pejorative and mentioned this to Goenka, who in turn said he was equally distressed and would speak to Arun Shourie. But RNG always drew a line between the editorial independence of his paper and personal friendship, even though he assiduously cultivated members of the judiciary the better to read their mind and mood. So while he deprecated the article in front of the judge, he did not prevent the rest of the series from appearing. Nor did he pull up Shourie.

It was RNG's view that the interest of better justice would be served were all judges of the Supreme Court permitted to serve until they attained sixty-eight years of age instead of sixty-five as obtains even today. He was on excellent terms with Rajiv Gandhi when the latter first became prime minister and canvassed the idea of extending the term of Supreme Court judges by three years and came away with the feeling that the prime minister was agreeable. Happening to meet Chief Justice Bhagwati, RNG mentioned that he should not be surprised if he got an extension of three years. However, some time later he told the justice with a tinge of bitterness that the prime minister was no longer of the same mind. He believed that the country had much to gain from the wisdom and experience of senior justices provided they were in good health and that premature retirement at sixty-five entailed a national loss.

Ramnath Goenka had great faith in the judiciary and saw in it a bulwark against tyranny and encroachments on freedom. He found in it a sure ally. He was time and again to get much-needed relief from the courts and was sustained in his incessant and prolonged battles with the Central and state governments in the knowledge that he was not alone. He was very particular that all important cases and judicial precedents should be properly covered in his papers as judicial literacy was a cornerstone of a truly democratic society.

When Justice H.R. Khanna once asked him how he managed to sleep at night with so many cases against him, RNG replied that he had never lost any sleep on this account. He had an amateur delight in jurisprudence and would hold his own while briefing the most eminent counsel who respected his pithy even if unconventional reasoning while discussing his briefs. Litigation was for him a joyful pastime and part of the art of living dangerously.

# 10

# A Wounding Time

The assassination of Indira Gandhi in October 1984 shocked Ramnath Goenka as much as it did the country. Enmity and resentment were soon forgotten. Deep down he probably remembered happier associations of times past. More immediately, his concerns turned on the imperative of national stability and solidarity as mindless public rage exploded in a most shameful pogrom against Sikhs in Delhi and elsewhere. The *Express* worked to heal those wounds both editorially and in terms of the relief operations it itself mounted and otherwise supported in the capital.

The election of Rajiv Gandhi as leader of the Congress party and his appointment as prime minister restored a sense of calm and assurance in the smooth accomplishment of a difficult transition. Though he had given up his job as an airline pilot to assist his mother after the death of Sanjay Gandhi, he appeared to be a guileless young man and reluctant politician, without any baggage. Here then was Mr Clean, keen to harness modern management and technology to his vision of the future, heralding a generational change in age and attitude and well suited to lead India into the twenty-first century.

Addressing the All-India Congress Committee on the occasion of the centenary of the Indian National Congress in Bombay in 1985, Rajiv Gandhi sounded a stirring call to rid the party and country of power brokers and manipulators. He inveighed against the underworld, corruption and black money. He spoke the language of peace and reconciliation with alienated groups at home and abroad. RNG was delighted. This was a transformation devoutly to be wished. The Congressman in him welled with new hope. In a Jack Anderson film entitled *Rajiv's India*, commissioned for release in India in collaboration with PTI, of which he was then chairman, he said, 'The country is in safe hands. I can now die in peace.'

*

Following Verghese's insistence on voluntary retirement, RNG had been looking for a replacement as editor-in-chief. Now with Rajiv Gandhi assuming office, it appeared to be a good idea to bring in Suman Dubey, who had been with the *Express* earlier and was highly regarded. He was now deputy editor at *India Today* and, moreover, a good friend of the new prime minister, having been in school with him. To RNG's way of thinking all of this made a nice fit. Dubey joined in June 1986. Seven months later, Arun Shourie was reinducted into the paper. RNG needed a 'race horse' back in his stable. He had had a love-hate relationship with Shourie and now, more than four years after his break with him in 1982, it was time to forgive and forget, and get a dynamic scribe and trouble-shooter back in harness. Moreover, with Suman Dubey disinclined to woo his schoolmate and friend Rajiv Gandhi on RNG's behalf, and with his own relations with the establishment clearly souring, RNG felt it prudent to prepare for guerrilla warfare. Gurumurthy had always wanted Shourie back, and was instrumental in persuading RNG that the time was ripe for his return.

Some months earlier, Pritish Nandy, editor of the *Illustrated Weekly of India*, had interviewed RNG. His answers were revealing.

> Q. What do you think of Rajiv Gandhi?
>
> A. He has certain ideas. New ideas. And he's doing a good job. He is certainly trying to change things for the better.
>
> Q. What do you think of the quality of the people around him?
>
> A. Opinions differ. But I think they are generally good. It will take at least a year to know, to find out.
>
> Q. Good? [Nandy demurred, naming members of the old guard.]
>
> A. Look here, there are many people around him whom I think are undesirable. But when undesirable things are thrown into the Ganga, the river purifies them. Rajiv Gandhi believes in removing corruption from the land, and he means it. Whether he succeeds or not, time alone will show. We must reserve our judgment about him for a year at least.
>
> Q. What about the future of the Opposition?
>
> A. I don't think very highly of it. [The people in it] have exhausted themselves . . . [As for the Communists], I have always been a Congressman in my heart and that is why I cannot agree with their attitude . . .[1]

The honeymoon did not last long. The prime minister's advisers sought to ensure a friendly press and cultivated a coterie. This bred discontent among others, including senior journalists who felt excluded. By 1986 the situation in the country had deteriorated. The Punjab and other Accords began to unravel and the press became more critical as scandals surfaced. By 1988 Rajiv Gandhi had decided that newspapermen were 'whiners and groaners' and introduced the Defamation Bill to curb tendentious writing. This draconian measure evoked fierce national and international opposition and had finally to be withdrawn. Rajiv Gandhi's press relations were in the mud.

The confrontation with the *Express* had developed even earlier and, before long, the gloves were off. It started with a falling out between Ramnath Goenka and Dhirubhai Ambani on an issue of corruption and business ethics. This soon sprouted several sub-plots and erupted in a bitter corporate war between Reliance Industries Limited (RIL) and Nusli Wadia's Bombay Dyeing, on whose side the *Express* came down with a well-documented exposé that showed that Reliance was the beneficiary of questionable governmental favours. Further exposures revealed what seemed a wide web of official corruption and intrigue that rocked Parliament, galvanized the Opposition and invited the wrath of the government on the *Express*.

Dhirubhai Ambani and RNG were both proud, self-made men, frontiersmen who rose from rags to riches by dint of hard work and steadfast devotion to a larger cause or vision. Neither would let anything come in their way. Both loved a fight, which often became greater than the cause. Both took calculated risks. Like RNG, Dhirubhai was prone to bet on people who were out of power as that, he felt, was a time to build relationships. Thus he had cultivated Indira Gandhi after 1977. In what was still a licence–permit raj, he thought it best to go along with the government and accordingly sought proximity to Rajiv Gandhi when he assumed office in succession to his mother. He was an unconventional businessman who was an innovator in two respects. He opened up the equity market for the small man to sell an investor-friendly corporate dream. Further, having cut his teeth in the Gulf among international oil giants, he defied the licence–permit mindset to establish what would be globally competitive mega-enterprises to tap economies of scale.

RNG and Dhirubhai enjoyed a warm and cordial friendship. Indeed, when Reliance made a rights issue in 1985, Dhirubhai obtained from RNG names of mediapersons who might be offered shares from the promoter's quota. Mulgaokar and

Girilal Jain were on that list. RNG bought some shares too. Then came the breach. The story goes that RNG and Dhirubhai were seated side by side on a Delhi–Bombay flight. In the course of conversation Dhirubhai apparently remarked that everybody had his price, even journalists, and, depending on his potential worth, he (Dhirubhai) would aim 'a silver or golden boot' at him. Those close to Dhirubhai deny any such crudity.

However, RNG was incensed when some time later he received a complaint about a story put out by PTI, of which he was then chairman, and was told by the general manager of the agency that the item had been planted (the details of this 'planted' story and its fallout are given later in this chapter, which quotes from an interview given by RNG to the newsmagazine *India Today*). Other such alleged plants followed on matters concerning RIL, one or two in the *Indian Express* and *Financial Express* as well. RNG was furious. He felt that if Dhirubhai could buy the *Express* and PTI he could buy the whole country and manipulate the media. The man had to be stopped. He decided to take on Reliance and investigate the corporate war between Bombay Dyeing and RIL, the two principal rivals in the petrochemical arena.

Enter Nusli Wadia, the urbane, young chairman of Bombay Dyeing, who had got to know RNG through Nanaji Deshmukh during the Emergency and had come to admire him for his indomitable courage. The two were poles apart in age and upbringing but were bonded by affection and trust. Theirs was an emotional relationship as between a 'second father' and something of an adopted son. Years later, Wadia was to say:

> . . . I think we both shared certain values and Ramnathji was a person who, if he adopted you, he adopted you. And we had a lot of things in common, surprisingly, considering that we were poles apart in everything. My background, my education, the way I dress, what I eat, everything about me was different. But poles, sometimes opposite poles, attract, you know.

> I found him a man of extraordinary character. But the other thing was [that] he was a person with tremendous depth of perception. He was also a man of great integrity. I'm not just talking of financial integrity. I'm talking specifically of mental honesty. If he believed in something, he believed in it. And if he felt that what he was doing was right, if the cause in which he was involved was right to him, he'd fight to his last breath. He was a fighter. He was a man who you could not help respect and admire . . . He didn't see the *Indian Express* as a commercial enterprise . . .[2]

Wadia too was a strong personality. Grandson of Jinnah, schooled in England, he came back to India as he wanted to be an Indian in every sense and participate in the country's development and future at a time when his father, Neville Wadia, was thinking of selling Bombay Dyeing and settling in Switzerland. Nusli, however, was determined to continue a 150-year-old entrepreneurial tradition and not just inherit a pot of gold. He prevailed and was back in Bombay, fired with zeal to build higher on the strong foundations of Bombay Dyeing.

Towards the end of the 1970s, Wadia and Ambani found themselves pitted against one another in a bid to gain ascendancy in the manufacture of certain polyester intermediates such as DMT and PTA. Reliance manufactured PTA whereas Bombay Dyeing was dependent on purchase of paraxylene from other producers or imports for the production of DMT. Both companies also held divergent views on the level of import duties to be charged on paraxylene, Bombay Dyeing naturally favouring lower rates. The turf war moved from the corporate boardrooms into the corridors of power. In the early rounds Bombay Dyeing found its licences blocked whereas Reliance appeared to be sailing with the wind. The approval given to Reliance for a Rs 900 crore debenture issue to set up a PTA plant at Patalganga stymied Bombay Dyeing's expansion programme, more so when it was later found that the capacity actually installed by Reliance far exceeded its licensed capacity. Wadia was possibly in bad odour as he had reportedly declined to fund Indira and

Sanjay Gandhi at the time of the 1980 elections. Certain key ministers did not appear well disposed towards him. Separately, the souring of RNG's relations with Rajiv Gandhi found him on the same side of the fence as Wadia.

In launching an investigation into the heady progress of Reliance, the *Express* was aided by documented information from insiders within the government. Combining a formidable array of data and citations culled from official files, with his own intimate knowledge of company law and finance, Gurumurthy put together a series of articles alleging that huge benefits had been showered on Reliance. It was a powerful indictment of the Ambani group, each instalment a hammer blow that embarrassed the government and caused commotion in Parliament.

RNG went on record in an interview with *India Today* in 1987:

> . . . I saw a clear gap between his [Rajiv Gandhi's] declarations and decisions. He declared his Government was not for sale. My first hand experience of his dichotomy was in regard to Reliance. When we wrote about 20 articles in the *Express* about the way Reliance Industries had manipulated the Government, the Rajiv Government did nothing about it at all.
>
> Q. But were the articles fair?
>
> A. Yes. We alleged fraud, smuggling and other economic offences of hundreds of crores. Despite our challenge to the Government to disprove us, we were never contradicted. Nobody told us why the persons complained about were not dealt with. There was no investigation of the offender; instead the punishment was on those who exposed the offenders . . . I am merely citing Reliance as one important example. The promises the young man made have all been falsified. I had a couple of meetings with Rajiv about 18 months ago in which he told me that necessary action would be taken against economic offenders. He mentioned Reliance and said no investigation would be held back.

Q. Did you get caught in the squeeze between two industrial houses—Bombay Dyeing and Reliance—and Nusli Wadia use your friendship to launch a campaign against his rival?

A. This is absolute nonsense . . . It is easy to say it is all inter-corporate war. Is smuggling a Rs 120 crore plant a subject matter of inter-corporate war? Or is forging a letter of credit for Rs 100 crores or drawing illegal loans of Rs 100 crores one? Whether import duty on yarn should be more or less may be an inter-corporate affair, but not crimes of this order.

Q. But are you not close to Wadia?

A. Dhirubhai Ambani was as close to me—even closer—as Nusli. He was generous. He always responded to me when I asked for donations for charities. I did not know Wadia till 1975. In fact, Ambani was my friend and I saw more of him in 1985 than I did Wadia. But Ambani was doing things to try and circumvent the entire government system.

Q. Did you feel sad about having to launch a campaign against a friend?

A. There was a reason for what happened. In October 1985, the *Economic Times* published a story about a CBI inquiry into the opening of backdated letters of credit by Reliance worth Rs 100 crores. Ambani sent a letter of rebuttal to PTI—the news agency I was chairman of—stating the news item was engineered by a DMT-producing textile company unable to produce quality DMT and in dire financial straits. The obvious reference was to Bombay Dyeing. When PTI ran the item, Nani Palkhivala, also on the PTI Board, called it to my attention and asked my advice as to what should be done as another company's name had been dragged in without evidence. So I had to write an apology. PTI had never before apologized to anybody. I also found that there had been pressure on the PTI desk to run the Ambani rebuttal. So I went to Dhirubhai and said, "You are pulling down a public institution—PTI. You should have some values." He gave me a reply that I would rather not go into with you, but that is where I felt his approach was highly prejudicial to the country. In fact that was the starting point of my investigations into Reliance's affairs.[3]

The titles of Gurumurthy's articles on Reliance Industries Ltd convey the gist of the story. The first was entitled 'A Rs 25 Crore Gift of a Power Plant'. The result? 'Poor Bharat Heavy Electricals Ltd [the public sector giant], which had been running from pillar to post in search of orders, was left at the end of a disconnected telephone line.' The second was 'Industry Ministry's Rs 34 Crore Foreign Exchange Bounty' for something, which by the government's own yardstick should have cost no more than Rs 16 lakhs. The third article, 'Petrochemical Plants without Licences', said the maxim in vogue appeared to be that 'what is good for Reliance is good for India'. It went on to say that not merely were the capacities licensed continuously increased but that this was done at the cost of competing public sector units such as the Bongaigaon Petrochemicals Ltd. A fourth article, 'The Foreign Collaboration That Is Nobody's Baby', asserted that a foreign collaboration approval for manufacture of paraxylene by RIL was approved without the requisite industrial licence or MRTP clearance and sanction, and without demur in respect of the unduly high know-how fees written into the deal.

Meanwhile, V.P. Singh, who had been Congress chief minister of Uttar Pradesh in Indira Gandhi's time and thereafter headed the UP Congress Committee, had been summoned to the Centre and appointed finance minister by Rajiv Gandhi towards the end of 1986. The prime minister had publicly denounced corruption, power brokers, middlemen and influence peddlers and it was this seeming determination to clean the Augean stables that had earned him the sobriquet Mr Clean. This had struck a chord with V.P. Singh, who took it as a directive and public commitment. A recent report on the role and magnitude of black money in India had aroused anger and disgust in the country. Now, it appeared, the government was, hopefully, resolved to ensure transparency and good governance.

Like others, V.P. Singh had followed the *Express* series on Reliance. His own inquiries revealed that there was substance in the allegations. Instead of the approved eight PTA units, Reliance had put up twelve units and had in addition installed a power plant that was outside the scope of the sanctioned project. The director of enforcement, Bhure Lal, acting in concert with the Revenue Secretary, Vinod Pande, was already following the scent and now determined to investigate these leads, some of which extended overseas. Bhure Lal too had been in touch with RNG as the *Express* was obviously an important source for the kind of intelligence he was seeking.

One of the issues Bhure Lal wished to probe was how Reliance's Patalganga plant was financed. Some clues unearthed by Gurumurthy led to eleven shell companies with paltry capital and strange names like 'Crocodile' and 'Fiasco' in the Isle of Man, a well-known tax haven. These were suspected to be Reliance fronts for money laundering. The trail from there led to the Bank of Credit and Commerce International (BCCI). Though headquartered in Belgium, BCCI had strong Pakistani connections and had acquired a dubious reputation, reportedly being used by the CIA for undercover operations. According to the FBI, BCCI was an acronym for Bank of Crooks and Criminals International! It appeared that BCCI was buying Reliance shares to build the market and, together with some other Indian banks, was engaged in soliciting NRI funds for purchase of RIL shares through the Isle of Man companies. The banking department apparently did not scrutinize these transactions too closely while RIL softened up key players within the system. BCCI's branch in Bombay was raided and some top executives were removed. Though the bank was otherwise uncooperative, it was later globally exposed and finally failed in 1991-92.

What precisely had Gurumurthy discovered? Three initial front-page articles analysed the mysterious course of events. In 1982 press reports appeared about misuse of the Non-Resident Indian Portfolio Investment Scheme that had been introduced by Pranab Mukherjee, Mrs Gandhi's finance minister, in order to attract foreign capital. Gurumurthy's finding was that a group of nonentities set up eleven shell companies in the Isle of Man, each with a capital of £200 (Rs 3000), and invested Rs 22.5 crore in RIL equity under the NRI scheme. Ten of them had a common ownership. Dividends had been paid and bonus shares and rights debentures issued to these companies whose investments were now valued at over Rs 100 crore and growing.

On 10 August 1985, ownership of the ten Isle of Man companies suddenly passed to 'Crocodile' and 'Fiasco'. Immediately thereafter, they metamorphosed to become Asiatic Multigrowth Investments Ltd and Asian Investments Ltd, etc., only to resurface in the Virgin Islands, an even more liberal tax haven in the Caribbean, as holding companies owning their Isle of Man namesakes that had become their subsidiaries through some subtle share transactions. These complex manoeuvres, completed within seventy-two hours, aimed 'to bury in anonymity the real facts of the ownership of the Rs 100 crore Reliance Industries shares ostensibly owned by NRIs behind the legal protection [against non-disclosure of ownership] under the International Business Companies, 1984 rules'.

Finding his trail getting cold, Bhure Lal decided he needed to collect evidence abroad. The problem was that the Directorate of Enforcement lacked a foreign agency or funds to undertake such a task. However, learning that Gurumurthy had recently visited the United States in pursuit of his own line of investigations regarding Reliance on behalf of the *Express*, the two got together. Gurumurthy had thought of engaging an American detective agency for the purpose and was directed to Fairfax, which had acquired a reputation for its part in the Watergate investigation. He met the head of Fairfax, Michael Hershman, who did some preliminary scouting and appeared willing to take on the assignment. But Gurumurthy then found that he would be unable to meet Fairfax's costs and fees. In the circumstances, he now suggested that the government might like to consider engaging Fairfax. Bhure Lal conveyed this back to the Revenue Secretary and Fairfax was engaged. This was not in the least improper, as other finance ministers later testified. However, what critics fastened on was the fact that nothing was put in writing and action followed oral approval by V.P. Singh, who had taken charge of the finance ministry in January.

Hershman needed some kind of official authorization that he could use to validate information gleaned from the US Customs and this was provided by Bhure Lal, who engaged Fairfax without payment but in terms of the Government of India's standard reward rules. Using this authority, Fairfax approached Du Pont for details of the plant it had sold Reliance. Before Du Pont could act on this, the Government of India transferred Bhure Lal out of the Enforcement Directorate and instructed Du Pont to ignore the query.

*

V.P. Singh had just drafted the budget for 1987-88 when the prime minister, also holding concurrent charge of the defence ministry, with Arun Singh as his minister of state, asked him to take over that portfolio full time. A delicate situation had quite suddenly developed following Pakistan's response to Operation Brasstacks, a mega-military exercise that the Indian Army had conducted in Rajasthan. The prime minister had earlier announced that middlemen would be barred in all defence contracts, but no sooner had V.P. Singh assumed his new charge on 26 January than a coded telegram landed on his desk, with a copy marked to the prime minister. The cable was from the Indian ambassador in Bonn, who said that the West German government had declined to renegotiate a lower price in a follow-up HDW submarine contract since 7 per cent commission had been paid to an Indian agent.

At the conclusion of a routine Cabinet meeting, V.P.

Singh informed Rajiv Gandhi of the message from Bonn and claims that the prime minister made no immediate response. Singh returned to his office, ordered a departmental inquiry into the insinuation of an agent into the HDW transaction, announced this in a terse press release and sent the file to the prime minister for information. Singh felt he had no option but to act as he did and the press release merely made mention of the 7 per cent commission without disclosing the weapon or source of supply.

The news hit the front pages of the morning editions the next day, 27 January 1987, and there was a storm in Parliament. The Opposition demanded a full statement from the defence minister but the proceedings were disrupted and the minister could do no more than reaffirm the contents of the press release. Rajiv Gandhi was perturbed and asked Singh how he could vouch for the truth of the contents of the telegram, and what would be the outcome of an inquiry, as HDW was unlikely to incriminate itself. Singh replied that the stated policy of the government had been violated and the inquiry would prove whether or not the contents of the cable were true. V.P. Singh was equally disturbed by this turn of events and decided to tender his resignation. There was pressure on Singh to remain and the prime minister met him twice. But by now the Fairfax matter had also begun to attract notice and K.K. Tewary, a minister, and Kalpnath Rai, another senior Congress functionary, said V.P. Singh had connived with the CIA and entrusted sensitive official matters to an American investigative agency. Singh replied that he would not have his patriotism questioned and declined to return to the government though he offered to undertake party work. K.C. Pant was appointed defence minister.

Bhure Lal had earlier investigated the Louis Dreyfus case in which Ajitabh Bachchan (Amitabh Bachchan's younger brother), Lalit Thapar and others with high connections had been named. Thapar was let off after an apology. The *Express* followed this lead and ran a story about Ajitabh Bachchan having acquired assets in Switzerland, including a house in Montreux, in violation of the Foreign Exchange Regulation Act. Since the prime minister had assured Parliament that he would leave no stone unturned to expose corruption, V.P. Singh wrote telling him that the *Express* report on Ajitabh Bachchan merited investigation. V.P. Singh was expelled from the Congress party the very next day.

Simultaneously, Bhure Lal was moved out of the Enforcement Directorate and put to pasture as Joint Secretary in charge of Currency and Coins, even as he was looking into the affairs of Indian diamond traders in Antwerp, among them a brother of Captain Satish Sharma, a minister and personal friend of Rajiv Gandhi from his flying days. The allegation was that these traders were engaged in benami transactions in India through invoice manipulation. Ramnath Goenka had met Bhure Lal and had provided him with useful information in furtherance of his investigations. Now, fearing Bhure Lal to be economically vulnerable, he assured him a job if sacked.

The *Express* rubbed salt in the wound caused by the Bachchan story. Arun Shourie claimed a bounty for revelations in terms of the Government of India's reward rules for actionable information on economic offences. On being turned down by the new enforcement director, Shourie published an open letter to him stating:

> I am now in a position to furnish definite leads and information which will cover the gamut of illegal foreign exchange activities of Amitabh Bachchan and his associates [and] point out the companies which have been used for secreting foreign exchange away . . . I am also in the position of helping your Directorate to identify a specific bank, as well as the specific officer within the bank in Switzerland, who has the information which will nail the FERA violations of Mr Ajitabh Bachchan.

*

All these developments were grist to the mill as the Rs 1700 crore Bofors 155-mm howitzer scandal surfaced on 16 April 1987 and took centre stage. Here again, the charge was that commissions totalling Rs 64 crore plus another Rs 250 crore had been siphoned into four or more secret bank accounts abroad for undercover payment to various parties through Win Chadha, a former Bofors agent in India. Among those named were the Hinduja brothers and Ottavio Quatrocchi, an Italian corporate representative in Delhi known to be a close friend of the Gandhi family. The *Hindu* took the lead in pursuing this story in Stockholm and Geneva through Chitra Subramaniam but abandoned it later owing to pressures and internal differences. It was left to the *Express* to take Chitra Subramaniam on board to pursue the story with great gusto, along with the *Statesman*.

The Finance Secretary asked Bhure Lal whether the Bachchans were among those whom he was investigating, but was requested to direct the query to the Revenue Secretary, Vinod Pande. Getting wind of this breaking news, Amitabh Bachchan rushed back from Europe, where he was holidaying, and proceeded to the Andamans, where Rajiv Gandhi was spending Christmas. In order to make the connection he flew via Rangoon, bending certain regulations by using a BSF aircraft. Remonstrance on this score by the Foreign Secretary, A.P. Venkateswaran, cost the latter his job. He was summarily removed and resigned in protest.

Rajiv Gandhi was in deep trouble. Nothing seemed to be going right.

*

As if all this were not enough, the prime minister was soon embattled on yet another front. The unfolding storyline seemed to attract an ever-growing list of superstars. For now in the limelight was Giani Zail Singh, President of India. And the impresario was once again none other than the *Indian Express*.

What had in some ways started as a manifestation of rivalry for commercial supremacy between Bombay Dyeing and Reliance had grown into a clash of egos between a larger-than-life media doyen and a leading business tycoon on issues of business and political morality. In the fallout of these alarums and excursions, the struggle now assumed the dimensions of a Mahabharata that threatened to engulf the great institutions of Government and State. The battle lines were drawn.

Giani Zail Singh was home minister in Indira Gandhi's Cabinet when elevated to the Presidency in July 1982. A backward-class Ramgarhia Sikh of humble origin with no pretensions to great formal learning or sophistication, he had risen through the ranks of ardent freedom fighters to become chief minister and head of the Congress in Punjab. He had earned a reputation as a shrewd politician who was approachable and believed in winning over people.

As home minister in 1980, he had intervened to shield Ramnath Goenka from official pressure, a gesture that earned him the latter's goodwill and affection. He soon found himself by-passed on Punjab affairs as Prime Minister Indira Gandhi preferred to deal with the chief minister, Darbara Singh, leading to the quaint situation that as home minister he was constrained to issue a directive to the home secretary that all Punjab files should be put up directly to Mrs Gandhi. Giani Zail Singh became President in 1982, but continued to be unhappy with the handling of the Punjab situation. He was anguished when Operation Blue Star was launched without any reference to him and, as he thought, was badly mishandled.

President Zail Singh was on a state visit abroad in October 1984, and had just reached the Yemen Arab Republic when he was informed of Mrs Gandhi's tragic assassination. En route home, he decided to appoint Rajiv Gandhi as the next prime minister. On landing, he immediately proceeded to the All-India Institute of Medical Sciences to pay homage to the departed leader. Rajiv Gandhi was there and, after offering his condolences, the Giani requested him to join him at Rashtrapati Bhavan, where he was sworn in even before being elected leader of the Congress party.

The Giani had high hopes in 'the young man' but faced an initial disappointment in the manner in which the anti-Sikh riots were handled. In the months to follow, relations between the President and prime minister were not what they should have been and the Giani soon got the feeling that Rajiv Gandhi was 'avoiding' meeting him, failing to brief him and keep him promptly and fully informed, even when specifically requested to do so. The prime minister suggested a hot line be established between them, which the Giani resisted, fearing that this would mean the end of regular personal meetings as was the practice. The President felt slighted and marginalized. In his memoirs, published after his death, the Giani wrote that Rajiv Gandhi even considered impeaching him but finding himself on weak ground thought to ease him out by sending emissaries with the suggestion that the Punjab situation could be brought under control if he would step down from the Presidency to resume office as chief minister![4] This extraordinary state of affairs had become a subject of political gossip and media speculation.

It was in this murky atmosphere that in 1987, the controversial 'god-man' Chandraswamy passed a message to RNG that the President wished to meet him. Gurumurthy went on his behalf and was straightaway led out on to the lawns, as the President feared that Rashtrapati Bhavan had been bugged. A three-hour conversation ensued, at the end of which Gurumurthy suggested that the Giani should write to the prime minister. There is no agreed version regarding the sequence of events thereafter. One account has it that the President requested Gurumurthy to draft the letter while the other is that the President had a letter drafted in his Secretariat and subsequently sent this to RNG for 'improvement'.

Gurumurthy reported back to RNG. Mulgaokar, editorial

adviser to the *Express*, and Arun Shourie were called to the Express Guest House in Delhi, at 130 Sunder Nagar. After much confabulation Mulgaokar volunteered to prepare a draft. Later, a draft was also received from Zail Singh, which was suitably 'edited' by Mulgaokar. The President received a final draft from the *Express* but toned down the language before dispatching it to the prime minister. The *Express* was not informed of the change and mistakenly published its 'final draft' dated 9 March 1987 on the front page of its issue of 13 March. The report convulsed the nation.

A report on the President's letter to the prime minister had actually appeared some days earlier in the Gujarati paper *Sandesh*, but had not attracted much attention.

The *Express* text also appeared in *Jansatta*, its Hindi affiliate. It read:

My dear Rajiv,

I find that some Hon'ble Members of Parliament during the discussion in the two Houses on the motion of thanks on the President's Address, referred to the relations between the President and the Prime Minister. While replying to the points raised, you said among other things that the President had been briefed on important issues of national interest.

I appreciate the spirit behind your observations, which understandably is to put the issue of the relations between the head of the State and the head of the Government beyond controversy. But as you are aware, the factual position is somewhat at variance with what has been stated by you.

The President–Prime Minister relations in our country are governed by certain well-established practices and conventions besides express provisions of the Indian Constitution. I am constrained to say that certain well-established conventions have not been followed. Before your visit abroad and after your return I have not been briefed. To quote a specific instance, after your visit to the USA and stopover at Moscow, and your discussions with top leaders of these super-powers, though I had requested you . . . to let me know your impressions . . . I was not briefed. I was given no briefing after the SAARC deliberations at Bangalore. In fact, I have not been briefed on foreign policy issues relating to such of our South Asian neighbours with which there are outstanding problems.

. . . Even on certain important domestic issues, I have not been kept informed on matters relating to Accords finalized in respect of Assam, Punjab and Mizoram. I was not briefed at any stage. On the other hand, when I had specifically requested you to meet me after my visit to Jammu and Kashmir last year, there was no response from you.

It is also distressing that constitutional provisions regarding furnishing of information to the President have not been consistently followed. I have brought to your notice that reports of some commissions of inquiry had not been sent to me even long after their receipt by the Government. I specifically raised this point with the Home Minister when he came to obtain my assent to the Commission of Inquiry (Amendment) Bill, 1986. I am yet to receive some of the reports promised by him.

You have also said in your reply to Parliament that the Opposition is politicizing the office of President. In fact the politicization was started by an Hon'ble Member of the ruling party in April 1985. I had brought it to your attention then that there was an emerging trend to drag the President's office into political controversy . . .

It is not my intention to catalogue all such instances, but I do feel that if relations between the President and the Prime Minister are maintained in line with the letter and spirit of the Constitution, keeping national interest paramount, there will be no room for comment or speculation from any quarter. This delicate relationship has to be nurtured by mutual trust, concern for conventions and an emphatic and free exchange of views.

As you have conveyed your views to Parliament, I felt I should convey to you the factual position on the subject.

With kind regards,

Yours Sincerely,
Zail Singh

The 'Hon'ble member' mentioned in the letter was K.K. Tewary, who had alleged that the President had been harbouring Punjab extremists in Rashtrapati Bhavan and had subsequently been inducted as a minister, 'perhaps as a reward for his labours'.

If the (draft) letter was blunt, the President, always accessible, was even more forthcoming in private conversation. He reminded one visitor that when at a press conference Rajiv Gandhi had been asked why he had not been meeting the President, the prime minister replied that he had broken hundreds of conventions. In his memoirs, Zail Singh said he had cited the constitutional provisions and Supreme Court judgements to the prime minister to establish that the President was not a 'cipher' and had well-defined powers. He also recalled:

> The President is the repository of the entire executive power of the Union. He has to be aware of what is happening in his Government. He is part of the Government and also of Parliament. The Prime Minister cannot draw a curtain of secrecy between himself and the President. The latter has the right to know how his Government is working . . . It is his constitutional duty to furnish the fullest information asked for by the Prime Minister.

Giani Zail Singh cited the example of the Governor of a state 'who had withdrawn his pleasure and dismissed a Minister', to which the prime minister had responded 'perhaps Governors have greater powers within their States in certain matters'. As to why only limited information was vouchsafed to the President, the prime minister observed that there had been leaks from Rashtrapati Bhavan, to which Zail Singh retorted that there had been far more and far graver leakages from the Prime Minister's Office:

> I asked Rajiv Gandhi, who was responsible to give official files to Arun Shourie, the exuberant Editor of the *Indian Express*, about my conduct as Home Minister in the matter of handling the Indian Postal (Amendment) Bill, in which it

> was alleged that I had mooted the idea of making the censorship of postal articles more stringent. In his write-up, Shourie had quoted from minutes and notings in the secret files of the Government, with page Nos. and dates. I reminded PM that all Ministers at the time of swearing-in took the oath of secrecy. Who was responsible then to place the secret files of the Government at the disposal of journalists to write articles? As the Prime Minister could not deny this, he said he would look into the matter and bring the guilty to book . . . His assurances of investigating the matter . . . carried little weight and were of no avail.

The Postal Bill had been sent to the President for his assent on 22 December 1984, within weeks of Rajiv Gandhi assuming office as prime minister. It was widely criticized as a draconian measure that entitled the government to intercept private mail in the interests of the safety and security of the state, public order or prevention of incitement to offence and other matters listed in Article 19(2). Arun Shourie had written in broad support of the Bill. However, the *Express* carried a letter by Ram Jethmalani stating that sufficient powers were already vested in the state which needed no more powers in this regard. Therefore, the key clause in the amending Bill, Section 26, 'should be scrapped and not merely rephrased as Mr Shourie suggests'.

The President sought reconsideration of the Bill, but since the government was disinclined to make any change he withheld assent until demitting office in July 1987.

Meanwhile, after the publication of the President's letter to the prime minister in the *Express* on 13 March 1987, events moved fast. Parliament demanded a debate on Zail Singh's letter and admission of a motion of privilege against the prime minister. Both were disallowed by the Speaker, leading to an Opposition walkout from the House. At 7.30 that same evening, fourteen officials of the Central Bureau of Investigation raided the Express Guest House in Sunder Nagar in Delhi. Gurumurthy was arrested in Madras and his office and residence raided. The government was clearly in panic. The CBI was obviously looking for evidence to establish how the leaks had taken place and what other surprises might be in store. The entire press corps was at Sunder Nagar, monitoring every move. The raid lasted four hours.

The *Express* carried a front-page editorial, 'It Won't Work', on 15 March 1987, advising the government to 'stop boxing the air, [and] answer the President'. It asserted that the *Express* would continue to examine all issues of public importance and issues arising 'from the doings of men holding high offices of state or buccaneers, with the independence that has been its hallmark'. It went on: 'Democracy rests on the principle that the people are sovereign and the press, like democracy, functions on the premise that the people have at their disposal all relevant information about how the Government functions. Accordingly we shall provide all the facts to the people on every matter of public concern.'

The CBI issued a statement charging Gurumurthy under the Official Secrets Act for possession of copies of official files, some of which had been quoted verbatim in his Reliance articles. It added that Gurumurthy had passed on some of this sensitive information available in government files to a 'foreign detective agency' (Fairfax).

The media by and large took the *Express* line that the CBI raids and threats constituted intimidatory tactics and an assault on press freedom. The CBI, however, did discover something it had not expected to find. Alive to the near possibility of a raid—and Gurumurthy had in fact been raided a few months earlier—the *Express* had conducted a clean-up operation and some papers were reportedly seen burning outside the Sunder Nagar guest house on 14 March. However, the officials found a single sheet that had been left behind in the drawer of an otherwise empty cabinet. It was a preliminary draft of a letter from the President with amendments in Mulgaokar's handwriting.

A photocopy of this draft letter happened to reach Dhiren Bhagat, a journalist, who called up Mulgaokar to ascertain the facts before publishing it. According to Bhagat:

> I telephoned Mr Mulgaokar. At first he declined to see me but when I told him I had the photocopy he said, 'I do not know which draft you have, the first or the second; but yes, I had marked certain corrections . . . I am neither ashamed nor embarrassed.'
>
> Others were not so sure. Two days after my piece appeared, the *Times of India* commented on this in a full page editorial, 'A Murky Affair'. The next day Mulgaokar replied on the editorial page of the *Express*. It was a sad performance by the grand old man of Indian journalism. Yes I did it, he seemed to be saying, but I am proud I did it. Why didn't he tell his readers about his involvement when he commented on the matter in the *Express*? And why didn't the *Express* reveal its involvement when it published the President's letter as a 'scoop'. Mr Mulgaokar said, 'I told one and all it was my handiwork.' Yes, but when? After the CBI had unearthed the document. And whom did he tell? There was no record of his admission in the public prints till I got hold of the photocopy. One can only conclude that here was something Mr Mulgaokar wished to conceal.
>
> What was that secret something? Mr Mulgaokar tells us he did not know the President, [and] that he was approached by 'a friend'. Who was that friend? And what was that draft doing in the *Indian Express* guest house, a place that he had no reason to visit except to call upon Messers Goenka or Gurumurthy? . . . Mr Mulgaokar won't tell. When the editor of the *Times of India* commented on this matter, saying Mr Mulgaokar had not told the whole truth, he received a short letter from Mr Mulgaokar. 'Of course I have not. I have told the truth only insofar as it relates to my part in the Zail letter to Mr Gandhi. But in doing so, I had to stop short where I might be giving up other people's confidences.' Well, well.[5]

Parliament continued to insist on debating the entire gamut of issues—the Zail Singh letter, Fairfax, Amitabh Bachchan, the *Express* case and the Reliance caper, but the government kept stonewalling. Parliamentarians, the media and public opinion were divided. The Congress rallied behind Rajiv Gandhi while V.P. Singh began to emerge as a rival focus around which the Opposition began to think it might regroup. The Reliance–Bombay Dyeing saga took a new turn with the Fairfax inquiry that the prime minister ordered to fend off the critics snapping at his heels. The *Express*, despite relentless government pressure to maim and silence it, continued to man the barricades, bleeding but unbowed. And speculation mounted as to what Zail Singh might do.

On 19 March 1987, the Speaker of the Lok Sabha and the chairman of the Rajya Sabha both disallowed any privilege motion against the prime minister. That same day Prabhash Joshi, editor of *Jansatta*, was assaulted by a mob of outsiders led by the *Express* Employees Union leader T. Nagarajan, in the foyer of the *Express* office in Delhi, in a foretaste of things to come. A couple of days later Arun Shourie wrote an article suggesting that the President exercise his powers under Article 86(2) which enjoins the House 'with all convenient despatch [to] consider any matter required by the message to be taken into consideration'. He felt fortified in recommending this course of action as Article 79 stipulates that Parliament 'shall consist of the President and [the] two Houses'.

In another article on 'The Speaker's Gag' on any privilege motion, Shourie chided Rajiv Gandhi for getting mired in the very bog of fixers and power brokers whom he had once reviled. He warned that he who resisted 'gentle pressures to reform, sets himself up to be hurled out'.

As the political temperature kept steadily rising, Rajiv Gandhi formally called on the President at Rashtrapati Bhavan for the first time in two years on 28 March 1987. They discussed their differences and came out smiling. The prime minister had been emollient. However, there was an acrimonious debate on the Fairfax episode in Parliament and it appeared that Congress MPs were seeking to put V.P. Singh on the mat for appointing a foreign investigative agency without Cabinet approval. In order to ward off snowballing criticism, the prime minister announced that a commission of inquiry would probe all aspects of the matter. The naming of a two-judge commission of Justices Thakkar (whose report on Mrs Gandhi's assassination had been held back by the government for months) and Natarajan, both selected by the Chief Justice, did not assuage feelings. The eminent lawyer Fali Nariman said that if a sitting judge agreed to be on a commission of inquiry, 'it must be on the specific term that the report when made should be published and the recommendations contained in it should be accepted'. Anything less than this would erode the supremacy of sitting judges whose orders in court become the law of the land.

Zail Singh was more caustic. In his memoirs he remarks:

> It became clear to me from PM's remarks [at their 28 March meeting] that the objective of constituting a commission of inquiry was to establish that V.P. Singh as Finance Minister had overstepped his brief and that he must be cut to size.

Arun Shourie wrote, 'Much depends now, as it so often does at crucial moments, on one man, and the man in this instance is V.P. Singh.' The minister of state for defence, Brahm Datt, sought to contradict his minister V.P. Singh's statement on Fairfax's role, suggesting that it was only that of an 'informer' rather than being an agency fully engaged by the government to assist its investigations. The purport of this perhaps became clearer in an editorial comment by the *Express*, which disclosed that 'the line along which Mr Gurumurthy was interrogated revealed the real anxiety of the Government: had the detective agency found anything about Amitabh Bachchan and company . . .?' The paper now pressed for a Parliamentary inquiry. Amitabh Bachchan in turn dismissed as lies and nonsense allegations about the Swiss connections of his brother, Ajitabh, who, he affirmed, had not taken Swiss nationality but only applied for Swiss residency. Even as the debate continued to rage, V.P. Singh resigned from the government on 12 April 1987.

*

When appointed editor of the *Indian Express*, Suman Dubey had had no intention of exploiting his friendship with Rajiv Gandhi to provide a conduit to the prime minister. As events unfolded, RNG and his closest advisers turned against Rajiv Gandhi and became shriller in their denunciations of the prime minister. Had an agenda been set in motion? The episode leading up to the drafting and publication of the Zail Singh letter was obviously distasteful to Dubey. He had earlier declined to publish three anonymous articles sent to him through RNG against Arun Nehru as he felt they were motivated. He now preferred to quit rather than carry under his imprint an editorial, the outlines of which had been discussed by RNG, Mulgaokar, Gurumurthy and Shourie in the wake of V.P. Singh's resignation. It took a while to decide on his successor. There was no consensus and it was almost a month after Dubey actually left that his name was finally removed from the imprint line, to be replaced by that of Arun Shourie.

The *Express* editorial of 14 April 1987 charged the prime minister with forcing out of office the one minister who had honestly pursued his directive to cleanse public life. It called on V.P. Singh to make a full disclosure of the facts to Parliament and 'reach out to those who want to reconstruct our polity'. Further, 'he must help forge the confederation of good men that our public life so sorely needs'. The paper had nailed V.P. Singh's banner to its mast.

More significant was the final exhortation that sounded like a trumpet call for regime change. 'The President must act', declared the *Express*. He was advised 'to consult the best minds in the country as well as leaders of all political parties to determine what must be done in this extraordinary situation.

Having done this, he must instruct the cabinet and inform the country about what needs to be done.' It was, the homily concluded, 'for him, as well as for everyone interested in arresting the cancer consuming us, the moment of truth'.

The din and dust had not subsided when on 16 April 1987, Swedish State Radio alleged that Bofors had bribed senior Indian politicians and key defence figures through secret Swiss bank accounts. Another uproar ensued. An official statement after a Cabinet meeting sharply denied any payoff in the Bofors arms deals even as Swedish Radio reiterated the charge in stronger terms. The Congress Working Committee went into a huddle and in a long, angry resolution denounced what it termed 'a grand design of destabilisation'.

> The Working Committee notes that the attack on the political system has proceeded in parallel with the attack on the defence system. All manner of phoney issues are being generated, including flagrant misinterpretation of clear constitutional provisions, to throw the delicate equilibrium of our polity into turmoil. The parties of Right Reaction have openly laid their cards on the table. After having being trounced in the general elections, they are engaged in sordid manoeuvres to topple the Government which has a massive popular mandate behind it, through trickery and fraud and through open incitement of lawlessness and subversion.

The *Express* kept up editorial pressure even as the general-secretary of the Youth Congress, speaking in Bhopal, accused President Zail Singh of being party to 'an international conspiracy to destabilise the Government of . . . Mr Rajiv Gandhi'. V.P. Singh meanwhile called for expanding the terms of reference of the Fairfax Commission to cover 'the real issue' of illegal funds being held abroad by Indians; Rajiv Gandhi told army commanders that the Swedish government had reassured India that no middlemen were involved in the Bofors deal; and the Janata Party proclaimed that Rajiv Gandhi had forfeited the moral right to continue in office. Matters did not improve with an ill-advised statement by Michael Hershman, the Fairfax chairman, that he would reveal information in his possession about Indian money held in Swiss banks if there was not a 'fair inquiry' into the Fairfax matter. The government's 'agreement' with Fairfax was promptly terminated.

The *Express* lent its columns to Ram Jethmalani, who started asking the prime minister ten questions every day on Bofors and other issues. Rajiv Gandhi dismissed the tirade with the remark 'Should I reply to every dog that barks?' But the questions persisted and when Jethmalani went abroad, they continued being posed by others in the *Express* 'war cabinet'.

In a May Day address in Kottayam, the prime minister accused a section of the press of trying 'to stage a coup against the elected representatives of the country' and warned against 'new interpretations of the Constitution'. The President's request for information on the Bofors deal was turned down and public discussion now encompassed not merely the President's right to information but his power to dismiss the prime minister. Strident speculation and leaks had become staple diet to the extent that on 3 May 1987 Rashtrapati Bhavan issued a formal communiqué in the name of the President denying in 'the clearest terms' 'persistent press speculation' that he intended to dismiss the prime minister. Things had truly come to a very sorry pass.

The Rashtrapati Bhavan disclaimer had a calming effect. Nevertheless, Zail Singh had not been coy in listening to 'advice' and sharing his thoughts with those disgruntled with Rajiv Gandhi. Some, like George Fernandes, wanted Rajiv Gandhi to step down in the interests of a fair inquiry into the many scandals abroad. Others, like columnist Rajinder Puri, sought the President's approval under the Prevention of Corruption Act to prosecute the prime minister on the Bofors deal. Still others, like Ram Jethmalani, advocated removal of Rajiv Gandhi and installation of a new prime minister at the head of a national government. Recording this in his memoirs,

Zail Singh states that he pondered over the propriety of granting permission to prosecute a prime minister who enjoyed an absolute majority in Parliament. He sought advice from several legal luminaries. All of them felt it was a borderline case. Asoke Sen, a legal luminary and former Congress minister, alone said the prime minister could be removed and anybody could be appointed in his place. He even offered his services if there were no other takers!

However, Zail Singh seems to have gone further. He himself wrote that with the Haryana elections going against the Congress, 'some people' were emboldened and canvassed specific names. A former Cabinet minister told V.P. Singh while he was still defence minister that the President would be prepared to dismiss Rajiv Gandhi if Singh was willing to replace him. V.P. Singh was aghast but was propositioned again, this time directly by Zail Singh. He firmly declined to be party to any such undemocratic action. Another interlocutor claims that Zail Singh had spoken of surprising Rajiv Gandhi by dismissing him late in the evening and swearing in a new prime minister before dawn, by when large crowds would have been brought to Vijay Chowk, the great plaza at the foot of Raisina Hill on which Rashtrapati Bhavan stands, to demonstrate in favour of the change.

The *Express*, which had been following these developments, appears to have changed its line and decided that it would not be in the national interest to convert a political impasse into a constitutional crisis that could undermine the stability of the state and the credibility of the highest functionaries in the land. RNG probably recalled that he was among the Founding Fathers who had signed the Constitution and could not now act in a manner that could lead to its undoing. Arun Shourie was accordingly sent to meet the President and informed him in blunt terms that the *Express* would oppose any move to dismiss the prime minister.

One last question remained. Would Zail Singh, whose term

expired in July 1987, seek re-election? The other possibility, around which the *Express* carried a speculative story, was that Zail Singh might precipitate a crisis by suddenly resigning his office with an emotional appeal to the nation. Neither event came to pass. The President assured the prime minister he was not interested in a second term, though it was known that he was not unwilling to stand. In the event, Vice-President Venkataraman was elected eighth President of India. An unsavoury chapter was closed. But the *Express* gadfly continued to buzz.

In his reminiscences after demitting office, R. Venkataraman had more to add:

> I was informed that my predecessor, Giani Zail Singh, apparently gave an interview to the press about this time, saying that Chandra Swami wanted P.V. Narasimha Rao to be made the Prime Minister when there had been speculation about the dismissal of Prime Minister Rajiv Gandhi. He had also stated that at one time I was agreeable to my being considered for that office. It was a pity that Giani Zail Singh gave that press interview when I had clearly stated that I would have nothing to do with political machinations. But I did not go to the press and contradict the statement as it would unnecessarily prolong the controversy.[6]

*

Fairfax had been cooking meanwhile. The Thakkar of the Thakkar–Natarajan Inquiry was the justice who had headed the commission that looked into Indira Gandhi's assassination, whose report Zail Singh had demanded to see and had been refused. The contents of that report did not long remain secret thereafter, for the *Express* carried excerpts of some of its central findings on 14 March 1987. Its publication embarrassed the government. The report said that the 'needle of suspicion' pointed towards R.K. Dhawan, then on the personal staff of

Mrs Gandhi and now a close adviser to Rajiv Gandhi. The government tried to rubbish the *Express* story but was compelled to lay the report on the table of the Lok Sabha a couple of weeks later. The document corroborated the *Express* version. RNG was triumphant and Gurumurthy recalls his exultant whoop of delight: 'Guru, we're the first paper again!'

The Thakkar–Natarajan Commission was attended by controversy regarding its appointment and terms of reference. The media and some jurists had raised a number of procedural questions. Further, V.P. Singh, among others, had asked that the terms of reference be widened to include a mysterious letter on Fairfax's stationery dated 26 November 1986 purporting to have been signed by McKay, its vice president, and addressed to Gurumurthy. The letter implicated the *Express*, Nusli Wadia and others but was soon shown to be a forgery. V.P. Singh insisted that the forgery be included in the commission's terms of reference. The government declined to do so nor was the commission inclined to be drawn into this matter which, it felt, would 'lead it astray'.

What did the letter say? The *Statesman* published the contents on 29 March 1987. It read:

> Dear Mr Gurumurthy,
>
> Dr Harris [supposedly a cover name for Michael Hershman] apprised me of his useful meeting in New Delhi last week with Mr R.N. Goenka, Mr N. Wadia, Mr V. Pande [Revenue Secretary], Mr B. Lal [Bhure Lal, Director of Enforcement] and yourself. Now that the group has been retained to assist the Government of India, we hope to expedite end result.
>
> We received only $ 300,000 arranged by Mr N. Wadia. As considerable efforts have already been made and expenditure incurred, it is advisable Mr Goenka arranges during his forthcoming visit to Geneva an additional $200,000. We shall refund both amounts on receipt from Government of India to F. Briner, Attorney, 31. Chemimchapeau Rogue 1231, Conchers, Geneva . . .

> We shall apprise Mr Goenka about the progress made on source of funds for purchase of Swiss properties of Mr Bachchan . . .

The letter was signed by Gordon McKay. The Geneva address was found to be that of Nusli Wadia's father, Neville Wadia, and R. Briner, it turned out, was an old friend of Goenka. It was widely believed, certainly in the *Express* camp, that the forged letter was a product of the government's department of dirty tricks and incidentally sought to fix Pande and Bhure Lal, who had worked with V.P. Singh.

Bhure Lal stated that the oral understanding with Fairfax was that the agency would only be entitled to receive up to 20 per cent of the value of authenticated evidence under the government's Reward Rules. Wadia declined to file any written statement in response to the commission's notice listing a number of questions but did make some applications that the commission heard. Hershman too was sent interrogatories but would not respond.

The commission in effect indicted Gurumurthy, V.P. Singh, Bhure Lal, Vinod Pande and Nusli Wadia, the last on circumstantial evidence, and did not find Fairfax's posture credible or its services effective. The commission's report stated:

> No written record existed about the alleged oral clearance or the alleged engagement of a foreign detective agency during the tenure of Shri V.P. Singh and all post-facto records came into existence much later, after some controversy arose and his shifting from the Finance Ministry to the Defence Ministry came about . . . The Government and even the Prime Minister were totally in the dark about these sensitive matters. The operations were shrouded in secrecy and surrounded by mysterious circumstances. And non-officials were being consulted and their advice or judgment was being trusted . . .

It however transpired that the Fairfax investigation was limited to Reliance Industries, L.M. Thapar and his connections with

Louis Dreyfus, a New-York-based edible oil supplier to the State Trading Corporation, and two NRIs in the United States who were alleged to be conduits for investments by Dhirubhai Ambani.

Not everybody was convinced by the Thakkar–Natarajan Commission's findings. Barring Nusli Wadia, no one—not V.P. Singh, Gurumurthy or anybody else—was issued 8B notices that would have entitled him to cross-examine witnesses. V.P. Singh described this as a singular injustice to him.

B.G. Deshmukh, Cabinet Secretary at the time, opined that the commission 'was a damp squib, exposing only the government's vindictiveness against V.P. Singh, Vinod Pande and Bhure Lal.' On the HDW matter, he recorded that the name of the Hindujas was associated with the affair by defence ministry officials. He then adds, 'I remember Arun Nehru telling me that Indira Gandhi was very annoyed with the agent involved in this deal as he did not pass on the promised amount from the commission to the Congress party and she refused to see him on her next visit to the U.K.'[7]

Arun Shourie pointed out that the circulation of the *Express* had gone up during the past few months and quipped: 'Rajiv Gandhi is our best circulation manager!'

In an editorial written while the commission was still at work, the *Express* reiterated the belief that the only result of the inquiry might be 'that Nusli Wadia ends up being framed before the Commission'. It said the best legal minds had warned sitting judges not to lend themselves 'to what was clearly a device to stifle debate in Parliament'. Messrs Thakkar and Natarajan had been summoning persons, recording their statements and settling procedures in private, ostensibly before they had formally taken up their work, it said, arguing that 'To be respected as judges, they must conduct themselves as judges must.' The *Express* concluded:

> Meanwhile, the duty of the press is clear. It must keep a hawk's eye over the functioning of the Commission, as it

> must over the functioning of any other institution. It must in particular excavate and publish evidence that a Commission would rather not look at. And it must in particular see if a Commission, whether unwittingly or with its wits about it, is lending itself to a government's political design. And it must not abandon this duty, this dharma, because some counsel waves some rule of contempt at it.

The commission also delivered itself of some obiter. The fact that two sitting judges had accepted the commission had been criticized. The commissioners responded that 'character assassination of a sitting Judge discharging his functions as a Commission is no less contempt of court than when a sitting Judge discharging the functions in a court is subjected to character assassination'. It also had some words of advice for the media, which it felt had been unfair to it.

> The time is more than ripe for the media to evolve a code of conduct for itself, in consultation with its conscience, keeping in mind the larger perspective of National Interest, realising the need for self-discipline. The media is an extremely powerful instrument that can promote national good. By virtue of the great power enjoyed by it, it can also do great harm. And the harm done by the media can perhaps never be wholly undone. The media expects the judiciary to protect its own interest by upholding the principle of freedom of expression and freedom of the press . . . The media expects the judicial institution to act with independence and fearlessness if the freedom of the press is invaded or threatened. The very same media cannot show scant regard for the doctrine of independence of the judiciary and the need to ensure that it can function fearlessly. When it indulges in character assassination of judges it thereby tarnishes the image of the judicial institution and undermines the authority of that very agency . . . To quote the memorable words of the Pope, uttered as recently as September 16, 1987 (as reported in the *Statesman*) in an outspoken speech to about 1600 executives, actors and policy makers in the television, radio, print, film and recording industries . . .

> 'In a sense the world is at your mercy . . . Your work can be a force for great good and great evil. You yourselves know the dangers, as well as the splendid opportunities open to you . . . Communications can appeal to and promote what is debased in people . . . You have untold possibilities for good, ominous possibilities for destruction. It is the difference between death and life . . . Communication leaders [owe] a great measure of accountability—accountability to God, to the community and before the witness of history. And yet at times it seems that everything is in your hands.'

The commission underlined the adage that the right to use (freedom of the press) does not mean the right to misuse (it). 'For the pen is not only mightier than the sword, but it can also be deadlier than the sword.'

Others too agonized about the media. Mulgaokar lamented the lowering of standards 'by rash judgements on insufficient evidence' and deplored the irresponsibility now witnessed. Everybody had been traduced, including the President and prime minister, but none so wantonly as V.P. Singh, with a campaign against him managed by those around Rajiv Gandhi. Amitabh Bachchan demanded more powers for the government to curb media 'irresponsibility' and hinted darkly at the coverage of the *Express*.

Meanwhile, matters came to a head in the *Express* when a handful of its employees backed by outsiders enforced a strike in Delhi in October 1987 on the issue of Diwali bonus. Loyal workers repaired to the Express Guest House to produce the paper. Several senior editors variously voiced concern regarding two matters. One was the induction of BJP activists to physically counter the striking employees. Girilal Jain, editor of the *Times of India*, argued that even if a majority of *Express* employees were desirous of resuming work, should they have taken the law into their own hands, with the editor, Shourie, taking the lead in this enterprise? 'The BJP cannot possibly fight the government in the streets . . . We journalists should not play politics. Our role is limited but not so limited as to suffocate us. Beyond that lies the treacherous path of temptation.' Nihal Singh endorsed that view but Prem Bhatia thought such criticism overblown. Rajendra Sareen said that instigating the President to dismiss the prime minister was illegitimate and warned that freedom of the press was threatened by pressures not only from outside but also from within. S. Sahay found the import of political cadres as strikebreakers to be 'wholly wrong'. He observed that 'A collective leadership that enlists the support of political parties to help it start the paper cannot really complain that the ruling party has initiated or encouraged the strike.' And Sunanda Datta-Ray, like Sahay a former *Statesman* editor, noted the *Express*'s 'curious isolation' manifested in the plaintive caption of one of its leading articles 'Why Are They Silent?' However, virtually all condemned the government's bid to crush the *Express*.

*India Today* noted that the *Express*, by giving Ram Jethmalani an office in its premises in Delhi while publishing his daily questions to Rajiv Gandhi, had acted in concert with him, leading even many *Express* sympathizers to feel that 'it had begun to stray from standards of fairness'. M.J. Akbar, editor of the *Telegraph*, commented that 'there has to be a difference between investigative journalism and allegation journalism . . . All these vicious cartoons—particularly the one on [Rajiv Gandhi's] running away to Italy. It's in thoroughly bad taste.'

After a cruel forty-seven-day ordeal of an engineered strike, raids, prosecution and persecution, the *Express* resumed publication on 2 December 1987. Far from being cowed down, it cocked a snook at the prime minister with an editorial. The caption: 'Good Morning, Mr Gandhi!'

# 11

# Last Roar of the Lion

Ramnath Goenka suffered a partial stroke towards the end of 1987. He was to describe the year just ending as 'tougher even than the Emergency'. This, he said, was because he was now older and the government had 'descended to levels even Indira Gandhi did not' in her time. He told *Gentleman* magazine that he had maintained his equanimity only because of the mental and physical training that came with association with Gandhi, Kripalani, Madan Mohan Malaviya and other great men 'who took nothing from society but gave everything to it'.

He felt he had judged Rajiv Gandhi favourably too soon. The prime minister could not tolerate an independent newspaper and had launched an unprecedented assault on the *Express*. But the paper was prepared to pay the price of freedom of expression and would continue to mirror the Indian reality. By 1989, RNG, at eighty-five, was suffering from respiratory and cardiac problems, hovering between life and death.

Even as he gamely fought the many cases brought against him in courts around the country, the *Express* kept up a withering fire that gave the government no respite. In July

1989, the Comptroller and Auditor General published a report on the Bofors deal that the government had stalled for two years and then sought to withhold from Parliament. The report indicted the government and irate parliamentarians called for Rajiv Gandhi's resignation. A shrill *Express* editorial denounced the prime minister's 'lies and calumnies' and exhorted the Opposition to get organized and prepare for a snap election or a postponement of the polls when due on some pretext or other.

Then in October 1989, the *Hindu* published the full text of the Swedish National Audit Bureau's report on the Bofors arms deal. This was picked up and thereafter doggedly pursued by the *Express*. The report confirmed that middlemen were involved and that payments had been made to Indians. It further established that the Swedish government was also involved and that the CBI had turned a blind eye to the information that the Swedish prosecutor was willing to exchange with it.

A National Front had by now begun to crystallize in opposition to the Congress, and V.P. Singh called for Rajiv Gandhi's resignation. The Opposition thought to force the prime minister's hand by threatening to resign en masse from the Lok Sabha. Soon thereafter, leakages from the diary of Martin Ardbo, former executive director of Bofors, showed how murky things had become. It was now alleged that Olof Palme, the former Swedish prime minister, who was later assassinated, was himself involved. Carl Petersen, a Swedish minister, Adnan Khashoggi, the Saudi arms dealer, Ardbo and some others had had a meeting in Vienna at which the Indian 'god-man' Chandraswamy and his associate 'Mamaji' Kailash Nath Agarwal were present, hinting at the global ramifications of the unfolding saga.

Later in October 1989, even as the Joint Parliamentary Committee kept stonewalling, the *Hindu* obtained further sensational documents on the Bofors case but was unable to publish these on account of official pressure. Since the *Hindu* was disabled, its correspondent Chitra Subramaniam was engaged by the *Express*, which broke the story in considerable detail. This exposed the intricate trail of dummy accounts held abroad, through which the Bofors pay-off was laundered. The *Express* was now outraged. A leading article declared, 'The truth will be delayed so long as Rajiv Gandhi remains in power. It will be out within the month of his being kicked out of it.' For the *Express*, the Bofors case had become a crusade.

Even as these events were unfolding, the text of a letter written in anguish by a former union minister, C. Subramaniam, to the President of India appeared in the press. After setting out the definitive nature of the evidence about the Bofors pay-off, he appealed to President Venkataraman to take steps to establish the identity of the offenders. This, he said, was what the people of India expected from their Head of State. This was not the last time President Venkataraman was to be approached to intervene.

Meanwhile, another storm was brewing. The publication of the Thakkar Commission's report on the assassination of Indira Gandhi should have given quietus to the speculation and rumours surrounding that tragedy. A writ for its early publication was instead followed by an ordinance on 14 March 1989, empowering the government to withhold the report from Parliament, creating the impression that there was something to hide. The reason given was that it could prejudice the ongoing case on the assassination and reveal sensitive information about the prime minister's security arrangements. This was unconvincing and scepticism was heightened when, many months later, the *Express* carried detailed excerpts from the commission's report stating that Justice Thakkar found the 'needle of suspicion' pointing towards Mrs Gandhi's aide R.K. Dhawan, recently re-inducted into Rajiv Gandhi's close circle of advisers.

RNG's delight at the scoop was in contrast to the frenzy it evoked in the government. The prime minister said the will of

Parliament had been betrayed and that the government would probe the leakage. Dhawan had been reinstated only after he had been cleared by the Special Investigation Team, of the 'observations' contained in the Thakkar Report, he said, and argued that withholding the report had not resulted in a miscarriage of justice in the assassination case. The *Express* retorted that the handling of the episode had disgraced the nation—Rajiv Gandhi had once again by-passed the President, this time, President Venkataraman, and the Cabinet in suppressing the Thakkar Report and therefore carried a heavy burden of responsibility.

*

At about the same time, events were moving towards yet another confrontation. In March 1989 the *Express* had published the report of the Grover Committee confirming Reliance's import of excess polyester yarn-making capacity. This had been kept under wraps and its disclosure now was an added official embarrassment.

The government did not take long to strike back. On 6 April it ordered the reopening of the *Express* Group's income tax assessments for all the years since 1972. The *Express* interpreted this as a clear act of reprisal. The government's vindictive attitude caused L.K. Advani to write an article in the *Express* seeking legislative protection for whistleblowers.

RNG went to court on the tax demand and secured a stay from the Bombay High Court on twenty-six assessments reopened in respect of the *Indian Express* Newspapers Pvt. Ltd. The plaint was that the income tax department had raised demands for over Rs 10 crore in regard to assessments for the past twenty-four months alone even as the banking department had 'advised' banks to put curbs on lending to the *Express* Group and had stopped rentals totalling Rs 3.2 crore. The obvious purpose was to strangle the company. It was further pleaded that persons doing any kind of business with the *Express* were being coerced into signing confessional statements implicating the company in various misdemeanours. An incident in Calcutta was cited as proof. The government had decided to teach the *Express* a lesson and compel it to desist from tormenting it any further.

Opening another front, the government sought to repel an implicit charge by the *Express* that its handling of the Indira Gandhi assassination case suggested a communal bias against the Sikh community. It accused the *Express* and its henchmen of exploiting communal sentiments and harming the secular ethos of the country. It particularly targeted Ram Jethmalani, standing counsel for the *Express*, who had an office in the Delhi Express Building and was currently defending some of those accused in the Indira Gandhi assassination trial. Never one to be cowed down, Jethmalani returned fire in the columns of the *Express* on 20 April 1989, vigorously defending himself against the charge of fostering Khalistan.

> Mr Rajiv Gandhi has obviously lost his equilibrium. His continuous ranting and raving against me personally shows I am succeeding in my current mission to topple a Prime Minister who combines the worst elements of Tammany Hall and the Sicilian mafia. He knows my relentless investigations in Sweden, Switzerland [and] Panama. He has not forgotten the unanswered four hundred questions, the Bachchan property documents and the Svenska lady, Virginia Rodrigues. Nor can he forget . . . his dear friend [Quatrocchi] with the Italian marble swimming pool.

Within days, the government struck back. RNG was implicated in a COFEPOSA (foreign exchange regulation) case. The home ministry accused Jethmalani of violating the Foreign Contribution (Regulation) Act in the course of his visits abroad. Arun Nehru, Rajiv's cousin, had fallen out with the regime, turned hostile and joined the Janata Dal, and now found himself answering charges regarding a Czech pistol deal that had surfaced when he was minister for internal security. Simultaneously, K.K. Tewary, who had earned notoriety as part of the Congress's 'shouting brigade' in Parliament that foul-mouthed those on the government's blacklist, was moved from the external affairs ministry, where he was minister of state, to hold independent charge of the ministry of information and broadcasting. It was surmised that he would there be better able to influence and control the media in general, and the official media in particular, in the run-up to the forthcoming general elections.

Meanwhile, the Janata Dal ministry in Karnataka, headed by S.R. Bommai, was dismissed following some controversial defections and the state was brought under President's rule. Yuva Janata and Janata Party activists broke into the Express Towers in Bombay and gheraoed the *Express* news editor. They submitted a memorandum stating that the paper's editorial had unfairly blamed Chandra Shekhar, the Janata Party leader, for being instrumental in toppling the Bommai government.

Even as these events were playing out, there were more developments on the Reliance front. In April 1989, the Public Accounts Committee had reported that it had found gross customs irregularities in the import of plant and equipment by Reliance Industries Ltd (RIL) for its Patalganga polyester filament yarn unit. RIL had resorted to unauthorized import of plant and machinery, wrongful declaration and under-invoicing of goods attracting customs duty of about Rs 120 crore. The customs authorities were 'blissfully unaware' of the alleged import of the additional machines. The finance ministry's explanation was that the equipment was imported in a dismantled condition in several consignments received over a period of time, thereby defying easy detection of the overall quantum. This defence was found unacceptable. Likewise, the favour shown to RIL in being permitted to pay a differential duty of Rs 31.28 crore in 138 instalments spread over two years was irregular and resulted in a loss to the exchequer.

Scarcely had the dust begun to settle on this episode when the *Express* opened a new front concerning the attempted takeover of the highly regarded engineering firm Larsen and Toubro (L&T) by the Ambanis. On 12 September 1989, the *Express* carried an article by Gurumurthy on the 'hijacking' of L&T, a process that had commenced a year earlier, in August 1988. The Reliance conduit here was said to be a new subsidiary of the Bank of Baroda by name of Bank of Baroda Fiscal Services Ltd or BOB Fiscal. The allegation was that Reliance had used four front companies to deposit in BOB Fiscal a sum of Rs 30 crore from the debenture funds it had raised for its petrochemical plant. The BOB Fiscal then or some time earlier, purchased 3.9 million L&T shares for Rs 40–45 crore from the LIC, GIC and UTI, all public sector units (PSUs). These transactions took place precisely on the days that Mukesh Ambani, the elder son of the RIL patriarch, Dhirubhai, and another RIL director, and some weeks later, Anil Ambani, Dhirubhai's younger son, joined the L&T board as nominees of the same PSUs! That done, BOB Fiscal transferred all 3.9 million shares to Trishna Investment & Leasing Ltd, a shell company fronting for RIL. Gurumurthy commented that it appeared RIL had proudly announced a marriage of 'L&T's professionalism with Ambani's entrepreneurship'.

This story was told by the *Express*, which collaborated with Manek Davar, editor and publisher of *Lex Et Juris*, the law magazine. By April 1989, Dhirubhai Ambani had become chairman of L&T and straightaway decided to invest Rs 76 crore in RIL shares from monies the company had raised as part of a Rs 93 crore debenture offer for its own capital expansion. Officially controlled financial institutions were alleged to have connived with these transactions under the eye of an indulgent government. An *Express* headline said it all: 'FIs Aid Creation of Frankenstein: Goodbye L&T, Hello Reliance'.

Another element was introduced into the picture when the

*Express* disclosed that relatives of a high BOB Fiscal executive owned a certain company associated with BOB, doing business exclusively for RIL at great profit to itself. Further, it had been funded by the Bank of Commerce and Credit International, which had an unsavoury reputation.

Parliament took up the matter. The government pleaded innocence and ignorance. The courts were seized of the matter when the *Express* published an article in April 1989 on a proposed L&T mega issue captioned 'L&T Sinks 76 Crore in RIL Shares: This Is How Rs 820 Crore Will Be Drained'. The *Financial Express* also ran an editorial to which objection was taken by Reliance. The *Express* was charged with contempt. Jethmalani argued the case and said that by unearthing a big fraud, the newspaper had served the cause of justice. This should be a matter of pride, not of shame as publication of truth could not constitute contempt.

Responding to the complaint that the *Express* had 'stolen' a letter from L&T files, Jethmalani argued that this was a 'commendable theft' as it proved embezzlement of public funds by RIL. He pleaded that it was the duty of every journalist to resort to all means to bring out the truth, especially when the regular investigative machinery of the state did not perform its duty to the public.

The *Express* described the verdict of the Bombay High Court on the L&T case as 'unconscionable'. In an editorial on 2 October 1989 it lamented that Justice Kotwal had not found any nexus between L&T and RIL even when the former had in its advertisements and affidavit to the court itself proclaimed that it had become a part of the Reliance group. The paper was stinging in its comment:

> . . . What is BOB Fiscal? A pot put together by a nationalised bank (for transferring shares to the Ambanis). And who set up this pot, 'BOB Fiscal'? The Bank of Baroda. And strange isn't it that the Ambanis have set up a factory for the son of the Chairman of the Bank of Baroda, a factory that enables

> him to rake in Rs 50 lakh a year on an investment of Rs 6 lakh . . .
>
> And strange isn't it that the financial institutions, having already surrendered seven per cent shares to the Ambanis via 'BOB Fiscal', are now set to be marginalised by the Rs 820 crore mega-issue?
>
> To maintain that all this is just 'a normal commercial transaction', as Justice Kotwal has done, is to maintain that a gigantic fraud is now a normal commercial transaction. To refuse to see a pattern in all this, as Justice Kotwal has so assiduously laboured not to see, is to announce that the courts will not come in the way when financial institutions are suborned . . . The judgement opens the way for buccaneers with a hold on the Government to acquire many a company via pots like 'BOB Fiscal'. A judgement, in brief, that must be appealed—in yet another attempt in the public interest . . . and also to unmask further the state to which our institutions have been reduced.

Mulgaokar, the *Express* editorial adviser, followed with an article dissecting the preceding events and the Kotwal judgement. Another contempt notice was slapped on the *Express*, this time in the Supreme Court, and an injunction sought to restrain the paper from publishing any articles on the L&T debenture offer until the closing of the mega-issue. The *Express* pleaded that this would be tantamount to a gagging order on a matter of public interest and would discriminate against the paper. It pleaded that the editorial entailed fair comment on the judgement and cast no reflection on the judge.

The expedition with which the L&T and other cases were heard caused a number of leading counsels to make a representation to the Chief Justice of India. The *Express* ran the story on 10 October 1989 under a four-column, two-deck headline: 'Speedy Justice only for the Ambanis, Thapars; What about the Common Man? Lawyers Ask CJ'. It commented:

> We are now witnessing a growing number of extraordinary cases of the rich and powerful of this country being heard and

> orders passed with such expedition that this Court has to sit at home on public holidays to do so.
>
> Very recently, this Court again entertained a petition filed by R.K. Amin on behalf of the accused in the Nusli Wadia murder conspiracy case on the same day as it was filed . . . The Court proceeded to grant bail to the petitioner without even knowing that the petitioner was not the accused. The CBI was directed to take over the investigation without even notice to the Bombay Police which had launched the investigation. The most recent and shocking example of extraordinary expedition shown in a case involving no great urgency is the case involving the Larsen and Toubro debenture issue . . .

The representation concluded with a plea for 'clearer guidelines' to determine 'when a judge can hold a hearing at his house or outside court hours'.

The *Express* kept snapping at the heels of Reliance. It wrote on 'How Ambanis Influence Govt. Decisions' with regard to excise duties on polyester staple fibre and filament yarn and welcomed the steps taken by an assertive L&T board not to extend Rs 840 crore of supplier's credit to Reliance Petrochemicals Ltd. The underlying target in all this campaigning was the 'arbitrary policies and rampaging corruption of the Rajiv Gandhi government'.

Even after the Rajiv Gandhi government was swept out in the 1989 general elections, the *Express* continued to pursue the story. Following V.P. Singh's assumption of office as prime minister at the end of 1989, Manek Davar wrote in the *Express* in February 1990, calling for redressal of the wrongs done, and an end to the vindictiveness shown towards a newspaper that had exposed the rot. Nevertheless, a year later, the Supreme Court upheld the Controller of Capital Issues's consent to L&T's Rs 820 crore mega-issue. But it had a word of caution for the financial institutions with regard to the procedures followed.

The *Express* next focussed on the alleged nexus between

Reliance and the BCCI through the early years of the Narasimha Rao government, when the bank came under the scanner in the United States. Manek Davar wrote a series of articles in the *Express* on this theme and on the continuing Reliance bid to take over L&T completely. The original sin was traced back to the preceding Congress regime.

*

Ever since the beginning of his disillusionment with Rajiv Gandhi in 1986 Ramnath Goenka had been marshalling his media, legal and political battalions for an assault on the regime, even as he held off the government offensive to crush him. He had reportedly turned to Adnan Khashoggi and Chandraswamy in a bid to pin down Rajiv Gandhi on Bofors. He had been emotionally upset by the arrest of his grandson Vivek Khaitan in Bombay, after a raid on the *Express* in March 1987, and by the persecution and arrest of Nusli Wadia in the wake of the Thakkar–Natarajan report. He felt personally responsible for their plight and was deeply concerned for their well-being, even as he nursed a heart condition and an unattended prostate problem.

At the same time he was bent on expanding his empire. He had undertaken a lightning tour of Calicut and Trivandrum from Cochin, to purchase land for what were to become two new centres of publication. He had driven from one place to another without rest in trying weather, despite all advice. The strain was beginning to tell and he returned to Madras ill and exhausted. He was admitted to the Trinity Acute Care Hospital in Madras in the early part of 1989, watched over with care and deepening anxiety by friends and associates. Saroj Goenka was on a visit to the United States, but rushed back. V.P. Singh kept calling over the phone to inquire about his health. Arun Nehru flew down from Delhi. Nanaji Deshmukh was at his bedside. They were soon joined by a distraught Nusli Wadia, who evacuated RNG to Bombay to be placed under the care of Dr Udwadia at the Breach Candy Hospital.

Wadia had taken Dr Udwadia with him to Madras and there chartered the entire first-class cabin of an Air-India airliner. This was fitted out as a mini-ICU and the patient flown to Bombay. RNG was all hooked up, with drips and oxygen, and the pilot took special pains in his ascent, routing and descent to ensure a smooth flight. It was touch and go. Fortunately, all went well. Goenka responded to the treatment at the Breach Candy Hospital and was slowly nursed back to health. The battle with the government was raging and victory hung in the balance.

Later, back at the penthouse in Express Towers, Gita More, RNG's devoted companion, housekeeper and nurse, and Maureen, Nusli Wadia's wife, watched over him with tender loving care. Drained but unbeaten, it was not long before the wily old fox was back, planning his next moves. Goenka had decided that this was no time to go!

*

Things had not gone well for Rajiv Gandhi from 1986 onwards, surrounded as he was by a self-serving coterie. The IPKF operation in Sri Lanka had gone terribly wrong. The Congress–National Conference misalliance and rigging of the Jammu and Kashmir election heightened alienation and provided a trigger for the insurgency that followed. In an ill-advised move, the side gates of the Babri Masjid leading to the makeshift Ram temple were opened on 1 February 1986, setting the scene for tragedy in Ayodhya. A foolish communal balance was then attempted by legislating the Muslim Women's Bill later that year to 'correct' the Shah Bano judgement. Rahul Pathak exposed the Balram Jakhar 'fodder scam' in the *Express* in May 1989. All this only succeeded in stirring up widespread dissatisfaction. The ghosts of several scandals haunted a harried prime minister.

V.P. Singh was on the rise. He had become president of the Janata Dal later that summer, and the *Express* saw something of a JP in him—a crusader against corruption, a political martyr and a suitable focal point for Opposition unity. Somebody in the Congress obviously concluded that it was time to fix him. That was the beginning of the St. Kitts caper. From out of nowhere a document that had been published in some Turkish and Kuwaiti newspapers surfaced in India on a simple, undated piece of notepaper signed by Alan E. Tonks and George D. McLean, managers of the First Trust Corporation of St. Kitts, a tiny Caribbean island. This stated that Ajeya Singh (V.P. Singh's son, a non-resident Indian in the United States) had opened a numbered account '29479' in September 1986 in which he had deposited a sum of $21 million over a period of six months, and listed Vishwanath Pratap Singh as the beneficiary. Tonks and McLean declared the statement to be a forgery. Tonks said his signature had been stolen and transposed on the document and that McLean had left the service of the bank a year earlier.

St. Kitts had been picked possibly because V.P. Singh was scheduled to go there for a World Bank meeting as India's finance minister. However, it so happened that the visit was cancelled. The plan miscarried. K.K. Tewary was then minister of state for external affairs.

Parliament took up the issue. The government said on 14 October 1989 that it was probing the matter and had no reason to doubt the genuineness of the document though there was as yet insufficient evidence to prosecute V.P. Singh under FERA. On 24 February 1990, the CBI commenced detailed 'verification' of the St. Kitts documents. That very day, the Delhi residences of Chandraswamy and his close associate 'Mamaji' Kailash Nath Agarwal were raided and the latter was arrested. Both were reportedly named by Indian diplomats for their involvement in the St. Kitts episode. Among the items seized was a photo album containing pictures of Chandraswamy with Adnan Khashoggi, the controversial Saudi arms dealer. Narasimha Rao, then foreign minister, was dragged into the affair and later made a co-accused.

The St. Kitts story was to linger. Chandraswamy allegedly contacted Michael Hershman of Fairfax to defame V.P. Singh in this case. Later, after V.P. Singh became prime minister, Chandraswamy fled the country in 1990. With the change of government, the CBI filed a case in March 1990 to get to the bottom of the forgery issue. But with V.P. Singh demitting office on 7 November 1990, the case officer, N.K. Singh, joint director CBI, was transferred and efforts were made by the next administration under Chandra Shekhar to close the case. Satish Sharma, R.K. Dhawan and many others did not desire the case to proceed.[1] A special court in Delhi finally acquitted Chandraswamy on 24 October 2004.

The *Express* had been zealous in defending V.P. Singh and in exposing the St. Kitts forgery. The general secretary of the All-India Congress Committee, Ghulam Nabi Azad, asked why: 'How is it that V.P. Singh and Ajeya Singh are silent whereas the *Indian Express* is going all the way to defend V.P. Singh, more than a lawyer?' The fact is that V.P. Singh had not been silent and had stated that his signature and that of his son, on documents subsequently touted around, were false. Azad alleged this was a quid pro quo for V.P. Singh's having helped the *Express* over a rental matter concerning the Minerals and Metals Trading Corporation (MMTC), one of its tenants in Delhi's Express Building, when he was commerce minister. The fact is that the CBI acquitted both V.P. Singh and the former MMTC chairman after investigating the matter.

RNG had used Chandraswamy earlier, but now concluded he was an imposter who needed to be exposed. Indeed, Chandraswamy had been a courier in the Zail Singh letter case and was present at the Express Guest House in Sunder Nagar when it was raided on 13 March 1987, the day the Zail Singh 'letter' was published by the paper. Rajat Sharma, then editor of *Onlooker*, with Pritish Nandy, editor of the *Illustrated Weekly*, in tow as his 'assistant Mr Sen', had jointly interviewed Chandraswamy in London. The subterfuge was necessary as the Swami was furious with Nandy for something uncharitable he had written about him in the *Weekly*. The interview was recorded. On the side, Chandraswamy boasted about his many important contacts around the world and allowed Sharma to leaf through photo albums that showed him with these personalities.

Two visitors were present when Chandraswamy read the published article in the *Onlooker* in the summer of 1987. One of them later told Rajat Sharma that an unnerved Chandraswamy had 'danced the *tandav*', exclaiming 'Mama, *dhoka ho gaya*' to his aide. Sharma subsequently narrated the story of his 'interview' to RNG, who found the exposure enormously funny and well deserved. Goenka had used Chandraswamy for his own purposes even if the Swami had thought he was using RNG! He was well aware that the man had led him a dance along false trails with the promise of conclusive evidence that would pin responsibility for the Bofors and HDW pay-offs and much else.

In the run-up to the 1989 elections, Rajiv Gandhi began to woo the religious right. An effort was mounted to see if historical and archaeological evidence showed a Ram Mandir beneath the Babri Mosque. This foundered. V.P. Singh said he would visit Ayodhya to find an amicable solution. This was reported to RNG, who convened a meeting with V.P. Singh, Bhaurao Deoras, the RSS chief's brother, Prabhash Joshi and Gurumurthy in the penthouse in Bombay, in a bid to mediate a solution. An outline proposal emerged, and Ashok Singhal was to issue a statement. But the government got wind that something was afoot and pre-empted that initiative by permitting the Vishwa Hindu Parishad to perform a token shilanyas, the laying of the foundation of the proposed Ram Mandir at Ayodhya in November 1989. Tensions rose. Rajiv Gandhi went to Vrindavan to meet Devraha Baba and received his blessings. Shilanyas was performed, though not without some confrontation.

On 11 November 1989, the *Express* editorialized:

> The *shilanyas* of the Ram Mandir in Ayodhya is an important announcement: the Hindus, the ceremony proclaims, will not put up with reverse discrimination . . . Four groups are responsible for this outcome. First, politicians like Bhindranwale and Shahabuddin . . . Secondly, politicians occupying offices of state. These have pandered to the little Jinnahs. Third, the 'progressives' [the Left] . . . Finally, the 'liberals', leaning over backwards to show that their hearts bleed for the minorities . . .
>
> If instead of adopting a rational solution . . . the controversy is seen as yet another occasion to prove who shall prevail, not just violence but militarisation of society is inevitable . . .

Some time before the polls were announced, Achyut Patwardhan is reported to have written to President Venkataraman suggesting that he should consider resigning in protest against the government's loss of moral credibility, presumably on account of the various scams in the news. According to one version, RNG favoured such a course. Be that as it may, Gurumurthy, Arun Shourie and Jagannathan drove down to Kanchipuram from Madras to meet the Paramacharya, and put to him the proposition that the President should resign. Apparently, the senior Shankaracharya merely heard them out, saying nothing.

Subramaniam Swamy, a maverick politician and loose cannon, later referred to this episode at a press conference in May 1992. He recalled it again two years later when president of the Janata Party, as reported by the *Hindustan Times* (25 July 1994).

Swamy was reported as stating that, having decided to build up V.P. Singh as an alternative leader, RNG and others persuaded President Venkataraman some time in 1989 to join a plot to force Rajiv Gandhi to step down from office as prime minister. His resignation as President a little before the Lok Sabha elections was to be the first shot to be fired in a protest campaign, with the blessings of the Dharma Sansad and the Paramacharya. However, the plan misfired as the election dates were advanced by a couple of months.

It was also reported that Swamy flaunted a copy of RNG's purported letter to the Paramacharya that was allegedly taken to Kanchi by his *Express* confidantes, Gurumurthy, Arun Shourie, N.S. Jagannathan and Manoj Sonthalia. But the pontiff rebuffed the overture.[2]

Venkataraman was contacted in Madras by UNI but declined to comment on Subramaniam Swamy's allegations.

The *Express* dramatis personae deny the veracity of this narration.

*

The general election of 1989 was preceded by a vilification campaign against V.P. Singh led by Kalpnath Rai, a minister who had described his former Cabinet colleague in the most derogatory terms. The *Express* compiled the list of epithets used: 'cobra', 'CIA agent', 'international fraud', 'paper tiger', and a 'bogus fellow' who should be 'hanged for treachery'. Civility had fled. The Opposition decided to boycott election broadcasts over AIR and Doordarshan following a decision by the authorities to censor any naming of those allegedly involved in the Bofors arms deal.

The *Express* lampooned the sixty-page Congress election manifesto, contrasting its high-sounding promises with what it described as its abject record in office. It quoted Rajiv Gandhi against himself. It recalled his ringing words at the Congress centenary celebrations in Bombay in 1985 denouncing 'the brokers of power and influence who dispense patronage to convert a mass movement into a feudal oligarchy'. For such persons, he went on, 'the masses do not count. Their life-style, their thinking or lack of it, their self-aggrandisement, their corrupt ways, their linkages with vested interests in society and their sanctimonious posturing are wholly incompatible with work among the people. They are reducing the Congress party to a shell from which the spirit of service and sacrifice have been emptied.'

The Congress ran a massive and aggressive Rs 75 crore advertisement campaign in all major newspapers. The text and illustrations had strong punch lines. The *Express* turned these around brilliantly in a series of illustrated and textual rebuttals, using the same cartoons and captions with telling additions. Rajendra drew the counter-cartoons while Shailaja Bajpai analysed the campaign 'Hearts of Darkness' thus: 'The advertisements, in black and white, are big, bold and ugly. The illustrations depicting snakes, scorpions, cocks, a dismembered doll and a host of Opposition leaders about to dismember each other, designed to hit the reader between the eyes. The idea seems to have been to create a sense of disquiet and distress—a doomsday vision—of what awaits the country should it fall into "wrong" hands.'

The Congress cartoon depicted a bullet surrounded by grenades with a caption reading 'Who does this remind you of?' Sample the counter-campaign with this rejoinder: The 3870 killed in Delhi. The 10 to 15 who are killed daily in Punjab? The 1150 soldiers killed in Sri Lanka? The ones being killed every day in Assam, J&K, Bihar . . .? The punchline: My heart trembles at leaving India in their hands!

Another cartoon showed the Congress symbol, a Hand. Beside it was the counter-caption: Have you noticed their Hand? A forked life line. A broken heart line. And no fate line at all. And the punchline: Before thinking up a new Ad, think up a new symbol!

The *Express* editorial on polling day was titled 'The Day of Judgement'. It concluded:

> In brief. Rajiv and his party must be booted out. And decisively so. That is today the one and only way to save democracy, and thereby save the country.

Inelegantly said, but precise in its injunction. The polls were hotly contested. There were allegations of rigging in Amethi, Rajiv Gandhi's constituency, where another Gandhi, Rajmohan, the Mahatma's grandson, opposed him. At Fatehpur, Congressmen opened fire on V.P. Singh as he entered the polling booth.

In the result, the Congress-I was voted out. The Janata Dal and its allies formed the hub of what was to become the National Front. The election of the leader was, as always, a messy affair with ambitions running riot. V.P. Singh was the front runner and had the complete backing of the *Express;* but both Devi Lal, leading the Bharatiya Lok Dal, and Chandra Shekhar thought their time had come, though the latter had only some months back declared that he was not a claimant to that office. However, he was advised that he would be unable to challenge V.P. Singh in a contest. Ultimately, a ruse was adopted. Devi Lal appeared to be the chosen leader, only to come to the parliamentary party meeting and propose V.P. Singh. Chandra Shekhar's thwarted ambition turned to undermining unity and stability and did not take long to manifest itself. George Fernandes made the point, oft repeated before and since, that prime ministers must be elected by the parliamentary party or coalition, and not selected and 'made' with a sense of obligation to a coterie. Such a democratic process would also remove or mitigate the grudge others feel about being cheated and denied a level playing field.

Devi Lal was made deputy prime minister and later acknowledged RNG's role in the formation and stabilization of the new government. But he too nursed his ambitions.

*

The government, in which RNG had invested so much energy and hope, got off to an unfortunate start with the kidnapping in Srinagar of Rubiya Sayeed, the daughter of the then union home minister Mufti Mohammed Sayeed, signalling the beginning of insurgency in Kashmir. The Congress gleefully went on the offensive, while internal divisions within the Janata Dal that had been papered over soon began to show.

Meanwhile, unrest was brewing within the *Express*. No sooner had V.P. Singh been sworn in at the end of 1989 than the *Indian Express* faced protests on its refusal to implement the Bachawat Wage Board Award. The Delhi employees' union struck work on 13 December 1989 and employees in other centres followed suit. A spokesman for the management explained that if the Bachawat Committee's recommendation that all newspapers in a group be regarded as a single unit were to be implemented, the *Express* would be compelled to shut down most of its editions. It argued that this particular recommendation was a legacy of the previous government that had wilfully targeted the *Express*. The paper had been making losses as it had been squeezed for advertisements, denied its rentals and normal bank credit, slapped with penal income tax assessments and hounded with trumped-up cases as part of a vindictive official policy. The *Express* union approached the prime minister. The management alleged intimidatory tactics by some workers, declared a lockout and filed a writ in the Bombay High Court.

Fali Nariman, appearing for the *Express*, was able to show what he termed to be palpable errors in computation and discrimination by the Wage Board. Further hearings were postponed. Meanwhile, the lockout was lifted on 27 January 1990.

As long as the Congress was in office, the charge was that the government was shielding those allegedly involved in a number of scandals while persecuting others. The Bofors actors, the Bachchans and Ambanis fell in the first category; while

V.P. Singh and Nusli Wadia in the other. The new government was expected to take a more balanced view. Certainly, investigations into the St. Kitts caper and the case regarding the alleged attempt to murder Nusli Wadia, allegedly by Reliance hirelings, were pursued more diligently, following court orders. In the latter matter, the Bombay Police was also instructed to continue to follow the case and the CBI director, Mohan Katre, to withdraw from it. The *Express* had brought on record Katre's son's connection with Reliance. The paper also kept hammering away at the Bofors and HDW submarine scandals. Chitra Subramaniam gave details of how the Bofors pay-off had been laundered and began to build evidence that some of the same suspects were at work in the HDW and Bofors deals.

The Ambani-dominated L&T board had proposed a resolution authorizing lending up to Rs 1000 crore to other corporate bodies. The *Express* inveighed against this 'incredible proposition'. Gurumurthy called it 'suicidal' for L&T shareholders. Presumably acting on the advice of the National Front government, the Life Insurance Corporation, a major L&T shareholder, announced that it had requisitioned an extraordinary general meeting of the company to remove the four Ambani directors from its board. The threat worked. Within weeks Dhirubhai Ambani, chairman of Reliance, resigned as chairman of L&T, to be succeeded by a former chairman of the State Bank of India. The impugned resolution was also withdrawn.

The *Express*, through Gurumurthy, said that this was but a first step in reclaiming L&T as an independent company. The matter was raised in Parliament where the finance minister, Madhu Dandavate, stated that the government was intent on finding out whether the financial institutions had colluded with an industrial magnate. He also announced that the board of directors of the Bank of Baroda had found some of the operations of BOB Fiscal 'fishy' and accordingly decided to wind up that subsidiary. Its chairman had been sent on leave and retired.

The Congress was chafing, and not alone in waiting to settle political scores. In April 1990, Chandra Shekhar, sulking as an MP, alleged that his residence was bugged. The National Front government denied that anything like this was afoot but ordered a CBI inquiry. It also informed Parliament that it proposed to amend existing postal and telegraph laws to bar tapping and bugging of communications.

Rigging in Meham, the Devi Lal family pocket borough in Haryana, during the 1989 elections had drawn considerable criticism. The *Express* had been outspoken on the subject, and Devi Lal was displeased. Arun Shourie then met him over the Meham controversy. In a candid conversation Devi Lal used the choicest abuse, littered with the vernacular equivalent of four letter words, to vent his spleen against his critics. Shourie ran a verbatim report on the front page of the *Express*. Devi Lal was livid and protested that a private conversation had been put on record. The defence was that it was necessary to show up the man as he really was.

Early in April 1990, Devi Lal publicly declared that he was ready for a repoll in Meham and elsewhere, and asserted that his party would win by a large margin. He then went on to state that big business houses like the Tatas and Birlas, assisted by newspapers like the *Indian Express*, the *Hindustan Times* and the Jain publications, were responsible for some of the recent turmoil in the country.

Devi Lal then wrote to Prime Minister V.P. Singh alleging various tax, FERA, customs and urban land ceiling violations by Ramnath Goenka. Congress members waved what purported to be a copy of the Devi Lal letter in Parliament, demanding an official statement. Circulated later outside the House by Congress members, the letter alleged

> . . . a conspiracy to destabilise the National Front Government, destroy the Janata Dal and push the country into chaos . . .

> This is a part of the Imperialist design, backed by some powerful capitalists of the country to dismember India . . . *Indian Express* and Mr Ram Nath Goenka are playing a crucial role . . . Mr Ram Nath Goenka wants to dominate the Government administration through his stooges for personal benefit.
>
> All of us welcomed their support in our fight against the Congress Government. Little did we realise that their aim was entirely different. Our just struggle was exploited by the *Indian Express* and Mr Ram Nath Goenka to implement their own conspiracy of destabilisation . . .
>
> Mr Goenka and *Indian Express* have started their game by smearing the image of leaders with a mass base. I am not at all surprised that I should be the primary target . . .

The Speaker disallowed any discussion on the letter but V.P. Singh directed the finance minister to look into the charges levelled against the *Express*. It was also stated that the cases against the *Express* were being pursued and none of them was being withdrawn by the new administration.

Devi Lal was to return to this theme.

Arun Shourie responded with an article titled 'That Criminal Silence' on 4 April 1990. He quoted Roman sources to cite Flavius, who conquered by delay. That, he said, was V.P. Singh's strategy—attrition; to wear down the opponent by inaction. He had employed that tactic successfully against Rajiv Gandhi and Chandra Shekhar. 'And since [then], he has not taken on Devi Lal. And Devi Lal, in one single month, [has] made such an embarrassment of himself that all those who were building their conspiracies on him are cursing themselves.' But, Shourie warned, the stratagem could consume the government.

Deeper anxieties could be discerned. The net appeared to be closing in on many who had guilt to hide or feared the consequences of lost political patronage. Where might the Bofors and HDW inquiries lead? Reliance stock values had fallen sharply. Those that lived off corporate patronage were equally worried. Their personal political 'futures' trading prospects were getting clouded. Many political forgeries were coming home to roost. And time was running out on the unconcealed political ambitions of some. Many believed they would be well served were the National Front government to fall. A coalition of interest appeared to be in the making.

On 31 May 1990, a signed front-page article by Arun Shourie in the *Express* said that Chandra Shekhar and Madhu Limaye had proposed the formation of a national government. It was to include the Janata Dal, Congress and CPI(M), minus V.P. Singh, Rajiv Gandhi and the BJP, and take office under Jyoti Basu. The proposition was said to have been debated by the central committee of the CPI(M) and was there denounced by many members. Jyoti Basu himself was opposed and not inclined to become a sacrificial goat like Charan Singh! The article, 'Open War', warned against the tactic of using disinformation to choreograph an 'issue' every other day that would grab the headlines and divert Parliament and thereby unbalance the government. It said that V.P. Singh should bestir himself and act, possibly dismissing Devi Lal, as he could no longer survive by practising his theory of 'managing contradictions'. In short, 'a leader must lead'.

Harkishen Singh Surjeet, the CPI(M) leader, and Madhu Limaye, both of whom had been named as prime actors, vehemently denied the story. The *Express* published their disclaimer but with a rider stating that the '*Indian Express* stands by its report'. The aggrieved politicians thereupon approached the Press Council which, after due deliberation, upheld their plea that the *Express* had carried the report without attempting to seek their verification and had subsequently reiterated the report in the face of their denials.

A couple of months later, Devi Lal's son, Om Prakash Chautala, assumed the triple offices of national general secretary of the Janata Dal, president of its Haryana unit and chief minister of Haryana. Shourie tore V.P. Singh apart for his indecisiveness and abject 'capitulation'. The Meham by-election had been rigged by Chautala, who had now been elevated before being cleared by the courts or facing the Meham electorate again, rather than being elected from another constituency.

In an article dated 7 July 1990, titled 'That Cruel Revelation Again', Shourie arraigned Prime Minister V.P. Singh, who had been held up as an exemplar of clean politics, for 'capitulation and dereliction'. Why? 'For Devi Lal, nothing has mattered except his son. And V.P. Singh has given in to him so that . . . the government may continue in office'. The same day, the *Express* carried an editorial, 'The Great Betrayal', in much the same vein. It concluded: 'No amount of rationalisation . . . can obscure the fact that the Janata Dal and V.P. Singh have dismally failed the country and the cause for which they were put in office. After such knowledge, what forgiveness?'

Within days, Devi Lal was berated at a Cabinet meeting for his endless sniping at the prime minister and for passing around a fabricated letter to get back at the commerce minister, Arun Nehru. There were demands for his removal. Janata Dal president S.R. Bommai's mediatory efforts failed when Arun Nehru refused to accept an apology coaxed out of Devi Lal.

Not all agreed with the tenor and style of the *Express* during this period. Madhu Kishwar, for one, writing in the *Illustrated Weekly* of 19 August 1990 commented that an opinionated *Express* was in danger of going overboard. It was widely rumoured that the forged letter had reached Devi Lal through the *Express*. That apart, she commented that

> What is not legitimate or acceptable is that the *Express* group should arrogate to itself the power to actually run the government, to decide who is to be in the ruling party and who is to be expelled, to use its clout as an all-India paper to run vindictive campaigns against politicians who don't fall in line, assume for itself the role of king maker and power broker, and plant stories and hatch conspiracies to bring down ministers or governments.

> Already V.P. Singh is being openly threatened for not having sacked Chautala at the first call of Arun Shourie. [Then quoting Shourie] 'How can a government run if it comes to be believed that a prime minister will not until he is flogged to do so?' . . . This is an attempt to become an extra-constitutional power centre appropriating, among others, the right to 'flog' the prime minister.

Not everybody might have agreed with that view of the *Express*. But the very fact that such a view was articulated at all was a caution. The circulation of the *Express* had begun to fall. Its stridency was beginning to tell.

Asked years later about what he thought of the treatment he received at the hands of the *Express*, Devi Lal replied that he had spoken to RNG many times over the phone, but being seriously ill he was not himself. At the time, however, Devi Lal's anger against the media was manifest. He used a press conference to warn of censorship against certain newspapers if they persisted in berating the National Front in general and himself in particular. He was later to deny having made such a statement.

Devi Lal, however, overstepped his limits in calling Prime Minister V.P. Singh spineless in an interview published in the *Illustrated Weekly*. He was asked to resign and was finally dismissed on 1 August 1990 when the Madon Commission was appointed to inquire into the Meham by-election, in which an independent candidate opposing Chautala had been murdered.

*

Two events now took centre stage. The Janata Dal manifesto had spoken of implementing the Mandal Commission's recommendation favouring 27 per cent reservation for other backward classes (OBCs) in government services. V.P. Singh moved to operationalize that commitment and convened an all-party meeting on 3 September 1990 to consider the matter.

The competition to garner the huge OBC vote bank had got under way. The Mandal formula was adopted, using caste as the basis of reservation without any economic criterion, dilution or exit policy. The nation was divided. V.P. Singh argued that unless the OBCs entered government in larger numbers they would not enjoy requisite social progress. He coined a pithy aphorism about 'capturing the Throne to command the Treasury'. The *Express* disagreed sharply. Agitators took to the streets and tragic self-immolations by angry and emotional youths were to follow.

The *Express* described the decision as 'one of the most momentous in the history of independent India'. In another editorial, it alleged that its purpose was to wean away OBCs from a rally that Devi Lal had planned in Delhi for a show of strength with massive rural (read Jat) support. It foretold a 'disastrous tragedy' if the Mandal Report was implemented.

Speaking for the Congress, Rajiv Gandhi said that the OBC concept had been given a dangerous and divisive caste connotation. He felt this was a gimmick before a snap poll that V.P. Singh planned to call, since the BJP was threatening to withdraw support from the National Front on the Ram Janmabhoomi issue. A barrage of articles and editorials followed in the *Express*, mostly critical of Mandalization and its consequences.

The anti-reservationist swell under the banner of the primarily student-youth Anti-Mandal Commission Forum threatened to engulf the country. The *Express* poured scorn on V.P. Singh's ambivalent pronouncements on dilution of the Mandal process by phasing it and calling for a dialogue. But it did also carry an article by Ram Jethmalani on 28 September 1990 offering a counter-view. Jethmalani said that 'India can never become a nation unless the high castes are prepared to make penance by willingly acquiescing in the State pursuing the policy of compensatory discrimination with persistence and generosity.' His introduction was significant:

> This article does not represent Editor Shourie's views. I am not sure it represents *Indian Express* views. It reflects my views and those of many others who are more in number than the anti-reservationists would like to believe.

Did it reflect the views of Ramnath Goenka?

The BJP and Sangh parivar, meanwhile, decided to pick up the gauntlet. Mandalization spelt polarization and would undermine Hindu unity in particular by promoting caste identities. Hence, the need for a cementing bond through Hindutva and a new cultural nationalism built around the Ram Mandir. An intensification of the Ayodhya movement was therefore programmed and Lal Krishan Advani set out on his rath yatra in the autumn of 1990. V.P. Singh retorted that the battle was now between 'Mandal and Kamandal', the masses and the classes, the high castes versus the rest.

Events were moving fast. On 30 September 1990 some forty Janata Dal MPs, meeting at Yashwant Sinha's residence, drafted a letter seeking V.P. Singh's resignation. They noted his unyielding stance against the anti-reservation movement, and charged him with mismanaging the nation. Devi Lal wrote to the prime minister tendering his resignation as an MP, while Chandra Shekhar talked of saving the country from a leadership that had brought it to the brink of disaster.

The Supreme Court was by now seized of the Mandal issue. But the prime minister said that high expectations had been aroused among the OBCs and any going back would give rise to violence. The *Express* saw this as 'interference' in the administration of justice.

The BJP formally withdrew support from the government on 23 October 1990, the day Advani was arrested in Bihar and his rath yatra halted. However, V.P. Singh declared that he would not resign but prove his strength when Parliament reconvened. The *Express* noted the tumultuous response to the rath yatra in opposition to the '*thekadari* of the minorities' assumed by 'pseudo-secularists' and was apprehensive of the consequences that might ensue from Advani's arrest. Feverish activity followed to avert a crisis. One formula followed another. The *Express* vented its disgust in yet another editorial and Shourie repaired to his den to write yet another long article on V.P. Singh's mishandling of the Ayodhya issue and his going back on his understanding with the BJP.

The article was sent over the teleprinter to all *Express* centres but did not appear. Goenka stepped in and removed Shourie as editor on 29 October 1990. His 'race horse' had run too far and too fast. He said later, 'The race horse was out to break my poor *tonga*.' The dismissal order was sent from the penthouse at Express Towers to Delhi on an open teleprinter circuit, as Shourie had ignored an earlier letter sent the previous day after talking to RNG.

The parting of ways was not exactly sudden. Though ill and bedridden for quite some time, RNG had been watching developments and been privy to the growing misgivings of his younger managers, Vivek Khaitan and other close friends and well-wishers. Though given to foul language himself, he felt that publication of the Devi Lal interview without suitable editing was in bad taste and had demeaned the paper. The anti-Mandal campaign had gone too far. The shrill and strident tone of some of what had been appearing and the inordinate length of Shourie's articles had become matters for concern. Illustratively, a readership survey in Kerala was to show that the circulation of the *Express* had fallen. It had lost credibility.

More than any of this, RNG felt that Shourie and even Gurumurthy, from whom too he began to distance himself, had presumed too much in usurping his powers and treating his paper as their own. He did not merely own the *Express*. He was the *Express*. He had his own values and had zealously fostered the *Express* as an independent voice. Now, he feared, it was veering towards the BJP. He was himself on good terms with the BJP and the Sangh parivar, and very close to Nanaji

Deshmukh and Rajmata Vijaya Raje Scindia. But his was not a pro-BJP organ, even if it had broken free from its Congress moorings.

Yes, V.P. Singh had proved a disappointment. But then, what would happen if he were ousted? RNG imagined that, for him, a second coming of Rajiv Gandhi could mean even greater torment than did the second coming of Indira Gandhi. He was now too old for new adventures and he would not have others undo his life's work to further their agenda. He had a legacy to leave behind.

Arun Shourie saw it differently. He believed he was the victim of a conspiracy by a cabal that wanted to take over the paper for its own ends. RNG was ill and disoriented, virtually senile. He had been fed with misinformation and his ears poisoned. Others had drafted the first 'dismissal' letter and he was not really aware of what he had signed. This was why, Shourie said, that when he rushed to show him the letter, RNG seemed bewildered and said nothing had changed. Therefore he had ignored the letter as RNG had seemingly disowned it.

In a formal statement to PTI, RNG said that 'in view of recent misunderstandings' he had told Arun Shourie that they had best part company amicably. Shourie confirmed to PTI that the letter said that the step was taken in the interests of 'morale and discipline' in the paper and so that the *Express*'s image and ability to fight misrule were not impaired.

The same Shobhaa Dé who had in a sense twitted RNG on Shourie's earlier ouster in 1982 wrote of his second dismissal in the *Daily* of Bombay on 1 November 1990. She was cutting: 'No one in the media is sorry to see him go.' He will be recognized 'as an opportunist who didn't know when and where to stop'.

Gurumurthy too had tried to intercede and rebuild trust. But it was too late. RNG seemed to come around only to change his mind. On 7 November 1990 the V.P. Singh government fell. A few weeks later, Gurumurthy, who had become an editorial adviser and editorial writer as much as a financial adviser and legal consultant to the *Express*, wrote to RNG stating that he would no longer tender any advice on editorial matters. Goenka in turn issued an office order that he alone would give editorial directions thereafter. With Shourie's departure, RNG wanted a replacement with balance and maturity to restore the paper's professional standing. He selected N.S. Jagannathan, editor of the *Financial Express.*

*

On 30 October 1990 kar sevaks stormed the Babri Masjid and damaged the domes. The rift within the Janata Dal now widened, with a majority of the party opposed to the formation of a secular front with the Congress. However, Chandra Shekhar and Devi Lal espoused such a move and called for V.P. Singh's resignation. Horse trading had begun. The end was near.

The prime minister moved a motion of confidence in the government. The Lok Sabha rejected this by a huge margin, with the Congress, BJP and various dissidents voting against. The fall of the National Front on 7 November 1990 saw the end of another political creation towards which RNG had contributed so much. The *Express* advocated a truly non-party national government that alone could 'save the nation'. It scoffed at the idea of a Congress-backed minority government led by Chandra Shekhar, but that is what came to pass after an agonizing wait. V.P. Singh remarked in an interview that 'the effort was to throw me out before the Bofors verdict'. Devi Lal was back in government.

The BJP leader L.K. Advani's planned rath yatra from Somnath to Ayodhya left a trail of communal violence countrywide in its wake. The Chandra Shekhar–led government was clearly hostage to the Congress. The backsliding on Bofors was evident in official interventions made in the Delhi High Court to derail a case that had been brought against the Hindujas for their complicity in the matter. The minister for law, Subramaniam Swamy, was criticized by the *Express* for this regression. Fortunately, the Supreme Court reversed what was seen as a perverse High Court order, a ruling that the *Express* commended.

However, when as commerce minister, a concurrent charge held by him, Swamy put paraxylene on the open general licence for import, he was invited to visit the ailing RNG in Bombay. The old man was glad as the decision benefited Bombay Dyeing. Swamy denied any favour and said he had acted strictly on merit. RNG had criticized Swamy as law minister but praised him as commerce minister. Whatever else he thought of Swamy, RNG admired the courage with which he had gone underground to fight the Emergency. In some matters, they were birds of a feather.

The Chandra Shekhar government fell a few months later, just before the ides of March 1991. The Congress pulled the rug from under its feet, as anticipated. It had barely lasted four months. There would soon be a fresh general election.

Perhaps the last senior editorial appointment RNG made was that of Prabhu Chawla. He was brought from *India Today* towards the end of 1990 as executive editor of the *Indian Express*, which became a pink paper in 1994. His coming to the *Indian Express* in June 1992, however, led to Jagannathan's resignation, causing Mulgaokar once again to be appointed editor-in-chief, with H.K. Dua and then Shekhar Gupta following him in succession.

The political turmoil caused by the fall of the Chandra Shekhar government in March 1991 was only the start of what was to be a tragic year. The mid-year general elections were still in progress when Rajiv Gandhi was assassinated in Tamil Nadu, on 21 May. The next phase of the polls was postponed to allow a stunned and sorrowing nation to recover from the shock of this terrible event. The Congress was returned to power. P.V. Narasimha Rao took office as prime minister in mid 1991. The licence–permit raj that RNG had never favoured would soon give way to an era of de-regulation, economic liberalization and reform.

This was something Ramnath Goenka did not live to see. His condition had deteriorated following a massive heart attack on 26 January 1991. Thereafter, he had been in and out of Breach Candy Hospital in Bombay, coming 'home' to the Express Towers in between. He reconstituted the *Express* board with close associates like Nusli Wadia and Venu Srinivasan and Vivek Khaitan, his grandson. He had formally adopted Vivek on 18 January 1990, through a registered deed of adoption witnessed by Achyut Patwardhan, Nanaji Deshmukh, Nusli Wadia and Gurumurthy. A religious ceremony was conducted later in Breach Candy Hospital in May 1991 following unavailing efforts to secure Saroj Goenka's presence. RNG's insistence on these rites flowed from his own deep and abiding belief in the significance of appropriate rituals and the rights they conferred. His purpose was to impart stability to the *Express* and ensure that its policy and traditional independence were maintained. Vivek Goenka's adoption was, however, to cause a family rift.

The penthouse was hushed and draped in gloom as the patriach of the *Express* lay on his deathbed. Rajiv Gandhi visited him there a little before his own tragic assassination. Otherwise, only those closest to him had access. Many kept vigil. On 5 October 1991, Ramnath Goenka breathed his last in the arms of Gita More. She had devotedly nursed and cared for him for nine years and 'mothered' him at the end.

# 12

# The Man and His Legacy

Ramnath Goenka died in Bombay, but the mortal remains of the Tamil Marwari were consigned to the flames in the city he had made his home—Madras, now Chennai. Family, friends and countless other mourners from far and near gathered at Hick's Bungalow, set in the palatial grounds of Express Estates, to pay their last homage to a man who had come there seventy years ago as a callow youth with 'no more than a *lota* and *dhoti*' but with fire in his belly. Vivek Goenka performed the last rites at the Gujarati–Marwari cremation ground at Choolai Pattalam. Thirteen days later, the ashes were immersed in the Ganga at Haridwar by a second grandson, Manoj Sonthalia. The doyen of the Indian press had departed.

The *Express* carried a black-bordered signed editorial by Mulgaokar. It hailed him as 'a magnificent rebel', a fighter to the end and a man of prodigious courage. *The Times* of London said he was acknowledged to be among the dozen most powerful men in India. Many political comrades-in-arms and bitter opponents were in the Lok Sabha when it condoled his passing. The Speaker, Shivraj Patil, said that in his death, the nation had lost 'a dynamic personality and relentless crusader of freedom of the press and democratic values'. He added that his 'incomparable services to the nation during the freedom struggle and, later, to journalism would be remembered for a long time to come'.

Obituary notices and tributes in memoriam came flooding in. The epithets summed up the man: a towering figure; fearless crusader; man of steel; path-finder; a phenomenon; a true son of India; an indomitable patriot; a heroic figure; a rishi with a difference; a peerless raconteur who would tell a story with great zest, replete with practical wisdom and guru-mantras.

RNG was a deeply religious man, though secular in outlook. He believed in karma. What was ordained must come to pass. Yet it was prudent to insure. He would consult astrologers and tantriks and had his horoscope read. He would visit a certain temple near Guruvayoor and break coconuts there, in keeping with tradition, to be rid of ailments and 'obstructions' in his path. He would likewise go to the nearby Kodunallur temple to perform shatru samharam, a puja for deliverance from the menace of his enemies. The joke was that he would first create the shatru or enemy and then offer puja for his own protection.

He was ruthless, petty and mean on occasion, but also extraordinarily generous and caring. For him, the ends justified the means, and duty and national interest were what he determined them to be. Like all strong personalities, he was both loved and hated, but he could never be ignored. He lived on the brink and danced on the razor's edge. He certainly walked with kings and, some would say, exaggeratedly perhaps, that he made and unmade them. Yet he never lost the common touch.

Gurumurthy, who knew him intimately, described him as a rich man with a poor man's austerity, who would see an advantage in every disadvantage and vice versa. 'His commitment to values was not always uniform. But his overwhelming commitment to the national interest, as he saw it, overshadowed his conduct as a businessman who stretched and strained his ethics. I loved him for things I would detest in myself.'

In December 1993, a statue of Ramnath Goenka was unveiled at a ghat and an ashram school named after him on the banks of the Mandakini River in Chitrakoot, a hallowed place of pilgrimage commemorating the forest region where Ram had spent his years of exile. Nanaji Deshmukh had taken the initiative, but RNG would have felt uncomfortable about such a display.

There were critics too. The *Blitz*, an old foe, doffed its cap, acknowledging that 'some of the country's greatest journalists and editors graduated from his *Express* group'. For that, it said

> a sizeable share of credit must surely go to him. He was not a proprietor who parachuted into the industry from shipbuilding or textiles. Within a framework of his own, he understood journalism better than most proprietors. More significantly, he understood the importance of good journalism, something very few proprietors do. [However] in no other newspaper group were so many editors sacked, transferred or otherwise humiliated . . . His attitude to law-breaking won him many admirers and much respect. But Ramnathji clearly considered himself well above the law . . . He will be remembered as the man who set an example of how the press should relate to authority. It may be a memory full of 'ifs' and 'buts', yet it will be one that will endure.

Others, including some who genuinely admired him, were more scathing. V. Gangadhar, a media watcher, said he was 'appalled at the lavish praise showered on a personality who ruthlessly used his newspaper chain to further his own interests'. One of his own Bombay editors, Darryl D'Monte, called RNG a 'pugilist of the press' and admitted that the *Express* was far more 'adventurous' than its rivals. 'But at the end of the day, you were never sure whether a story that appeared was correct or not.' It lacked credibility. Further, 'much of what is appearing as news is editorial. It's twisted.' P. Venkateswara Rao, former editor of the *Andhra Prabha*, said something similar. 'Our group of newspapers started to identify with parties. This was not good for the organisation as objectivity and credibility were lost. We should concern ourselves with values and not with political parties.' Another assessed that when the *Express* was not involved in bringing down a government, it was almost a part of it or a faction within it. 'His closeness to Jayaprakash Narayan and his antipathy towards Dhirubhai Ambani was reflected in his papers beyond the demands of journalism.' He subordinated the autonomy and independence of his papers to the causes he held dear. Yet another lamented that he lacked balance. He was a bundle of contradictions, more picturesquely put as 'an oxymoron on two feet'; a man with a corkscrew mind.

In an irreverent but affectionate tribute, carried in the *Express* soon after his death, Shobhaa Dé speculated about how RNG was faring in Swarag Towers, planning his new venture, the *Celestial Express*, with God as editor. She suspected he would soon run out of staff and might have to make a quick trip to Hell to recruit some devils, 'if only to keep God in check and maintain a balance'. The old man was exasperating but lovable!

The *Express* became an activist newspaper and, on occasion, a participant rather than an observer, using guerrilla tactics to ambush its opponents. It made news as much as reported it. Pamphleteering and hectoring, sometimes in collusion with political actors and legal activists, compromised objectivity and created a perception of partisanship.

Yet for all that, as the *Deccan Herald* said of Goenka, 'The many vices that he had will not live after him; but the good will, because his vices were personal and the good that he did was social.'

He was a true newspaper publisher, not just a businessman in the newspaper industry. There were those who would compare him to some of the great press barons and media tycoons the world has seen, men like William Randolph

Hearst, who combined print and politics, Beaverbrook and Murdoch, all of them ruthless and ambitious, yet visionaries of a sort. In some ways, RNG went beyond this characterization. He was a freedom fighter and nationalist who saw his newspapers as the sword arm of freedom, democracy and national unity. RNG reflected Churchill's view of the man who built the *Daily Express*: 'Beaverbrook is at his best when things are at their very worst.'

Goenka's credo echoed Pulitzer's famous words about the United States:

> We are a democracy and there is only one way to get a democracy on its feet in the matter of its individual, its social, its municipal, its state [and] its national conduct, and that is by keeping the public informed about what is going on. There is not a crime, there is not a dodge, there is not a trick, there is not a swindle, there is not a vice which does not live by secrecy. Get these things out in the open, describe them, attack them, ridicule them in the press, and sooner or later public opinion will sweep them away.

RNG did not use the newspapers he owned for self-glorification. He barred his papers from publishing news reports or photographs of himself or any member of his family. When the *Express* was sent a picture of one of his granddaughters' wedding, he withheld its publication on the ground that a family wedding did not make news. But when it came to what he considered to be the national or public interest and freedom of the press, there would be no compromise. He was possibly the only proprietor to join the celebrated journalists' march from India Gate to the Boat Club along Delhi's Raj Path in protest against the 1988 Defamation Bill to curb the press.

He gave his editors considerable freedom within a broad policy framework, allowing for regional variations, as he believed that the bedrock of India's unity lay in respecting its diversity. This was why, though a staunch and devout Hindu, he did not cling to any kind of religious fundamentalism or exclusive cultural nationalism. Ultimately, spirituality mattered more than ritual or religiosity. Though he drew close to the BJP and RSS on the rebound from the Congress, and was closely associated with some of their leaders, he wished the *Express* to be truly independent and never become or be seen to become an organ of any particular party. During the Emergency, for example, he was particular that official news should not be suppressed merely because it was not to the liking of the paper. The people must know and had a right to know. Likewise, he was very agitated when, on one occasion, the Delhi edition of the *Express* failed to carry the news of a raid on a large industrial house whose scions were close to him. He ranted that he would be accused of accepting favours to cover up corruption and could tolerate anything but that!

The *Express* had a certain élan and panache that owed something to his editors and reporters but perhaps more to his ideas and ideals and the strong editorial backing his staff could expect from him. Narasimhan, who emerged a hero during the Emergency, said as much. Where RNG failed was as a manager and conservator. He did not consolidate what he had so painstakingly created. There was neither delegation, not even to Bhagwandas, nor professionalism in the management. And as he was ruefully to admit to Saroj Goenka rather late in the day, the *Express* continued be run like a 'Marwari shop'. He was a stingy paymaster and unable to keep the best talent that the *Express* attracted. He also believed in creating an element of tension among his senior staff, playing one off against the other, so that they would turn to him and he might reign supreme. He would listen to gossip and had 'four ears but only two eyes'. In politics as in life, he always kept a line open to his adversary. Prudence demanded having an exit.

He was a lonely man who lived a lonely life, wanting to be loved but unable to give the love of a father or grandparent that would have provided the spark of family warmth that was missing in his life. His involvement in public life from a remarkably young age and the peripatetic routine his multi-centred newspaper chain and sometimes corporate interests entailed, here today, there tomorrow, kept his body and mind in a constant whirl, leaving little quality time for the family and especially its younger members. Of course, he was always there, a stern paterfamilias who provided for them. He cared in his own way. But it was the *Express* that became family and the penthouse and the Sunder Nagar Guest House his home from home.

He sought attractive young women and sported with them, feeding them with ice cream and taking them to the cinema. It fulfilled a yearning for filial affection and gave release to his libido, till illness and worry aged him.

Among the tributes paid to RNG after his passing was one from a Shubha Khandekar that appeared as a letter in the *Free Press Journal*. She recalled that with some other college girls she had once thumbed a lift in Delhi from an old man driving a nondescript Fiat. Introductions over, one of the girls inquired what he did at the *Indian Express*. 'Oh, I generally hang around,' he quipped and then amusedly asked if they would care for a cup of coffee. 'We readily assented and he took us out of his way to Lodhi Woodlands, the Mecca for lovers of South Indian food, and let us eat idlis and dosas to our heart's content, while he just sat and watched.' There was obviously a sadness and longing behind that spontaneous gesture.

*

Ramnath Goenka wrestled with the problem of succession for years. He was a self-made man who had struggled and staked all, time and again, to build a proud media empire. His children and their children had been born with silver spoons in their mouths. He was never sure that his progeny would rise to his expectations though he had pinned a fugitive hope in his son. Bhagwandas's death was therefore a shattering blow. Now hope lay in his grandsons, granddaughters and grandsons-in-law. He tried them all, finally narrowing down the field to Vivek Khaitan and Manoj Sonthalia. They had variously managed the Bombay and Delhi centres and the Madras and Southern editions.

He toyed with the idea of forming a trust and inducting a broader-based public interest board of directors, going beyond family and loyalists, but too late and too tentatively to take hold and make a difference. Here too, he was not sure of its practicability. Deep down, he felt that the succession must follow his blood. There was a gnawing desire to adopt a son after the death of his firstborn. The lack of a direct male line in the family over four generations was a cruel deprivation. Bhagwandas was the one exception. But when he too died, adoption seemed the only available course of action. He saw surrogate sons at various times in Arun Shourie, Gurumurthy and Nusli Wadia. He would for some time publicly speak of Ajay Mohan Khaitan, Vivek's father, as his 'second son', but formally sought to adopt others. He himself was the adopted son of an adopted son.

RNG had long back requested his daughter-in-law, Saroj, to adopt Vivek Khaitan when he was very small. But she was disinclined. After Bhagwandas's death, he again tried to persuade her to adopt a son. Sushil Goenka, a grandson of RNG's brother and the first male child in the extended family after Bhagwandas, was a potential choice. Saroj said that she was running an orphanage and could adopt any one of those children if she wanted. She reasoned that if she adopted an infant that would be little use (for the purpose of an immediate succession) whereas an adult would probably be attracted by the inheritance. In any case, she regarded her sons-in-law and nephews as her sons, though later she was to rue that they had turned away from her.

RNG had been very close to the TVS family over three generations and in 1989 told Venu Srinivasan that he would like to adopt him. Saroj Goenka had agreed, but Venu demurred. RNG had treated his father, Cheema, as an adopted son, and the old man was grief-stricken when he suddenly passed away. Venu Srinivasan knew and understood RNG's belief in the seminal place of a son according to the shastras, but felt it would be wrong to deprive RNG's own blood of their patrimony.

The future of the *Express* was a worrying concern. RNG had not been able to build foundations for the future. Members of the family had begun to jostle for position. A lot of people had their eye on the *Express* and the power it represented. RNG had had a heart attack in 1989 and yet another in January 1991. Mulgaokar was not happy with the direction the *Express* had taken in RNG's last years, and was of the view that the independence of the paper was more likely to be protected by an independent editor than by an independent proprietor. But where are such editors, RNG would exclaim! However, realizing that time was running out, he decided to act and formally adopted Vivek Khaitan, his grandson by his eldest daughter, Krishna.

The necessary religious ceremony was performed on his birthday (according to the Hindu calendar) in the presence of Gurumurthy, Prabhash Joshi, Nusli Wadia, R.V. Pandit and Vivek's wife Ananya's parents. His grandson was now his son who would be there to perform his last rites. Saroj Goenka, abroad at the time, was taken aback.

After the death of Bhagwandas, the shareholding of the *Express* Group had undergone a series of changes. First, the property companies were separated from the newspaper companies, most of the former passing under the control of Saroj Goenka. This reorganization led to RNG becoming almost the sole owner of the newspaper companies. Thereafter, in successive stages, the pattern of stockholding was changed to vest 62.72 per cent with Vivek Goenka, 37.12 per cent with Manoj Sonthalia and 0.16 per cent with Radha Sonthalia, Manoj's mother and RNG's younger daughter.

In between, family disagreements had led to Manoj Sonthalia returning his holding to RNG. Other options were explored. Gurumurthy suggested an equal split, bestowing anywhere between 45 to 49 per cent of the shares to each of the two grandsons, with the balance of 2 to 10 per cent being held by a trust. This did not find favour. In the event of family friction, the trustees would hold the balance of power and be in a position to dictate terms and virtually take over the organization. RNG thereupon convened a conference with Achyut Patwardhan, Gurumurthy, Nanaji, Nusli Wadia and Venu Srinivasan in Delhi in 1990, at which it was decided to form a trust comprising Patwardhan, Deshmukh, Wadia and Srinivasan that would own 51 per cent of the shares, the balance being divided between the two grandsons, Vivek and Manoj. Blank share transfer forms were signed and given to Nusli Wadia for safekeeping. However, on a more careful reconsideration, RNG decided to scrap the idea of a trust and transfer the shares in the proportion of 62.72 per cent to Vivek Goenka and 33.12 per cent to Manoj Sonthalia, with Radha Sonthalia holding the balance of 0.16 per cent as before. Nusli Wadia honoured that commitment after RNG's demise.

Subsequently, Manoj Sonthalia and Saroj Goenka went to the Madras High Court. They challenged the redisposition of shares at a time when they believed Ramnath Goenka was in no position to take an independent or coherent decision in view of his critical medical condition. Saroj Goenka failed to get any relief and finally settled all issues in March 1997. This left her, as before, with a large part of the property but with no share in the newspaper business. Vivek Goenka's contention was that at the time of the transfers, Ramnath Goenka was in full possession of his mental faculties. He had been active and had flown to different destinations, participated in PTI board meetings, called on the prime minister and other leaders in a bid to secure a mediated settlement of the Ayodhya matter, and had attended to other work.

The court did not give Manoj Sonthalia any relief either. But he and Vivek Goenka finally entered into a settlement in 1995, which was duly approved by the *Express* board. Basically the compromise entailed a partitioning of control over the newspaper companies. Manoj Sonthalia took charge of the Madras, Bangalore, Hyderabad, Cochin and other Southern editions, while Vivek Goenka retained possession of the Delhi, Chandigarh, Bombay–Pune and Gujarat centres and the *Financial Express*. R.V. Pandit was instrumental in brokering the deal. Vivek Goenka and Nusli Wadia drifted apart.

There was concern over the move to partition the *Express* into a Northern and Southern group, the latter to be named the *New Indian Express*. A clutch of sixteen prominent media, legal, academic and public figures separately issued a statement over the signatures of Justices Sarkaria, Krishna Iyer and C. Subramaniam. Their appeal in defence of the integrity of the *Express* said:

> . . . It is our firm conviction that any splitting of the *Indian Express* will not only be unfortunate and undesirable but will undermine what has developed into a national media institution.
>
> On more than one occasion, Ramnath Goenka himself stated that he regarded the newspaper as a national asset, not as a business or property. Whatever may be one's response to the views projected by the paper, the great tradition of fearless journalism that Ramnath Goenka upheld during the struggle for Independence and against the Emergency imposed in 1975 would be subverted by any move to bifurcate the *Indian Express*.

That sentiment was widely shared.

*

Much has happened since Ramnath Goenka departed. Television has grown immensely. Community radio seems poised to burgeon.

The Web has spurred new experimentation in decentralized communication, and newspapers can be read on the Internet. Ever-new technologies are influencing media production and trends. There has been significant change in the mainline newspaper business too. With economic reform and the opening up of a market economy and its impact on investments and advertising, an increasing number of newspapers are being market driven more than reader driven. Huge new vernacular media conglomerates have appeared on the scene. In some notable cases, newspapers are being managed rather than edited. The editor is in decline. RNG's lament was that the 'missionaries' had gone, leaving behind 'mercenaries'.

Speaking at a Ramnath Goenka centenary celebration in Delhi in 2004, Prime Minister Dr Manmohan Singh wondered what Goenka would have thought of the media scene today.

> As India moves into the new millennium we see all around us signs of restlessness and ferment at the grassroots that heralds a new awakening in this vast, plural society of over a billion people . . . At this time we need to ask ourselves what kind of media does India need and deserve? . . . Should the market define the media or the media define the larger market of ideas, values, goals and information needs both for the classes and masses.
>
> The media to a great extent defines the daily national agenda. What should our agenda be? . . . I see the power both of God and the Devil in the new technologies of the media. I am often disturbed by the messages we are transmitting. Have we no larger mission in hand? Of nation building, of caring for the underprivileged, of seeking better governance, of making ours a more humane, prosperous, creative, free and liberal society.

Dr Manmohan Singh urged the media to engage in the battle for values and ideas with the passion and fervour of Ramnath Goenka. 'The Journalism of Courage, however,' he added, 'must be combined with commitment and compassion.'

*

For RNG the *Indian Express* was more than a newspaper chain. He envisioned it as a national institution, a custodian of the people's freedom and their right to know. It had always been an instrument for national service, not commerce. Its financial prop was prime real estate, now worth several hundred crores of rupees. Published and read in all regions and in seven languages it was for all its frailties a force for unity, truly the Fourth Estate and vox populi. Not for nothing did the national motto, *Satyameve Jayate*, hold both deep meaning and a promise for him. The *Express* emblazoned 'The Journalism of Courage' on its masthead 'Because the Truth Involves Us All'. Rhetoric? Maybe. Great ideals might never be fulfilled. But, as Tagore said, enduring achievement lies in 'tireless striving that stretches its arms towards perfection'.

In the late autumn of his life RNG remarked that he had played his innings and had no regrets. Another generation follows and there is always a second innings and further innings thereafter. The nation remembers. Bombay's City Fathers named after him one of the roads radiating from Nariman Point. An old epitaph reads, 'Tread softly, lest ye disturb this Old Warrior resting between Battles'. Those walking down Freedom Fighter Ramnath Goenka Marg in the shadow of the Express Towers may, if they listen carefully, hear these words blowing in the wind.

But ultimately, RNG will be remembered not by streets named after him, nor by any epitaph recording his words and deeds, Ozymandias-like. His legacy will remain alive by the united exertions of his progeny who involuntarily divided the institution he built with his lifeblood but failed to hold together the *Indian Express*. Many more battles remain to be fought and won. The burden lies on those that follow him.

The bifurcation of the group has hurt and in some ways diminished the *Express* at a time when the best of Ramnath Goenka's kind of journalism is needed, perhaps more than ever before. Can the two sides reunite to serve a larger cause? More than the *Express*, RNG himself became the institution he left behind. But with it he left a legacy that could recreate the enduring institution he strove to build. That would be a fitting tribute to the man who, despite many failings and foibles, strode the scene like a colossus.

# Notes

**Introduction**

1. Sir Edwin Arnold. *The Song Celestial* or *Bhagwad-Gita*. From the Second Book. Being a discourse between Arjuna, Prince of India, and the Supreme Being under the form of Krishna. London: Kegan Paul. 1945.

**1. The Making of a Marwari Tamil**

1. T.J.S. George. *Pothan Joseph's India*. Delhi: Sanchar. 1992.
2. *The World of Tamil Journalism*. Volume 39, December 1980.

**2. Getting Rooted in Madras**

1. *Bhavan's Journal*. 30 November 1991.
2. Jawaharlal Nehru. *Selected Works of Jawaharlal Nehru*. Second Series, Volume 13. Edited by S. Gopal. pp. 138-39. 15 September 1949. New Delhi: Jawaharlal Nehru Memorial Fund. 1992.
3. Rajmohan Gandhi. *The Rajaji Story, 1937–72*. Bombay: Bharatiya Vidya Bhavan. 1984.
4. Ramnath Goenka. Letter to Lala Sri Ram. 7 December 1951.
5. Khasa Subba Rao. 'Easier for a Camel to Enter the Eye of a Needle'. *Swarajya*. 4 July 1953.
6. *Swarajya*. 'Sidelights'. May 1959.

**3. Taking Wing to Bombay**

1. N.J. Hamilton. *Troubled 'Times'*. Keynote. March 1982.

**4. A Capital Move**

1. G.N.S. Raghavan. *PTI Story*. Delhi: Press Trust of India. 1987.

2. M.O. Mathai. *Reminiscences of the Nehru Age*. Delhi: Vikas Publishing House. 1978.
3. Prem Bhatia. *Of Many Pastures*. Delhi: Allied Publishers. 1989.
4. Ajit Bhattacharjea. *Unfinished Revolution: A Political Biography of Jayaprakash Narayan*. Delhi: Rupa. 2004.
5. B.N. Tandon. *PMO Diary–I: Prelude to Emergency*. Delhi: Konark Publishers. 2003.
6. A.S. *Who Killed L.N. Mishra? An 'Indian Express' Investigation*. Bombay: Popular Prakasam. 1979.

**5. Business Bubbles in Calcutta**

1. Nantoo Bannerjee. 'IISCO: The Coup That Failed'. *Business Standard*. 22 November 1981.
2. Prakash Tandon. *Banking Century*. Delhi: Viking. 1989.

**6. Dark Days to New Freedom**

1. Affidavit of Ramnath Goenka before the Shah Commission. Delhi. 1977.
2. K.K. Dass. White Paper on Misuse of Mass Media during the Internal Emergency. Appendix 1. Delhi: Government of India. 1977.
3. D.R. Mankekar and Kamla Mankekar. *Decline and Fall of Indira Gandhi: 19 Months of Emergency*. Delhi: Orient Paperbacks. 1977.
4. K.K. Birla. *Indira Gandhi: Reminiscences*. Delhi: Vikas. 1986.
5. *Onlooker*. 15–30 April 1977.
6. Nani Palkhivala. *We, the Nation: The Lost Decades*. New Delhi: UBS Publishers. 1994.

**8. Managing a Growing Empire**

1. N.D. Sampath, Malathi Rangaswamy, and N.V. Kasturi (eds). *Kasi Diaries. Excerpts from the Diaries of N.D. Varadacharirar (1903–1945)*. Madras: East West Books. 2004.
2. 'The Dark Lady', *Society* November 1980, and 'The Express Empire', *Gentleman* July 1982.

**9. Litigant Par Excellence**

1. Nicholas Coleridge. *Paper Tigers*. Extracted in *Sunday*. 20–26 June 1993.

**10. A Wounding Time**

1. 'Autumn of the Patriarch'. *Illustrated Weekly of India*. 24 November 1985.
2. 'I Am Proud to Be Jinnah's Grandson'. *Illustrated Weekly of India*. 2–8 October 1993.
3. 'On the Firing Line'. *India Today*. 30 September 1987.
4. Giani Zail Singh. *Memoirs of Giani Zail Singh, the Seventh President of India*. New Delhi: Har-Anand. 1997.
5. 'The Contemporary Conservative: The Plot to Oust Rajiv'. From the *Spectator*. 6 February 1988. Included in *Selected Writings of Dhiren Bhagat*. Viking. 1990.
6. R. Venkataraman. *My Presidential Years*. Delhi: Indus. 1994.
7. B.G. Deshmukh. *A Cabinet Secretary Looks Back*. New Delhi: HarperCollins. 2004.

**11. Last Roar of the Lion**

1. N.K. Singh. 'St. Kitts Rewind: On the Trail of the Flying Godman'. *Indian Express*. 27 October 2004.
2. 'Swamy: RV Party to "Oust Rajiv Plot"'. *Hindustan Times*. 25 July 1994.

# Appendix

## Persons Interviewed under the Biography Project

Abdullah, Farooq
Abraham, T.
Acharya, *Dr* Vijayalakshmi
Agarwalla, L.P.
Aiyer, Swaminathan
Aramugam
Assomull, Mathuradas T.

Bajaj, Ramakrishna
Bajoria, B.P.
Bajoria, S.L.
Balakrishnan, M.G.
Bansidhar Lala
Bansilal
Bhagwati, *Justice* P.N.
Bhargava, G.S.
Bhatt, *Dr* H.S.
Bhattacharjea, Ajit
Birla, B.K.
Birla, G.P.
Birla, K.K.
Birla, S.K.
Bose, *Dr* Sisir
Buch, Arvind
Burnier, Radha

Cama, R.M.
Chakraborti, Nikhil
Chander, Jagpravesh
Chandola, Harish
Chandran, N.R.
Chandra Shekar
Chengalvorayan, P.
Choraria, I.C.
Chudasama, Nana
Cunchitapatham, M.

Daddha, Siddha Raj
Dadha, S. Mohanchand
Dalmia, K.K.
Dalmia, S.N.
Dalmia, Trilokchand
Dalmia, V.H.
Damani, V.S.
Dandavate, Madhu
Daniel, *Mrs* H.
Dharia Mohan
Das, Sitanshu
Dass, Shobhakant
Dave, Harindra
Deora, Murli
Desai, Hitendra
Desai, Kanti
Desai, M.V.
Desai, Manubhai
Desai, Morarji
Desai, Narayan
Desai, Chandrakant,
Deepak
Deshmukh, Nanaji
Deshpande, Govindrao
Dhanuka, Devi Prasad
Dhar, A.N.
Dhar, Vijay
Dharia, Mohan
Duggar, N.M.
Duggar, S.M.
Dilip Kumar
D'Monte, Darryl
Dua, H.K.
Dubey, Suman

Fernandes, George

Gadgil, V.N.
Gadkari, Madhav
Gandhi, Hasmukh
Gandhi, Pravinchandra
Gandhi, Rajmohan
Ganeriwal, R.G.
Ganesan, Shri Sangu
Ganz, Peter
Godrej, S.P.
Goenka, A. Lal
Goenka, Santosh
Gokani, Usha
Gokhale, Vidyadhar
Gomti, Prasad
Gopalan, P.S.
Gopalakrishnan, M.
Goray, N.G.
Govindaraj, *Mrs* S.
Goyal, *Dr* B.K.
Grover, R.K.
Guha, Samar
Gujral, I.K.
Gupta, *Justice* A.C.
Gupta, Gordhandas
Gupta, Vinod
Gupta, Vishwabandhu
Guy, Randor

Haja Shariff, K.S.G.
Haksar, P.N.
Harvani, Ansar
Hegde, Ramakrishna

Irani, C.R.

Jagannathan, N.S.
Jain, Girilal
Jain, J.C.
Jain, J.K.
Jain, L.C.
Jain, P.C.
Jain, Shantilal

Jain, Ramesh
Jaisingh, Hari
Jatia, Mohanlal
Jatia, M.P.
Jethmalani, Ram
Jha, Prem Shankar
Jotwani, *Dr* Motilal
Jog, Leela
Jaipuria, Ashok

Kailasam, Soundara
Kalidas, V.
Kanoria, Kantilal
Kanoria, Nandlal
Kapoor, Virendra
Karanjia, B.K.
Karanjia, Russi
Karlekar, Hiranmay
Karunanidhi, *Dr* M.
Karuppiah
Kaul, Sumer
Kejriwal, Ghanshyam
Kejriwal, Hari Kishore
Khan, Arif Mohammad
Khanna, *Justice* H.R.
Khaitan, Ajay Mohan
Khaitan, Rajesh
Khurana, Madanlal
Killa, Hari Shankar
Kohli, K.D.
Kohli, Mohan
Kohli, S.K.
Kokaje, Tukaram
Kothari, G.D.
Krishna, G.
Krishnamurthy, Lakshmi
Krishnamurthy, S.
Krishnaswami, M.
Kulkarni, B.V.
Kuppuswamy, V.

Lakhani, Geeta
Lakhotia, R.N.
Lal, Bhure
Lal, Devi
Lal, Phyllis
Lalbhai, Arvindbhai
Lalbhai, Nirajan
Laxman, R.K.
Limaye, Madhu
Lodha, K.M.

Mahadeo, T.S.
Mahadevan, I.
Mahadevan, R.N.
Mahalingam, *Dr* N.
Maheshanand
Manjubhashini, *Mrs*
Masani, Minoo
Mathew, K.M.
Mathuradas
Mehta, Ashwin
Menon, Leela
Miller, Harry
Mittal, R.P.
Mukherjee, S.N.
Murali
Murjani, Jamnadas
Murlidhar, N.
Murti, Gayatri

Naik
Nahata, S.N.
Nair, K. Sankaran
Nanda, H.P.
Narasimhan, V.K.
Narayan, C.A.
Narayan, L.L.
Narayan, V.N.
Narendra, K.
Nath, Rajendra
Naqvi, Saeed
Nayar, Kuldip
Nehru, Arun
Nevatia, Rajeshwar
Nijilingappa

Padmanabhan, R.A.
Pai, M.R.
Palkhivala, Nani
Pandit, C.S.
Pandya, Anand Shankar
Pant, K.C.
Parthasarathy, Prema
Patel, Chimanbhai (CM)
Patel, Chimanbhai (ED)
Patil, Veerendra
Pattabhi Raman, C.R.
Patwardhan, P.H.
Phumbra, Ramanlal
Pichai, S.

Pinglay, D.D.
Poddar, R.K.
Puri, Rajinder
Puri, Ranvir & Usha
Purohit, Trilokchand

Radhakrishna
Raghavan, A.
Raghavan, D.S.
Raghavan, G.N.S.
Ramakrishna K.G.
Rajagopal, S.
Rajaram, K.
Ram, Bharat
Ramadurai Indira
Ramakrishnan, P.R.
Raman, B.V.
Ramanujam, K.S.
Ramaswamy, P.V.
Ranga, N.G.
Ranganathan, V.
Rao, Bala
Rao, Binod
Rao, Muturi Satyanarayan
Rao, Venkateshwara
Potturi
Rao, P. Venam
Rathi, Jai Narain
Ravindran, Sheela
Reddy, C.A.
Reddy, C.G.K.
Reddy, C.N.
Reddy, Neelam Sanjiva
Reddy, *Dr* Pratap
Rindani, *Dr* T.H.
Ruia, Nirmal Kumar
Ruia, Radhakrishna
Rungta, P.N.

Sadasivam, T.
(M. Subbalaxmi)
Sahay, S.
Sankaran, P.
Samant, Datta
Sarkar, Aveek
Sastry, S.N.
Saxena, Pilloo
Seervai, H.M.
Seksaria, K.N.

Seshadri, N.
Sen, Bhola Nath
Sen, K.K.
Sengupta, R.N.
Seth, *Dr* R.K.
Shah, Shantibhai
Shah, Viren J.
Shakerwade, Shobha
Sharma, N.D.
Sharma, V.S. Ganapati
Sharma, Rajat
Sharma, Renu
Sheth, Asha
Sheth, Ratilal
Shetty, P.S.
Shivaram, K.
Shourie, Arun
Singh, K.R.
Singh, K.V.
Singh, Khushwant
Singh, S. Nihal
Singh, Randhir
Sinha, Tarkeshwari

Sivaraman, A.N.
Sanghvi, Vir and Malvika
Sonthalia, Radhadevi
Sonthalia, Sant Kumar
Srinivasan, K.
Srinivasan, R.
Srinivasan, Radha
Subramaniam, C.
Subramaniam, *Dr* Swamy
Subramaniam, T.S.
Sunil's Grandmother
Sunder Rajan, K.R.
Swaminathan, K.
Swami, C.S.A.

Talwalkar, Govind
Tapadia, Chauthamal
Tarneja, Ram
Tharayan, P.
Thakur, Umakant
Thiruvengadam, K.V.
Tiwari, P.L.

Tulzapurkar, *Justice* V.D.
Thakur, Janardhan
Thyagarajan, T.K.

Upendra P.
Unnikrishnan K.P.

Vaidya, Triguna
Vardhan, K.S. & Kamala
Varadhan, K.S.
Varier, Kottakkal
Varier, P.V.C.
Vasu, T.T.
Vedprakash
Venkataraman, R.
Venkataraman, V.S.
Venkatasubramaniam, S.
Verghese, B.G.
Viswanathan, A.P.
Viswanathan, S.
Visvam, S

Yunus, Mohammed

Zakaria, *Dr* Rafiq

# Index